Organized Interests
and the European Community

edited by
Justin Greenwood, Jürgen R. Grote
and Karsten Ronit

SAGE Publications
London • Newbury Park • New Delhi

Editorial arrangement and Chapters 1 and 8 © Justin
Greenwood, Jürgen R. Grote and Karsten Ronit, 1992
Chapter 2 © Volker Schneider, 1992
Chapter 3 © Justin Greenwood and Karsten Ronit, 1992
Chapter 4 © Alan Cawson, 1992
Chapter 5 © Jürgen R. Grote, 1992
Chapter 6 © Luca Lanzalaco, 1992
Chapter 7 © Jelle Visser and Bernhard Ebbinghaus, 1992

First published 1992
Reprinted 1994

SAGE Publications Ltd
6 Bonhill Street
London EC2A 4PU

SAGE Publications Inc
2455 Teller Road
Newbury Park, California 91320

SAGE Publications India Pvt Ltd
32, M-Block Market
Greater Kailash – I
New Delhi 110 048

British Library Cataloguing in Publication Data

A catalogue record for this book is available
from the British Library

ISBN 0 8039 8701 3

Typeset by The Word Shop, Bury
Printed and bound in Great Britain by
Biddles Ltd, Guildford and King's Lynn

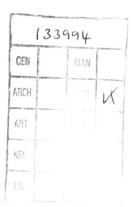

Contents

Contributors

Alan Cawson is Professor of Politics at the University of Sussex. He has written extensively on corporatism (including *Corporatism and Welfare, 1982* and *Corporatism and Political Theory*, 1986). Since 1985 he has been researching the European consumer electronics industry, and he is the co-author of *Hostile Brothers: Competition and Closure in the European Electronics Industry* (1990) and author of a new unit on high tech industry for the Open University course D212, *Running the Country*.

Bernhard Ebbinghaus is a Lecturer in Sociology at the University of Mannheim, and is currently completing his PhD thesis on 'European Trade Unions and Social Change' at the European University Institute in Florence (Italy). He is involved in an international comparative research project on the Development of Union Systems in Western European Societies since 1945 (DUES) at the University of Mannheim (Germany). He is co-author, with Jelle Visser and Winfried Pfenning, of a data handbook on the historical development and structure of trade unions in 12 European countries, to be published in 1992 by Campus Verlag.

Justin Greenwood is now Senior Lecturer in Public Administration at the Robert Gordon's University, Aberdeen, and recently held a Senior Lectureship at Teesside Polytechnic. Following completion of a PhD thesis in 1988, he has researched and published in a wide variety of public policy domains, including government/industry relations studies involving pharmaceuticals and biotechnology, and in the fields of tourism, welfare, and the voluntary sector. He is currently researching and publishing articles examining interest groups and the European dimension.

Jürgen R. Grote is Research Associate at the European University Institute (Florence) where he is also completing his PhD. He has previously held Lectureships at the Universities of Genoa and Siena and at ISIA–Florence and is also working as a consultant to IRES, the Institute for Social and Economic Research in Tuscany. He has published in the fields of European regional development policies and in problems of transnational collective action by interest associations.

Luca Lanzalaco is a post-doctoral fellow at the Centre for Comparative Politics at the Bocconi University in Milan (Italy). He has written several articles about business interest associations, industrial relations and political theory. He recently published a book about the Italian Confederation of Industry from a comparative and historical perspective.

Karsten Ronit is attached to the Centre for Public Organization and Management in Copenhagen and lectures at the Department of Socio-Economics and Planning, Roskilde University Centre, and at the Department of Political Science, University of Copenhagen. He is currently completing doctoral research and has published on business associations and collective action theories.

Volker Schneider is Research Fellow at the Max Planck Institut fur Gesellschaftsforschung in Cologne (Germany). He has published several books and articles on public policy-making, network analysis and technological development. He is currently involved in a study on long-term institutional changes in the telecommunications sectors in the United States, Japan, Germany, Britain, France and Italy.

Jelle Visser is Associate Professor in Sociology at the University of Amsterdam (Netherlands), Department of Sociology. He has published several books and articles on trade unions, industrial relations, labour time reduction and social policies. His most recent book, *In Search of an Inclusive Unionism* (1990) was published by Kluwer. He is one of the coordinators of the DUES (Development of Union Systems in Western European Societies since 1945) project in Mannheim (Germany), and international consultant to the Organization for Economic Co-operation and Development in Paris (France).

Preface

The editors would like to thank the European Consortium for Political Research which first brought them together in a workshop on transnational forms of deregulation and reregulation in Paris in April 1989. Thanks to the ECPR, we then received funds for our own workshop on organized interests and the transnational dimension which we co-directed in Rimini in September 1990 during the conference on 'The New Europe'. Second drafts of papers collected in this volume were then presented during a meeting at Teesside Polytechnic in June 1991. The generous support of its Department of Health, Social and Policy Studies, which provided us with outstanding hospitality, contributed significantly to the final version of this volume.

1
Introduction: Organized Interests and the Transnational Dimension

Justin Greenwood, Jürgen R. Grote and Karsten Ronit

This book is about organized interests and the transnational dimension. It is about complex and reciprocal influences exerted between organized interests and processes of economic and political internationalization.

A very topical expression of the internationalization of markets and policies is the drive to create a single European market, and all of the contributions in this volume address the organized interests–EC dialectic. Yet our choice to highlight this specific issue neither came about by accident, nor was influenced by the current countdown to 1992 alone. The forces of economic internationalization may well be influenced in some domains by the actions of organized interests, and the material presented by 1992 provides the opportunity for illustrative and topical case studies. This may well increase our understanding of the processes of economic internationalization *per se*. Bookshelves are sagging under the weight of studies around the theme of '1992' and the completion of the internal market under the Single European Act. Yet amidst this explosion of print concerning the economic, political, strategic and management dimensions of 1992, relatively little attention is being paid to the impact of organized interests upon the 'Europeanization' of markets and politics, and, in turn, of the effects of such 'Europeanization' on organized interests. However, in undertaking this exercise we do not assume that studying organized interests at the level of the Community can, or should, be an end in itself. Interest associations are but one amongst a vast set of alternative governance mechanisms (Campbell et al., 1991; Schmitter, 1991).

It is a relatively easy task to chart the increase of Euro interest groups. Butt Philip, for instance, records some 300 in 1970 (Butt Philip, 1985a) while Grote found 654 in 1986 (Grote, 1989b). The Commission has been keen to see representative outlets with which to reciprocate since the 1950s (Butt Philip, 1985a), and remains today anxious to accelerate the formation of these. Thus, there were some 429 groups formally recognized by the Commission in 1980 (Grote, 1990) and 525 in 1990 (Mazey and Richardson, 1991). Kirchner (1986a) has interpreted 'interest group development at the European Community level as an indicator of integration'. However, the issue here concerns more than just the sheer volume and growth of interest group activity, or the simple equation between volume and possible output dynamics, but rather the dialectic of influence between representative outlets and other forces of internationalization. More than this, however, it is our contention that representative interest outlets should be regarded in a much wider sense than the traditional idea of an 'interest group' as a formal association. Although these outlets are concentrated in the functional business domain, our concern also has social and territorial dimensions. Another idea is that the tools we have traditionally used to recognize expressions of interests at the national level should be set aside, perhaps temporarily, in the hope of taking a fresh look at the transnational dimension. In part, this is a recognition that the transnational level will exert a qualitatively different set of dynamics from those of the national level. In this respect, we cast our net as wide as possible by including as representative interest outlets those collectives best described as associational, whether 'peak', 'sectoral' or other domain based; coalitions, clubs, clans and networks (Schmitter, 1990); and individual firms, which, when of sufficient size, can themselves possess resources far greater than some EC member states. Thus, while Lanzalaco (chapter 6), and Visser and Ebbinghaus (chapter 7) elaborate on the prospects for building encompassing European peak associations of capital and labour, and on the emergence of interorganizational agreements, Schneider (chapter 2), Greenwood and Ronit (chapter 3) and Cawson (chapter 4) concentrate on arrangements in individual sectors. Grote, instead, analyses the organizational formats of an intersectoral category of associations, namely those populating the policy domain of small firms (chapter 5). Together, these display a rich diversity in the associability of organized interests.

Another characteristic of the contributions is that none is exclusively concerned with the analysis of one level alone, be it the subnational, national or European. Elsewhere, there have been attempts to argue that the important focus is not the European level of organization, which itself presents some important obstacles to collective action, but more the way national interests respond to the enhanced competence of the EC (Averyt, 1977; Grant, 1990; Sargent, 1985; 1987). This is an argument which we would reject as an unsustainable generalization, but would nevertheless wish to

retain national as well as subnational elements among the ingredients, as well as the collective 'Euro strategy'.

Traditions and Approaches to the Study of European Interest Groups

The tradition within this volume is partly one within the broad area
of 'interest group theory'. This is an exciting area within itself,
particularly given the new challenges posed by economic internationalization, and in this respect the volume is also an attempt to
'bring the interest group dimension back in'. The concept of 'private
interest government', for instance, has mainly been applied to the
national level; much less to the transnational level. However, the
transnational dimension of such a study is inevitably linked to areas
such as integration theory, international politics and international
organizations, organization theory and state theory. Contributions
on the European or transnational dimension of interest groups can
be found under such labels. However, there is not yet any coherent
or established tradition or common research agenda to test or
proceed from. Rather, there are a number of disparate contributions, broadly split between integration theory (including European
studies and international relations), and organized collective action
theory derived from organization theory. These branches have to
some extent pooled their resources to examine the phenomena we
are now considering (see, for instance, Caporaso, 1979; Keohane,
1984), although there is still some scope for a text drawing upon this
tradition, particularly since the passage of the Single European Act.

There is certainly a tradition of studying interest groups at the
European level. The first shot came from neo-functionalist theory.
It was anticipated that groups could play a significant role in
propelling integration, and that they would contribute to the 'spill
over' of integration into other domains and sectors, partly with the
idea that one step paved the way for the next. The possibility was
raised of this compensating for the lack of direct contacts between
EC institutions and the citizens of member states, and strengthening
the role of the Commission vis-à-vis Council and the European
Parliament by relying on, and exchanging information with,
transnational groups (Haas, 1958, 1964). The degree of how
automatically this 'spill over' effect was supposed to work has been
discussed ever since, and it has been argued that factors such as
deliberate political actions and leadership must be duly taken into
account (Lindberg and Scheingold, 1970). In this way, doubts about
the 'spill over' effects have been raised.

There have been a number of other attempts to try to investigate the role of interest groups in the internationalization of markets and policies in the shape of the EC. Some of these exercises have the character of mapping out parts of the (mainly) associational landscape – undoubtedly a most valuable task – without deliberately attempting to test the existing but sparse literature, or developing a new one (Butt Philip, 1985a; Kirchner and Schwaiger, 1981; Meynaud and Sidjanski, 1971). Others have voiced scepticism concerning the emergence of a too autonomous bureaucracy (Caporaso, 1974), and/or have emphasized the strong role of national associations, explicitly or implicitly (Averyt, 1977; Grant, 1990; Sargent, 1985, 1987; Schmitter, 1990; Streeck, 1989b). Here, we would share the focus of those such as Platzer who have sought to focus upon the dialectics between national and transnational interest representation (Platzer, 1984). A clear focus of this volume is thus to analyse which levels play the most important part, to clarify why a shift has taken place, and the conditions under which this has emerged.

There have been difficulties in assessing the importance of associations. It seems likely, for instance, that the role of peak associations of business and of organized labour has been somewhat overstated (see, for instance, Meynaud and Sidjanski, 1971; von Voss, 1980). But this is also a result of the general optimism of the role of interest groups found in neo-functionalism. Our analysis shows that the peak associations do have a role to play, but present in all the chapters is a recognition that less grand levels of aggregation are politically active too. The emphasis put upon encompassingness, intraorganizational coordination and control, hierarchical order in the classical sense of neo-corporatism can only partly be found here, in that the collection of chapters provides evidence of a wide variety of appropriate responses.

Although the difficultes of the 'spill over' hypothesis of neo-functionalism led to a decline in fashionability of the theory, there may be some grounds for guarded optimism in the renewed recognition of the value of a recast neo-functionalism (Keohane and Hoffman, 1990). At the heart of this must be a recognition of the substantial differences that can occur between domains and sectors, rather than in expecting a simple 'spill over' effect. In this respect, it is one of the ambitions of this volume to challenge some recent tendencies to generalize about relations and processes between regulatory authority and interest groups on the EC level, whether they are characterized as 'pluralist' or 'corporatist' in character. Perhaps surprisingly, a number of those who have put forward the 'pluralist' hypothesis have been those associated with the neo-corporatist tradition (Grant, 1989, 1990; Sargent, 1987; Schmitter,

1990; Streeck, 1989b). Paradoxically, references have been made by writers associated with the neo-pluralist school to a 'quasi-corporatist' relationship between farming interests and DG VI (Agriculture) (Butt Philip, 1983a, 1985a; Lodge and Valentine, 1980; Mazey and Richardson, 1991).

There are a number of grounds for challenging generalized claims about relations and processes between regulatory authority and interest groups on the EC level. One is that both neo-corporatism and pluralism lack a theory of the 'state', and generalized claims to processes being one thing or the other can therefore not be sustained. Generalized claims of the 'pluralism at the EC' type are particularly surprising, in that both classical and neo-pluralism variants stress the fragmentation of the state; here, pluralism has been characterized as an 'anti theory' (Jordan, 1990), and to be regarded more as an 'image' (Cox, in Jordan, 1990). We would also regard as unconvincing any attempt to revive the 'macro corporatism' once popular in the 1970s, which focuses attention on the tripartite relationships between peak representatives of capital, labour and the state (Streeck and Schmitter, 1991). From this emerges another challenge, namely that the focus and value of neo-corporatism since the 1970s has been in explaining sector-level arrangements, carrying with it the recognition of the extent to which arrangements can vary in differing domains. Indeed, it is clear from the studies presented in this volume that arrangements do differ considerably at the European level. Grote (chapter 5), Lanzalaco (chapter 6) and Visser and Ebbinghaus (chapter 7), for instance, do not find much evidence either for the emergence of private interest government, or for that of corporatist forms of intermediation. However, Greenwood and Ronit (chapter 3) and Cawson (chapter 4) demonstrate that neo-corporatist-style relationships involving expressions of organized interests do exist in certain domains or sectors at the EC. That is, there are exchange- and power-dependence relationships involving private interests, organized by an agency in the economic division of labour, and EC institutions; and that such a relationship extends into the territories of policy formulation and implementation, involving some element of the 'private' interest 'crossing the boundary' and becoming 'part of the state'. From here the next task is to seek to understand why differing arrangements seem to prevail.

The 'pluralism at the EC' thesis represents also a prevailing view of Euro interest associations being weak 'federations of federations', often unable to agree and act upon meaningful common positions (Averyt, 1977; Grant, 1989, 1990; Kirchner and Schwaiger, 1981; Sargent, 1987). There may well be a number of illustrations of this, but there are also examples where 'super federations' (federations of federations) can act coherently and decisively (see, for instance, chapter 3). In addition to this challenge, however, is the evidence from a number of chapters which are illustrative of neo-corporatist relationships in domains where the representative format is not the 'super federation' but one which approximates to one of the variety of formats already identified. Taken together, these not only provide an important challenge to the 'pluralism at the EC thesis', but are also illustrative of the symbiotic relationship between the EC and interest groups. In drawing attention to the importance of this dimension, we are seeking to demonstrate its contribution to understanding the processes at work in the internationalization of markets and policies.

Although the emphasis has been more upon national and cross-national research, it is clear from the brief references so far that there have been important works in the tradition of neo-corporatism which have given importance to the international dimension. Kreile, for instance, in comparing policy networks of foreign economic policy in West Germany and Japan, related the effectiveness of such policy to the existence of corporatist patterns of policy formation (Kreile, 1978). Another, more comprehensive study raised questions concerning whether foreign policy decisions would be affected by the degree of neo-corporatist intermediation within modern industrial societies; whether there are characterizations of international relations involving the interpenetration of states and encompassing interest associations; and whether such neo-corporatist elements would be more capable of promoting consensual forms of international relations than other varieties which exclude organized interests (Forndran, 1983). On the transnational (European) level, there has however been a shortage of work done on collective action (Greenwood and Ronit, 1991a, b). Nevertheless, some studies have usefully applied the neo-corporatist perspective to transnational arrangements at the meso level. Here, we would mention work by Kenis on the Community's multi-fibre agreement (Kenis, 1986); the analysis by Kenis and Schneider in characterizing the Community as a corporate actor in its external relations in chemical control; and Grunert's study of associational responses to the restructuring of the steel sector (Grunert, 1987). The Kenis/Schneider corporate actor model is a debate to which we return later in this Introduction in the context of conceiving the nature of the EC itself, but for the present context it appears to be too strongly tailored to the specificity of foreign relations to be of value. The Grunert study, on the other hand, is of some importance to us, because it anticipates some of the arguments brought forward by the contributors to this volume.

Grunert conducted a comprehensive study of European steel crisis management in the 1970s and 1980s, demonstrating that 'the institutional framework and the decision-making process in Community steel policy is eminently suited to reveal the neo-corporatist pattern of procedure at a supranational level' (Grunert, 1987: 295).

In part, this was attributed to the substantial regulatory capacities with which the Commission was endowed under the terms of the European Coal and Steel Community (ECSC) Treaty; to the search for cooperative solutions in the political climate of the era concerned; and because corporatist arrangements already existing at the level of domestic states could be extended to the supranational level without too many difficulties. Also of importance was that the steel crisis

> definitely furthered neo-corporatist traits in the structural and behavioural patterns both at national and – even more so – at supranational level. The Commission also succeeded in exploiting favourable institutional conditions and strengthened neo-corporatist tendencies in its management both by the substance as well as by the way in which its policy was transmitted. Both have to be regarded as elements promoting integration. (Grunert, 1987: 298)

Grunert's study is of particular interest because it may be possible to compare the powers of the Commission in this instance with those it is assuming in some other, mainly growth, sectors. Our starting point is to begin at the level of analysing particular policy domains and sectors, but without running into the functionalist trap of predicting 'spill overs' of any kind, be they pluralist or corporatist in nature. In this sense, we are not concerned with forecasting the likely future course of the integration process, although particular kinds of arrangements may prevail in domains or sectors which might increase our understanding of the dynamics likely to contribute to particular types of policy processes or of collective forms of action addressed to the transnational level. Thus, our interest is not to prove the existence and prevalence of either pluralist or corporatist forms of interest intermediation at the level of the overall Community system, but rather to show how associations may insert themselves into the more widely known and appreciated mechanisms of sectoral governance, such as markets, hierarchies, communities and public authorities.

At the national level, the contribution of interest groups to policy domains has been well recognized. Indeed, no modern government can govern without the assistance of organized interests. The reasons for this have been well documented. They include the dependence of governments upon the expertise of private interests; their dependence upon them for policy implementation; their need for cooperation in order to facilitate governance; and the 'overload' of government. These factors give rise to a number of power-dependence relationships, in that power is essentially a concept of resource exchanges. There is no reason why these power dependencies cannot equally apply to the European level. Although transnational arrangements cannot be predicted by applying what is known about exchanges between governments and interests at the national level, there would appear to be little to prevent a fruitful hypothesis about power dependencies arising from the relationships between these parties at the transnational level.

Internationalization and the Single European Act

The Single European Act (SEA) seeks to give expression to one of the original intentions of the Treaty of Rome. One of the principle aims of the SEA is enshrined in Article 8A and defines for the first time what a common market actually is. Article 8A provides that:

> the internal market shall comprise an area without internal frontiers in which the free movement of goods, persons, services and capital is ensured in accordance with the provisions of this Treaty.

The impetus provided by political leadership, as well as by more direct economic forces, itself provides a challenge to the neo-functionalist concept of the 'spill over' effect. Beyond this, the creation of an internal market has required dismantling, abolition or revision of a large number of national regulation devices. Although political change often lags economic change, our preference is nevertheless to regard politics and markets as a dialectical process rather than to posit a one-way influence of economics upon politics. Similarly, the issue as to whether the European level represents either deregulation or reregulation is a complex one. It cannot be seen in straightforward terms of capital turning to the transnational level for 'deregulation', and states and labour interests seeking 'reregulation'. At its most simple level, this can be seen in the embrace of 'deregulation' by some left leaning parties in EC member states. Another distinction which is difficult to sustain is that between types of 'interests', in that sometimes states have sponsored certain industrial concerns, or where responsibilities are shared in certain policy domains, or where there is some other form of mutual dependency relationship. Where there is a recognition of common interests, a dual strategy can be effected for influencing events in Brussels by working both through national government channels in Europe and private interest channels, both domestically and transnationally.

Cerny likewise counsels against thinking in terms of 'deregulation' and 'reregulation' at the transnational level (Cerny, 1991). In essence, his argument is that so-called 'deregulatory' responses have themselves created new sets of 'reregulation', and might more accurately be thought of as restructuring. Similarly, there are 'knock on' effects (often unseen) of making various changes which may themselves lead to a new set of demands, particularly as a result of the increasing interconnectedness of private and public life. Other dimensions to be considered include a change likely to be effected in political relationships between interests and regulators, while another concerns the creation of new dynamics within international capital itself. Thus 'deregulation becomes a complex maze, with sectoral, macroeconomic and transnational consequences far removed from the original intentions of policymakers' (Cerny, 1991: 27).

It is in this sense that we believe that changes incorporated by the Single European Act ought to be regarded. Streeck maintains that European integration will become linked to deregulation through mutual recognition (Streeck, 1989b, 1990b), a position that seems to be partly confirmed by the findings of chapter 7. Majone, on the other hand, regards mutual recognition as an insufficient basis for the achievement of an internal market (Majone, 1989a, b), partly confirmed by the sectoral chapters in this volume (chapters 2, 3, 4).

European integration and the formation of encompassing European interest groups is not a smooth process equally penetrating all sectors. Wallace draws a distinction between informal integration, involving economic development and technological progress, and formal integration where deliberate political decisions are taken to achieve something more specific (Wallace, 1990). The drive to create an internal market contains both elements, but the extent to which these two forces are present differs within and between sectors and other types of domain. The chapters in this volume suggest that both formal and informal integration can be influenced by the actions of organized interests. This clearly differs for sectors and domains, and cannot be seen in the rather straightforward way suggested by early neo-functionalist theory. Rather, an examination needs to be made of each set of arrangements as they arise, and in this respect this volume contains a series of selected studies of sectors, domains and regions, as well as categories such as 'capital', 'labour' and 'peak' levels. A recognition of this differentiation means that we are not able to, and thus do not, attempt predictions as to the future direction of the Community in the way of earlier neo-functionalist attempts.

Levels, Sectors and Territories

The Variety of Levels

The focus of neo-corporatist ideas has long been directed towards less grand levels of aggregation than nation states. One contribution which corporatist approaches have had to confront is the thesis of 'disorganized capitalism' provided by Lash and Urry (1987). This posits the breakdown of organization which is implicit in neo-corporatist theory, and draws attention to the level of disorganization, competetiveness and 'deregulation' on the one hand, and weakening unionization of the labour movement and vanishing labour party hegemony in most of Western Europe on the other. In an article published in 1990, Schmitter, who doubts that this reversal has been as dramatic as suggested, suggests that reports about the generalized demise of corporatism may be quite premature, and that organized capitalism may still be a more likely outcome than disorganized, that is, neo-liberal, capitalism (Schmitter, 1990). The rethinking being required to solve this puzzle 'involves a shift in the level of analysis away from an exclusive concentration on the national economy both downward to particular "sectors" and upwards to supranational and global "regimes"' (1990: 10).

This raises the possibility of identifying a number of 'levels'· at which interests are voiced and negotiated in a European context. There are a number of related dimensions to these. A starting point is to distinguish between the global, the European economic space, the EC, the national, the regional and the subregional.

The transnational level is more than simply an additional layer. Loyalties guaranteed over time in national associations can hardly be transferred to transnational associations. Coherence in European associations is thus challenged to another degree and we cannot simply expect that the idea of designing federal associations, if it works in a national context, can be applied to a new and higher level. This does not necessarily mean that associations cannot be established, for they may well be formed and then perform nothing but ritual functions and have fraternal purposes (chapter 4).

Grote (chapter 5) shows how a 'prime example' of a private interest government, the case of German Handwerk, might make impossible the emergence of similar patterns of governance of the small firm economy at the level of the Community. In turn, this raises interesting questions about whether corporatist-like forms of interest intermediation in Brussels have to be understood as an extension of existing patterns of this kind in some of the member states, or whether domestic arrangements would have to be dismantled to enable effective participation at the transnational level. Similarly Grote, Visser and Ebbinghaus (chapter 7) can see few signs 'of a remake at the transnational level of what is now disappearing at the national level'. Greenwood and Ronit, however, find that transnational arrangements mirror national ones in the case of pharmaceuticals (chapter 3), resulting partly from common features in the regulation of medicine supply across member states. As such, this is similar to the case of steel described by Grunert (see p. 7 above).

Another way of approaching levels is to consider the macro, involving peak associations, the meso (involving domains, sectors and regions) and the micro (involving individual, larger firms or local areas in responding to their specific concerns). These latter levels are to some extent interwoven with the first (that is, territorial) in interest organization. For instance, sector associations can influence the internal market when aggregated on a national, EC, European or international level.

The existence of a transnationally organized peak or sectoral association cannot be regarded in each case as an absolute prerequisite for successfully influencing Community decisions. This can be achieved in a number of ways. A domestically organized association with a sufficient degree of encompassingness in terms of membership and coverage of issues might suffice for achieving access to EC decision making centres and for co-determining the latter's outcomes. More than that, an exclusive focus on associations as the most efficient organizational device to capture regulatory agencies at EC level, or, less negatively, to influence the directorates of the Commission in the interest of a specific category of firms, would be quite misplaced. Collective action by business takes various forms and this variety, we maintain, is even larger in the case of the Community where public institutions have to cope with an incomparably higher number of 'rent seekers' which try to capture special treatment than in the case of national agencies. The decision by business (labour is a different case) to combine in the form of a transnational association is neither the only available rational option nor is it determined by the relevance of a particular policy domain or the capacity of EC institutions to regulate markets in specific product areas or domains. As Schmitter has shown, the range of options for business to solve its collective action problems include such strange animals as clubs, clans, networks, alliances, hierarchies, communities, private interest governments, joint ventures and the like (Schmitter, 1990). Business interest associations are but one among an even greater set of domain governance mechanisms built up to achieve competitive advantage on economic and political markets.

Schmitter's idea of 'supranational and global regimes' is of course quite different from a disaggregated focus involving sectors, large firms and regions. One qualification we have already made is that between different forms of interest aggregation, from associations to large firms. It follows from an identification of these that an attempt to posit a kind of 'mega corporatism' at the EC where the focus is upon the macro level of peak associations would be misleading. Similarly, there would be few today seeking to examine interest intermediation at the EC level where the focus is restricted to tripartite arrangements involving exchanges between peak organizations of business and labour. Given that it is clearly possible to discern a number of quite different trends and arrangements in different domains (Butt Philip, 1985a; Grant, 1989, 1990; Greenwood and Jordan, forthcoming; Greenwood and Ronit, 1991a, b; Jordan, 1991a; Kirchner and Schwaiger, 1981; Mazey and Richardson, 1991; Sargent, 1985, 1987; Sidjanski, 1982), it is not possible to identify processes at the EC as one type or another. Nevertheless, an examination of interest intermediation at the EC does require at least an inquiry into events at differing levels, and in this respect two chapters in this volume (6 and 7) include an examination of peak Euro associations. Lanzalaco (chapter 6), and Visser and Ebbinghaus (chapter 7) make clear that examples of exchanges involving peak associations of business, labour and EC institutions, cannot be regarded as forming some kind of macro system, nor would the level of organization evident in peak associations make this possible. There have been, in fact, a number of attempts to posit the existence of a Euro tripartism centred on the Economic and Social Committee (ECOSOC) (Lodge and Herman, 1980). In the 1990s, the continued marginalization of the Economic and Social Committee within the EC would seem to make the proposition of an emerging tripartism unsustainable, although there has been at least one recent attempt to suggest just this (Andrews, 1991). Visser and Ebbinghaus show in chapter 7 how European business associations are not authorized by their national membership to represent employer interests of capitalists; business will thus be more likely to pursue their sectoral interests as producers, rather than their class interests as employers (Lanzalaco and Schmitter, 1992). There may thus be exchanges between domain/sector based interests and the ECOSOC which are worth considering as exchanges and influences, particularly over points of detail or more specialized issues. It is unlikely that positions on the ECOSOC would continue to be taken up by interests if it did not provide some degree of access to policy processes in the EC.

A somewhat different question is the idea of the EC as representing a kind of system as a whole. Wallace illustrated attempts to interpret the EC in terms of an 'overall regime within which Euro governments cooperate to manage a wide range of issues within an established framework of rules, norms of behaviours, and decision-making procedures' (Wallace et al., 1983: 404), quoting Stanley Hoffman as one of the proponents of this kind of approach. These attempts have been criticized, not least because of the qualitative differences between intergovernmental collaboration on the one hand, and the idea of a Community with significant capability of generating (albeit disparate) policy-making processes (Wallace et al., 1983). What it might, however, be possible to do is to conceive of sectoral policy regimes, and territorial policy regimes, within the wider context of the EC. Lindberg (1990) has interpreted the transnational European Monetary System (EMS) as an example for the transformation of a sectoral governance regime at the level of the member states of the EC. In very general terms, the first three chapters of this book describe 'sectoral policy regimes', while the last three deal with forms of 'territorial policy regimes'.

Regions and Small Firms
Within the existing nation states and within the Community regions may be a disaggregating factor complicating interest aggregation at a common European level. It has been demonstrated that regions may be of importance in organizing interests (Coleman and Jacek, 1989a), although strong variations prevail. In this respect, as with sectors, it seems to make little sense to investigate these systems in their entirety.

It would appear that regimes can be conceived of as transnational, whereas others can be characterized as domestic in that some continue to have their organizational and regulatory 'epicentres' at the domestic level while in others comprehensive systems of rules and norms may have been established and, in some cases, been legally institutionalized at the level of the Community. These can afford additional points of access for interests to the Commission.

In territorial policy regimes, the question of cohesion and disparities (of the single market) does not only arise with regard to the relative position, strength and property of individual sectors but to the location and industrial resource endowment of European territories like regions and subregional units. Of particular importance in this context is also the average size of firms populating these territories. There are dramatic examples of regions which are not only characterized by high concentration rates of declining sectors, but, in addition, by firm sizes which do not reach the critical minimum necessary for staying in the market. Regional properties of this kind are very unevenly distributed across the member states of the Community (Grote, 1992a). In chapter 5, Grote demonstrates that responses of organized business in the small firm domain to processes of international integration crucially depend upon the type of 'territorial policy regime' chosen for achieving compliance within the domain. Cases such as the German one, where these regimes appear to be strongly regionalized and backed up by comprehensive national regulations, may make the emergence of a European policy for that domain difficult, if not impossible.

Grote does not advance a 'Europe of the regions' type hypothesis, and indeed the prospects for such an arrangement seem to be rather remote (Anderson, 1990b). However, he does see a transformation of nations into regions of the supranational EC, who, together with subnational regions, form a supranational economy. Due to the uneven endowment with institutional assets, and the resulting differences in forms of interest aggregation of them, Grote's chapter suggests it would be misleading to expect organized business, and particularly associations representing small artisan firms, to converge at the transnational level. Encouragement to associative action on the basis of (small) firm size is thus neutralized as a result of cross-national and cross-regional incompatibilities, whether economic, organizational or cultural.

Large Firms

Levels disaggregated below the macro also include the micro, mainly involving the study of political action by individual firms or subregions. Our preference is to see large multinational firms as significant and collective actors, particularly as they can command more resources than some member states. It follows that the 'micro' is thus an important level of interest intermediation to study in the transnational context.

There is in fact a rich tradition of studying the impact of multinational firms upon national autonomy, particularly in the less developed nations of the Third World. Here, the focus has been upon the manipulation of prices and trust regulation, labour conditions, dumping, and interference with national planning. There have also been studies of political action taken by multinational firms in western economies (Bornschier and Stamm, 1990; Braithwaite, 1984; Martinelli, 1991), although the focus has generally been much more upon the internationalization of the economy than the internationalization of politics.

There are examples, such as the Vredeling directive, where the EC has aimed policies at multinationals across sectors. These corporations, which seem to have had a significant impact on propelling the whole internal market project, have thus been challenged to accommodate new patterns of policy. So, the 'corporate elite' approach has pointed to the existence of networks and cross-sectoral coordination at the cross-national, and even European, levels (Fennema and Schijf, 1985; van der Pilj, 1989), but without considering the dialectics between organized interests and the EC. It may well be that reciprocal relations between single large corporations and various EC institutions could be thought of in terms of 'micro corporatism', that is a level of interest intermediation between the state and privately organized interests. In chapter 4, this level is clearly evident.

The value of a disaggregated focus involving sectors, regions and firms is that it can illustrate the diversity of dynamics involving organized interests. Differing arrangements and differing organizational formats clearly produce differing outcomes, although it may be possible to detect which sets of arrangements might influence outcomes in particular sets of directions. In this volume, the 'sector ' and 'firm' studies are all devoted to the high technology domain. These are: telecommunications (chapter 2); pharmaceuticals and biotechnology (chapter 3); consumer electronics (chapter 4). These are domains involving both informal integration (with particular respect to technological development), and formal integration where the EC has itself established major scientific and technological programmes (Eureka, RACE, FAST, SPRINT, VALUE, SCIENCE, ECLAIR, FLAIR, HUG, COMETT, BAP, BRIDGE). These programmes partly reflect the importance which the EC attaches to new technologies as strategic concerns, particularly vis-à-vis the United States and Japan. They help illustrate the example where high technology domains might be thought of as a genuine transnational policy domain regime. The EC has an overall negative balance of trade of -0.67% (EFPIA, 1988), a deficit which would be of colossal proportions without the contributions of new technologies where, in some domains, Europe leads the way. Consequently, a significant amount of formal integration effort has been devoted to areas involving new technologies. Peterson (1991), noting the greater involvement of the EC in high tech domains than with the chemicals industry, writes of an EC level 'meso corporatist technology policy', at considerable advantage to such firms in terms of the receipt of public funds. The combination of both informal and formal integration forces thus appears to make the new technologies ideal candidates through which to study both the impact of organized interests upon the internationalization of markets and policies, and vice versa.

Another reason for examining arrangements in high technology domains is that they are areas where political inputs are rapidly developing, and in some cases unfolding before our eyes as the technologies themselves mature. For instance, applications involving the new biotechnologies only emerged in the 1980s as arrangements for the internal market were unfolding. Because states and scientists had played a significant role in the development of biotechnology, organized interests had hardly progressed beyond the status of loose and fragmented federations which only partly involved industrial concerns. Consequently, the important level of both development and organization has largely been the European one. The opportunity exists therefore to study developments now as they are evolving, which may itself provide clues as to the nature of organized interest aggregations at the European level in the future. In the case of biotechnologies, the full range of interest aggregations is evident, but the important point is that the significant ones appear not to be unions of national interests, but more genuine European (that is, transnational) forums (chapter 3). This may suggest that there is a need to leave behind the traditional baggage with which scholars have approached the organization of interests at the European level, where the focus is more upon the national level as a result of the perceived difficulties of collective action by a number of previously existing national federations. There are, however, high tech industries such as pharmaceuticals which are relatively well established, both in their operations and political representation structures, where a more traditional pattern of organized interest activity can be observed. This means that high technology concerns provide the opportunity for comparative studies which display the full range of responses by organized interests. These range from the Euro 'super federation' where national strategies have been reproduced at the European level (chapter 3) to 'policy networks' in telecommunications (chapter 2), and, at the other end of the spectrum, large multinational firms who can be considered collective actors by virtue of their size (chapter 4).

One recent study has claimed that the role of interest groups in high technology domains is negligible (Hilpert, 1991). Here, the role of the state has been postulated to be of such importance that interest groups are assigned an almost negligible role. This is a claim which does not appear to fit the evidence presented in the following three chapters. Nevertheless, it may reflect a more generalized tradition whereby the 'interest group dimension' has not been fully taken into account in high tech domains (Audretsch, 1989; Duchene and Shepherd, 1987; Zysman, 1983). There are, however, some contributions where the associational dimension has at least been considered, such as that by Sharp (Sharp, 1985a, b; Sharp and Holmes, 1989).

An EC 'State'?

One of the main interlocutors of interest groups is the state. This immediately presents a problem on the EC level, in that it is clearly not the case that a new and compeletely formed 'state' has evolved. Policy implementation, for instance, rests largely in the hands of member states, and it may thus be better to conceive of the EC as an aggregation of member states with representative transnational institutions. Nevertheless, the process of integration is undoubtedly constructing a powerful transnational agency which can act as an interlocutor with interest groups, through the Commission, in ways resembling those occurring in nation states.

The most important starting point is to recognize the diversity between and within the different institutions which comprise the EC, and in this respect it does not seem helpful to think of the EC as a whole as a kind of 'corporate actor', or indeed as some form of unitary state. The European Parliament, Economic and Social Committee, Council and Commission are of course very different types of agencies, whose approaches and perspectives contrast markedly. In agencies such as the Commission, perspectives also vary markedly. There are examples of these in this volume. Chapter 3 emphasizes the importance of divisions between DG XXII (Science, Research and Development), DG III (Internal Market and Industrial Affairs) on the one hand, and DG XI (Environment, Consumer Protection and Nuclear Safety) on the other in domains such as new technology, which are not always resolved by attempts at coordination such as the creation of task forces. In chapter 7, Visser and Ebbinghaus show how the compartmentalization of the Commission into 23 separate Directorates General (DGs) works to the disadvantage of collective labour movements. Similarly, Peters suggests that 'the 23 Directorates General appear to be developing their own organizational cultures and approaches to policy' (1990: 38).

These differences once again commend the advantages of adopting a disaggregated approach to the study of interest interme-diation and the transnational dimension, in that arrangements have to be examined separately for each case. In turn, this means that the uneven process will exert different dynamics upon the way in which private interests are organized, and the impact of private interests upon the integration process.

Kenis and Schneider (1987) have not conceived of the EC as a whole as a corporate actor, but have rather thought of parts of it acting in this way in relation to foreign policy, where the possession of resources and institutional self interest make it an actor in its own right on the international stage. This is a somewhat different type of debate from the one which we engage in here, and may be of value in conceiving EC interactions in this domain. However, expressions of self interest are difficult enough to conceive of in even the smallest units (Colebatch, 1991). 'Mission statements', for instance, can be articulated by an organization but may not carry effective meaning throughout the organization. Organization theorists like Salaman have shown how the articulated goals of an organization can represent little more than the goals of the few at its helm, whose task is to persuade other members of the organization that their personal goals coincide with collective organizational ones (Salaman, 1979). Since it is possible to conceive of those within an organization as having very different interests, it is in fact rather misleading to talk of collective goals. The larger and less unitary in purpose the organization is, the more potential there would appear to be for such conflicts to arise, and for disagreements to occur over both the meaning and implementation of 'goals'. Firms, for instance, can easily specify an overriding goal – profit maximization. Public sector agencies, on the other hand, may have some difficulty in stating an overriding 'goal'. The Commission, for instance, will have a variety of ambitions which embrace the interests of firms, workers, citizens and consumers. Some of these multi-goals may well conflict. It would thus seem unhelpful to conceive of the EC, or indeed the Commission, as a corporate actor.

Expressions of 'rational action' are also difficult to apply to the Commission in terms of interorganizational politics. Exchanges between member states and interests, member states and the EC, interests and the EC all contribute to a rich diversity of experiences. One expression of this is the growth in the number of advisory committees of the Commission, which now number 1,000 and include some 5,000 representatives from member states and private interests (CEC, 1990a). There have been some bizarre examples of these, such as the Committee on Management of Bananas (Grote, 1989b). The corresponding increase in interest representation is likely to contribute to the fragmentation of the Commission's actions. For instance, a significant level of exchange may be between national officials working in the Commission, and domestic interests, private and public. Similarly, there is evidence of private exchanges with national permanent delegations at COREPER resulting in influence being exerted through the European Council (Greenwood and Jordan, forthcoming). Indeed, the very premise of interest groups exchanging with authorities at the European level presupposes a variety of exchanges which would make the notion of the Commission as a corporate actor difficult to sustain. As we have already identified, these varied exchanges can lead to a variety of different outcomes.

A recent contribution by Colebatch warns against thinking in terms of distinct players such as 'the EC' or 'business' (Colebatch, 1991). Rather, there is an interpenetration of business and regulatory agencies, in which 'government' becomes an arena for action rather than a distinct single actor. This approach rather discourages us from thinking of organizations as coherent, instrumental and hierarchical. Although we cannot carry this argument as far as the level of organization of a business interest group, where a degree of coherence can arise as a result of unitary purpose (the pursuit of profit), there is more than a ring of truth about it as applied to the EC, or indeed to the Commission.

It is clear that the EC must be considered as a fragmented arena. Nevertheless, these points should not be taken as implying that the EC is somehow directionless. Acts of informal and formal integration, for instance, can collectively create the conditions for economic internationalization, and, no matter how incomplete, 1992 will see the creation of an internal market more complete than it otherwise would have been without the passage of the Single European Act. Indisputably, the EC now contains a higher degree of competence than before the passage of the SEA. However, the relationship between this and an increase in the activity of interest groups at the European level cannot be automatically assumed *per se*. Here, Jordan makes the point that participation by interests in collective forums occurs not so much as a result of predicted 'rational action' but through the possibility of a sponsorship or clientelistic relationship with bureaucratic authority (Jordan, 1991a).

There have been a number of deliberate attempts to coordinate the activities of the Commission in some domains, such as high level working groups comprising the relevant DGs in the Commission. One example of this is given in chapter 3, in the case of biotechnology. Once again, the point is not to expect a uniformly high or low level of coordination throughout domains. For instance, Agriculture and Fisheries have for years been forming parts of a coordinated EC policy whereas regulation of the likes of financial markets, transport and shipping are of more recent origin. One ingredient in this diversity is to study the groups who are themselves the targets of formal integration, that is, the actions of organized interests. It is clear from the evidence presented in this book that exchanges between the EC and interest groups do exert significant influences upon both policy domains and the organization of interests within that domain. This makes possible the a priori assertion of an agent with authority for interest groups to reciprocate with. Indeed, the neo-corporatist structures which have emerged in certain domains would not be possible without something like a 'state'. Whilst fragmented, the EC is certainly not directionless, and it is in these senses that the EC might be thought of as a reciprocating 'state' agent. Indeed, cohesion and comprehensiveness in transnationally organized associations will generally result where there are powerful public institutions (or competing private groups) against which established properties and power positions are to be defended, or with which reciprocation can occur in a mutually beneficial fashion.

Many of the chapters which follow particularly emphasize the 'logic of membership' of collective action. In part, this is because of the difficulty in conceiving of the concept of 'transnational stateness' at a time of institutional infancy. The patterns of 'logics of influence' are in part dependent upon the future form and nature of EC institutions, and in this sense the concluding chapter refers to some scenarios for the emergence of the new type of governance and domination represented by the Community. Schmitter has conceived of the EC

> as an extreme manifestation . . . of trends that are endemic to the modern state in advanced industrial societies and that are everywhere undermining its 'stateness'. From this perspective, the EC should be thought of as a proto-type, a sort of supranational testing ground for new forms of organized political domination that are also and already emerging at the national and subnational levels. (Schmitter, 1991: 3)

Here, part of the argument submits that different levels of government and governance, ranging from the subnational (provincial, regional, industrial districts etc.) through the national to newly emerging forms of transnational regimes, are confronted with essentially the same kinds of problem. The fact that the capacity of the traditional state to act in a unitarian fashion is currently in a process of dissolution – partly as a result of demand overload or of ungovernability, partly as one of increasing internationalization of core policy areas – does not imply that it would now re-emerge at alternative levels. The 'not anymore' of traditional forms of domination and rule does not correspond to a 'not yet' of this domination at other, particularly transnational levels. Governance at any of these levels may thus be conceptualized as a kind of simultaneous process of forces which are both disintegrative and integrative. Thus, we have attempted to avoid using models which have been offered to describe the Community, such as the idea of the EC as a system of intergovernmentalism (most recently, Cameron, 1990), which gives relatively little attention to the activity of supranational institutions, be it that of a new 'super state', or functional equivalent of the latter, which would be able to assume responsibility for an increasing number of policy domains and which would be based on new European identities and loyalties.

Actors, Associability and Access

The importance of disaggregation into domains, sectors, firms and territories to study interest intermediation and the transnational level is partly accounted for by the sheer range of types, and volume of players, involved. It is certainly a multi-player game, but the sheer number does not necessarily imply competitive relationships and pluralism.

A number of categories can be distinguished in the representation of private interests. A starting point is to distinguish between categories of private interests which are capital, labour and consumers. A study of their responses to economic internationalization in Europe partly reveals the range of actors involved, the types of associability and the access points to the transnational stage.

Capital

Perhaps unsurprisingly, 'capital' includes the most developed forms of political representation at the European level. The goal of firms is profit maximization, which provides capital with an overriding sense of unity and purpose within domains/sectors. Capital has a history of international movements and exchanges which have also provided an impetus to organization which goes beyond the national level. Multinational firms are actors which have developed experiences of exchanges with national and international regulators in the operation of markets. Economic cooperation can foster interaction and the establishment of codes of practice, both within and without associations. For these reasons, it would not seem unreasonable to expect capital as a whole to display the most sophisticated form of transnational interest representation. Where a sector is particularly concentrated there are also less actors to organize, and in these cases transnational representation may not be excessively complicated (but see chapter 4). On the other hand, it might be that collectives of business which experience difficulties at the trans-national level are those in domains where economic internationa-lization is weak.

The 'orthodox strategy' for national interests in securing a route to the European level was outlined by Averyt in 1977. This concerned the formation of Euro interest groups, partly encouraged by a Commission keen to liaise with single collectives of national interests. However, Averyt goes on to suggest that the problems posed by this – not least the difficulty of securing meaningful agreement upon the 'lowest common denominator' – meant that this had to be supplemented by direct relationships with national interest groups (Averyt, 1977). In this sense, both Averyt and Jordan posit the continued survival and vigour of national interests for European representation despite earlier attempts to organize collectively at the European level (Averyt, 1977; Jordan, 1991).

The same issue is approached by Sargent in a rather different way. Here, commenting on the experience of Britain's first decade of membership of the EC, Sargent talks of a 'learning curve' for interests where, although she found a concern to maximize available channels of influence, a distinct preference was found for using national government contacts (Sargent, 1987).

There are a number of reasons why interests should use the 'national route' to Europe:

1 The reliance upon member states for policy implementation affords considerable possibilities for influence. This has been extended with the offloading of public functions to private actors in a number of member states.
2 The national route represents very much the 'tried and tested' grounds for interests (Grant, 1989). The presence of long established 'policy communities' which all parties feel comfort-able with can be used for 'European' as well as 'domestic' concerns.
3 The national level is more amenable to smaller concerns. Having more than a token presence in Brussels is extremely expensive (Grant, 1990), and may not be a realistic option for many enterprises.
4 Large firms will often be valued at the national level as national champions, and can rely upon the support of national govern-ments.
5 There may be circumstances where it is easier, and perhaps essential, for national interests to act alone than with others. Here, Greenwood and Jordan use the example of national

agricultural interests, which are often in opposition to each other (Greenwood and Jordan, forthcoming).

6 Firms may be more concerned with losing their case in national capitals than in Brussels. If a case is lost with the national government the chances of winning in Brussels may be remote, particularly if the government concerned is lobbying for a counter position (van Schendelen, 1992).

7 Access to the Council can, in the main, be secured only through the national route.

8 There may be established networks between national governments, national interests and their citizens who work inside the Commission.

The importance of the 'national route' to Brussels has thus been emphasized amongst writers who have investigated the impact of organized interests upon EC policy-making and implementation. Here, the tendency has been to see Euro groups as weak, fragmented, unable to agree on meaningful common positions (Grant, 1989, 1990; Jordan, 1991b; Sargent, 1987; Schmitter, 1990; Streeck, 1989b), and whose existence is seen as more for purposes of fraternal contact (Grant, 1990). It is this view which has led to the rather premature generalization amongst many of these authors of policy processes being more 'pluralist' in character. There may well be some examples of the Euro 'super federation' (that is, federations of national federations) being unable to act convincingly, but there are nevertheless also examples of this format operating successfully. Interestingly, Grant himself provides an example of this, in the shape of the European Spice Association successfully excluding herbs and spices from the scope of amendments to the Unit Pricing Directive (Grant, 1989). Another, more illustrative, example is given in chapter 3. Here, the key components appear to be a multinational industry which faces similar issues throughout the economic environments in which it operates, enabling the replication of a near common national strategy to the EC; and the experience of an industry well rehearsed in international political action. Also underlying the 'pluralism at the EC thesis' is a view of neo-corporatist structures being dependent upon the development of the trade association, an issue which we have already disputed.

The importance of the national route appears in fact to have been somewhat overstated. At the very basic level is the idea that business is concerned to keep open a plurality of channels for political representation. The evidence of this book suggests that there is an increasing confidence and familiarity with the European level, and that the 'Brussels strategy' (that is, working through

European organizations or approaching EC agencies directly or thorough appointed agents) is increasingly being taken. The Commission can best be reached as a target through this route, and indeed it has previously expressed a preference for engaging with collective European voices rather than a series of national ones. It is not difficult to see why the Commission has been keen to see the formation of encompassing Euro groups since the 1950s (Butt Philip, 1985a). Some of the reasons will be familiar to scholars of policy communities at the national level – the possibility for expertise, information and cooperation in formulation and implementation with significant economic interests who contribute much to European economic performance. Other reasons, however, are either unique or more acute in relation to the European level. Although many governments face the problem of overload, there are only some 3,500 senior administrators in posts in EC institutions (Mazey and Richardson, 1991). This makes reciprocal relationships with interests a necessity rather than simply desirable, and in this sense there may be an increase in the number of self regulatory arrangements at the European level from the relatively small number which presently exist.

Another reason for the growth in importance of the Commission as a target for interests is because of the uncertainty of outcomes and loss of control by taking the national route, in that interests may be negotiated away at the Council of Ministers, through COREPER negotiations or ministerial exchanges. Interests are also less able to rely upon the exercise of a veto by their national government following the introduction of the majority voting procedure for matters concerned with the creation of an internal market.

It is, however, the enhanced competence of the Commission that provides one of the major reasons for the development of the 'Brussels strategy' among private interests. It is clearly not just the Commission which benefits in exchanges with interest groups, and interests are increasingly finding themselves involved in power-dependence relationships with the Commission. The depth of these may increase if Grote is correct in his assertion that there are signs that the Commission is increasingly becoming involved in policy implementation (Grote, 1989a, b). In a direct sense, the Commission is involved in policy implementation through referring cases concerning the observance of Directives to the European Court; more indirectly, it is involved through 'licensing' self regulatory agreements.

There are now increasing points of access with the Commission, as compared to a relatively inaccessible Council where there is no direct input for interests and where some national delegations are wary of exchanges with interests. Here, Mazey and Richardson, among others, comment that the Commission is a relatively open bureaucracy compared with those of some member states (Mazey and Richardson, 1991). This, too, must surely have influenced the development and attractiveness of the Brussels strategy, not least because it makes it amenable to a variety of forms of interest representation. Hence, it is quite possible for the range of non-associational actors identified (for example, individual firms and informal networks), as well as more formal and traditional aggregations of interests such as European-level interest groups, to develop fruitful reciprocal relationships (chapter 4).

It may be significant that domains which have developed in parallel with the enhanced competence of the EC display a greater use of the 'Brussels strategy' than they do of the domestic strategy (see, for instance, the case of biotechnology in chapter 3). This may well represent a pattern of the future, particularly where there are no significant levels of national interest organizations to inherit. Interestingly, the biotechnology domain contains one of the very first direct firm membership Euro forums, albeit a very peculiar type in that membership has until recently been by invitation only. It may well be that the direct membership Euro group will become a recognizable feature of interest intermediation at the European level.

Membership of Euro 'super federations' may well not be the ideal answer to a sector or domain's Euro needs for political representation, particularly if there is difficulty in acting beyond the 'lowest common denominator' position. Indeed, Olson has claimed that the most 'rational' perspective for the individual firm is not to join collective associations, but to 'free ride'. However, Jordan wonders whether Olson may in fact have 'over intellectualized' the membership decision (Jordan, 1991). A wide variety of benefits can accrue to the individual member of a collective group, not least in the implementation of policy (chapter 3) and in contact with the citizens of member states. Butt Philip argues that

> the Commission, for its part, both wants and needs contact with the many interest groups in Europe. It too needs information about the variety of positions and aspirations of Euro groups and national pressure groups, as well as factual information which may be slow in arriving from national governments. Such information will often be essential material upon which to construct proposals and policies which will have a community application. (Butt Philip, in Jordan 1991: 16)

Commenting on this, Jordan argues

if this is the spirit of the relationship that operates then the calculation of participation is likely to be skewed much more in favour of a membership than Olson presented. For little investment companies can expect to get the bureaucracy to act as its advocate; the bureaucracy is predisposed to assist. This surely pushes the logic towards participation. (Jordan, 1991b: 16)

Other benefits may not be so apparent. They include status (King, in Jordan, 1991); listening posts for likely developments (Grant, in Jordan, 1991); fraternal contact (Grant, 1990) and trading opportunities (Jordan, 1991b). Elsewhere, Jordan and McLaughlin (1991) have also identified another benefit of membership, namely the ability to influence the direction of the trade association in line with the interests of the firm. Such a dynamic may encourage membership of Euro groups, in that the costs of non-membership may be greater than the costs of joining. Such arguments can also be abstracted one level beyond firm membership decisions, that is to the 'super federation' made up of national associations. Similarly, the rapid development of the internal market may in fact mean that it is too costly for firms and associations, who may have remained members of super federations for 'fringe' reasons, not to be able to reach agreement on positions. Where there is near complete associational membership through the super federation, the benefits for both the Commission and the domain interests can be substantial in providing an effective mechanism of policy implementation. Here, the same advantages which apply to both parties in private interest government arrangements can operate (Baggott, 1986; Greenwood, 1988; Streeck and Schmitter, 1985).

There are also examples where firms, perceiving the Commission to look more favourably upon associational than individual firm contact (Sargent, 1987), act through 'front' or 'fig leaf' organizations which are more 'legitimating devices for the big firms rather than . . . powerful bodies in their own right' (chapter 4). In the case cited by Cawson, the industry concerned, consumer electronics, is highly concentrated. In these, where large firms are evident, a degree of divergence in Euro interest organizational format would appear to be possible, involving networks and informal alliances as well as large firms.

The increasing confidence of interests in using directly the European level – both as a target in the case of regulators/administrators and as a level of organization for themselves – is further illustrated by the increasing use of the European Parliament as a target for lobbying. In turn, this may reflect its increasing importance, particularly with the new cooperation procedure under the terms of the SEA where a second reading is provided for through the Parliament on a selected range of issues, most notably those connected with the internal market (Bates, 1990). Any position adopted by the Parliament requires a unanimous vote at the Council of Ministers to overturn it. The effect of this has been to increase the involvement of the Parliament to prevent conflicts arising as late as the second stage, and in this sense the Parliament has become an important actor in the policy formulation stage (Bogdanor, in Mazey and Richardson, 1991).

A further dimension in examining the responses of capital is the extent to which interests represent themselves at the transnational level or hire the services of the professional lobbyist. This may once again reflect the extent to which interests are changing their behaviour to accommodate the European level. For instance, Sargent notes a Britsh domestic preference for interests to self represent (Sargent, 1987), whereas Grant notes considerable use of lobbyists for representation in Brussels, largely on the grounds of the barrier presented by establishing more than a token direct presence in Brussels (Grant, 1989). In Britain, there is already a small community developing of firms such as Burston Marsteller, Access Parliamentary Public Affairs, and Kingsway Rowland Public Affairs, who specialize in political representation at the European level (Greenwood and Jordan, forthcoming). This new development is also commented on by Mazey and Richardson, who note 'an explosion of professional lobbyists, financial consultants and law firms locating in Brussels' (Mazey and Richardson, 1991: 6).

These authors cite one estimate of 3,000 such actors in existence in 1990, thought to represent a threefold increase from 1987/8. Such a rapid growth has been sufficient to place the issue of a register of lobbyists on the EC policy agenda.

Another dimension to consider is that of interests securing European influence through political parties, either using lobbyists or through self representation. A considerable degree of research effort has been devoted to assessing the impact of influence exerted through political parties upon domestic politics. Much less is known about any impact upon the European level, apart from domestic influence exerted upon representatives at the Council of Ministers. No doubt this reflects the avenues of power in the EC (that is, as residing more in the Commission and the Council), although more research is clearly needed to determine the impact of exchanges with political channels, such as those centring on the Parliament.

A matrix of issues has thus been established in conceptualizing business access to European channels. Here, there are three main dimensions, and an identification of these reveals the complexity of actors involved. One is the route, which can be national or Euro transnational. Another concerns the outlets, which can be associational, individual collective, or other collective type (for example, clubs, clans, networks). The voice dimension can be through self representation (whether interest group or individual firm), or through the commercial lobbyist.

The final dimension which can be added to the 'matrix' concerns that of targets. These would of course include the Commission, Council, Parliament and the Economic and Social Committee. They would also include, however, individual parts of these, such as COREPER (Council), working groups and advisory committees, and individual directorates within the Commission who deal with rather different affairs.

Greenwood and Jordan have conceived of the 'matrix' in the diagrammatical representation shown in Figure 1.1 (Greenwood and Jordan, forthcoming).

Organizational Form of Corporate Activity	Route	Voice	Target
1 Individual collective (eg Philips)	Try to determine policy at national level	Self-representation	Commission and directorates
2 Coalition (functional, territorial)			
3 National Trade Association	Influence Europe via national contacts		Council of ministers
4 National Federation			
		Commercial lobbyist	Working Group
5 European specific coalition (eg direct firm membership, informal collective)	Brussels strategy		Parliament Economic and Social Committee
6 European Federation of National Federations ('super federation')			

Figure 1.1   *Interest groups influencing the European level*

It may well be that the development of the 'Brussels strategy' is confined to capital representing the interests of large firms. Small (and possibly medium-sized) firms may find cost to be a prohibitive factor in securing more than a token presence in Brussels. There are generalist, 'peak' associations of small business operating in Brussels, who are able to voice the interests and needs of small business *per se*, but there may be difficulties in representing sector interests presented by cost, expertise, diversity and communication.

Where small enterprises join trade associations in domains and sectors characterized by large firms, they may find their interests sacrificed to accommodate those with greater muscle – assuming they can bear the cost of the membership of these associations in the first instance. However, it may be that some associations – fig leaf or otherwise – are keen to be seen to be acting collectively for the purposes of impressing the Commission through their apparent ability for encompassingness. In this scenario, small firms may be presented with an opportunity for a 'Euro voice', and there is in fact some evidence that alliances are made between small and large firms in this way (chapter 4).

The alternative to such an unsure strategy would seem to be to use national governments for representation. This is partly dependent upon the organization and representation of small firms, which in any event may be weak, or the extent to which governments can pursue their causes without jeopardizing the interests of large firms within the domain. In these senses, the 'national route' to Brussels may not present an effective route either. However, a 'national route option' may be available for small firms or small firm collectives through support offered by peak associations of business, who provide significant training resources for firms with Euro lobbying needs (Mazey and Richardson, 1991).

An effective route to Brussels for small firms may in fact be presented by the regional level of organization, where small firms have the opportunity to be effective members of regional forums of business, or to use local and regional government as the route to voice in Brussels. There is evidence of significant use of this tier of organization (chapter 5).

This brief review of the position of small firms is once again a reminder of the difficulties of treating units such as 'capital' as a whole, and it is important not to reach generalized conclusions. Small firms may have considerable difficulty in matching the representation of large firms in Brussels, a problem also often encountered by labour organization.

Labour
It has been argued that there are significant differences in the logics guiding collective action of capital and labour (Offe and Wiesenthal, 1980; Traxler, 1987) in national contexts, although attempts

have been made more recently to modify this principal assumption (Streeck, 1989b). One idea is that capital is liquid and mobile and that this basic feature has a strong impact on the organization of interests. For instance, the transnational nature of capital (informal integration) assists the transnational level of organization (formal integration). Capital can also be organized within the narrow orbit of individual firms, whereas labour would seem to need to form associations, that is, trade unions (Crouch, 1985). Labour thus displays less of the diversity in the organization of interests than does capital, and the idea of encompassingness would appear to be more crucial to labour organization than to capital. Nevertheless, trade unions started life as international collectives, and there is in principle no reason why transnational collective action by labour should not be possible.

The European Trade Union Confederation (ETUC) was not established until 1973, as much as anything a response to the organization of capital at the European level. It has never been charged with functions as significant as some of its national counterparts, which took part in the tripartite arrangements of the 1970s. Consequently, there may have been less of an influence upon development at the European level. Indeed, the social dimension is certainly a 'latecomer' issue, and the initiatives which have arisen appear to have come as much from the Commission and individual member states as from organized outlets of labour.

Few 'Euro observers' can have failed to notice the considerably greater degree of disagreement between member states over the social dimension when compared to the internal market. This may partly account for the relative underdevelopment of the social dimension at the European level. However, the distinct power differentials between organized capital and labour throughout member states would also appear to be a significant factor. Nevertheless, there are examples on a regional basis of capital and labour establishing some *de facto* coalitions fostering technological progress and social welfare.

Differences in national density, and cleavages within the European trade union movement, on functional, political and religious grounds, make it difficult for labour organization to have a degree of overall coherence at the European level. In chapter 7, Visser and Ebbinghaus show that less grand levels of organization, such as individual unions or networks of unions, have not been without influence. The contrast between the evidence they provide on these, and the influence of the peak association ETUC, would again seem to confirm the value of the perspective which informs this book, namely the need for a disaggregated approach.

Nevertheless, there are also reasons as to why the micro and meso levels cannot be regarded as alternative scenarios for future labour organization in Europe (chapter 7). The access points for labour to the EC reflect the relative disorganization of these groups. Some authors (for example, Greenwood and Jordan, forthcoming; Sargent, 1987) have written of business undergoing a 'learning curve' in seeking access to Europe. One of these contributions has identified a growing confidence in seeking access to the EC, seen as expressed in an increasing tendency to use the 'Brussels strategy' rather than to rely upon the 'tried and tested' national channels (Greenwood and Jordan, forthcoming). This confidence is not evident in the case of labour organization.

Where the national government of a member state is regarded as sympathetic it would appear that taking the 'national route' to Europe is a tempting strategy, either via the Council or through government contacts with the Commission. However, the Council may not represent a viable option because of the use of vetos by other national governments hostile to organized labour. Contacts with the Commission may in fact be a significant access point for interests generally. A different picture evidently emerges, however, where the national host government is generally regarded as unsympathetic (Britain, for example), where unions themselves may have had to develop their own routes direct to Brussels. Although this may be via other national governments through contacts with filial associations in other member states as well as direct to the Commission, it does still mean that development of collective ties has to occur beyond national boundaries. It may therefore be that, paradoxically, the greatest development exerted on unions to take the 'Brussels strategy' may in fact be the degree of hostility of the host government. It follows that this has also been a factor leading to the uneven development of unions taking the 'Brussels strategy', given the relative differences between member state governments in their attitudes to working with representatives of labour.

Although Visser and Ebbinghaus make it clear that there is evidence of some relatively well-established contacts between representatives of labour and certain parts of the Commission, it may well be that the easiest general access to an EC institution is afforded by the Economic and Social Committee and the Parliament. It is possible that organized labour has made a relatively higher use of these channels than has business, where at least some degree of access is afforded to Euro decision-making process. Here, the enhanced competence of the Parliament can only be good news, both for labour and consumer interests.

Consumers

The position of the consumer has been at the heart of some approaches to collective actors, not least in that branch of public choice theory associated with the 'new right' (Dunleavy, 1990). Here, the assumption is that organized expressions of self-interest have to some extent acted as barriers to public choice and in doing so have prevented the rule of the consumer through the free expression of market choices. These have, however, mainly been applied to public sector professionals and to organizations of labour. Collectives of business have been regarded as a problem in new right public choice approaches largely in respect of anti-trust perspectives or, in the case of large firms, in monopolization of markets.

Birkinshaw et al. have most recently drawn attention to the problems of accountability presented by normative accounts of neo-corporatism (Birkinshaw et al., 1990). Although this is a dimension of the tradition which we have deliberately avoided, even the most cursory description of closed, symbiotic interest group relationships needs to at least acknowledge the potential for 'squeezing out' the consumer. However, early neo-functionalist accounts of interest intermediation at the European level in fact cast interest groups in the role of a 'bridge' between the EC and its citizens, where the hope was expressed that they could at least partly make up for a lack of contact between these groups. Although satisfactory contact might be established in this way with the business community as a whole, particularly with the drive towards an internal market, there are clearly considerable gaps. Labourers without capital interests are one, while the more generalized 'consumer' is another.

The obvious places for consumer representation in the EC are through the Economic and Social Committee (ECOSOC), the Parliament and DG XI (Consumer Protection) in the Commission. The first of these provides the most direct line of representation, which, given the relative unimportance of the ECOSOC as an institutional actor of the EC, may not be of great significance. Nevertheless, the ECOSOC does afford representatives of interests, whether capital, labour or consumers, the ability to be able to exercise influence over technical issues.

Further problems for consumer interests are those of the representation of such a broad and diverse group, and the position of consumer groups on the ECOSOC as one of a collective of groupings which includes capital and labour. Although there may be the potential for alliances where the interests of capital and labour do not coincide, there may also be cases where either one of these agents finds it difficult to align their interests entirely with the 'consumerist' cause. The pharmaceutical industry, for instance, often uses the word 'consumerist' to describe groups it regards with hostility (chapter 3).

Collective action by business and labour are clearly possible as a result of the ability to identify common interests. These are much more difficult to identify in the case of the consumer, and groups claiming representative functions may consequently find themselves being far more reactive to the EC agenda than proactive. Similarly, the relative weakness of consumers as an interest collective, particularly vis-à-vis business interests, may mean that the latter have a relatively challenge-free path to their aspirations in the creation of an internal market. This is a scenario which could be envisaged in the cases described by chapter 2 (telecommunications), chapter 3 (pharmaceuticals, but not biotechnology where opposition in some member states has been relatively organized) and chapter 4 (consumer electronics).

The problem for consumers is clearly aggravated by the problem of size and diversity. The European level, greater in both these respects than the national level, therefore presents considerable difficulties for the 'consumer interest'. Nevertheless, there are international expressions of consumer collectives, such as the International Organization of Consumer Unions (IOCU), which might be described as a 'peak' consumers' association. This may paradoxically be the greatest level of organization of consumers, in that it possesses a world headquarters with a secretariat and premises. The European Organization of Consumer Unions (EOCU), based in the Hague (rather than Brussels) is in fact a partly autonomous subdivision of the international unit. In turn, this suggests that consumer interests themselves lack a firm transnational (European) identity.

Sectoral representation of consumers, theoretically easier than peak organization by virtue of size, is in fact notoriously patchy. The greatest degree of development of consumer representation at the national level appears to have been where users consume a service provided by a near monopoly supplier, often in (or recently in) the public sector, such as with rail or postal services. An alternative level of organization has been where a small number of users have been unusually and severely affected, such as the victims of adverse reactions to medicines. This latter type of group are only created in a highly reactive and specialized environment, often for a limited period, and are unsuited to wider EC representation which is sustained and semi-permanent. Only the first of these two categories of sectoral consumer representatives have in fact been invited to serve as representatives to the ECOSOC. In these cases, it is not clear what specialisms, for instance, a post office users representative from Ireland can bring by way of interest representation to, for instance, potential victims of chemical pollution. The diversity of the environments in which consumers operate means that it would not be possible to provide across-the-board representation. It may also be that these representatives find it easier to express their own interests in terms of capital or labour. For these reasons, it may well be that only the peak level of organization, with its professional consumer representatives, can be appropriate in a European environment.

The European Parliament has provided the consumer with an effective voice over specific issues, and its significance is now greater with its enhanced competence. For instance, the Parliament organized, together with DG XI (Environment, Consumer Protection and Nuclear Safety), a proposal that all products arising from the application of the new biotechnologies should prove their social and economic use prior to market authorization. The biotechnology issue has been the focus of significant consumerist activity in Germany and Denmark (see chapter 3), and the Parliament represents an obvious forum where environmental groups can exert influence. In the event, however, the proposal has been defeated, partly arising from collective action by business interests in the biotechnology domain (chapter 3).

Another arena for consumer representation in Brussels is afforded by the existence of DG XI within the Commission. This has developed a sound reputation within the Commission as the consumers' champion, to the extent that a wide variety of business interests have taken the trouble to cultivate contacts. Here, DG XI has responded by talking also to the less organized sectors of business representation, such as small firms in certain sectors where cleavages are apparent (see, for instance, chapter 3). This has provided one strategy in dealing with the greater power of larger business interests. However, there are cases where these have sought to marginalize DG XI within the Commission, most notably through the creation of high level task forces consisting of a collection of DGs to coordinate policy within a particular domain. DGs with a more favourable outlook to business can thus counteract unwelcome consumerist representation (chapter 3).

The 'national route' to Brussels may also be problematic in the representation of consumers in that it is no less easy to detect significant levels of organization at the national level. However, the governments of some member states, most notably Britain, may see themselves as the champion of the consumer in the sense of public choice theory, and here a form of generalized sense of representation may occur. However, this may not be carried forward into domain or sector representation, particularly when national governments also have needs in championing the causes of significant economic concerns. Once again, the need to examine arrangements for each policy domain is emphasized.

Policies
The distinctive argument of this volume is of the need to disaggregate levels of study, in that arrangements differ between, and sometimes within, domains. We have thus sought to avoid making generalizations in examining the dialectics of interest intermediation at the transnational level. Thus, Cawson argues in chapter 4 that 'the logic of influence (in the sense of how to organize to affect outcomes) is dependent upon the logic of policy, and . . . this varies according to the policy at stake'.

In this sense, it is clear that a study of interest group–EC dialectics needs to focus upon arrangements as they prevail within particular policy domains. Different domains will be underpinned by differing dynamics, which in turn influence the dialectic of interest intermediation. Hence, Cawson (chapter 4) invokes Theodore Lowi's dictum that 'policies make politics', explaining that

> Lowi (1964) was concerned to show that the type of policy under consideration affected the political process which underlay it; for example, the struggle to influence distributional issues was quite different from that around regulation . . . we cannot divorce the interpretation of interest group politics from the policy-making institutions and domains at which it is targeted. 'Who governs?' is a more critical question for the study of EC policy-making than 'who speaks?'

In this account, it is thus possible to explain the relative level of advancement of the organization of capital as compared to other groups by reference to the dynamic influence exerted by the progress towards the internal market itself. Political developments tend to lag economic developments – a justification for this book is the idea that rather less attention has been devoted to the completion of the political market. In turn, this directs attention to the influences exerted by market conditions upon regulation, and from there to the extent of political organization within a domain. Nevertheless, there is not a mechanical link between the degree of regulation and the extent of interest group activity and organization, not least because of the difficulty in distinguishing between 'regulation', 'deregulation' and 'reregulation' (Cerny, 1991). However, the very idea of these concepts must be framed within a consideration of the economic conditions which underlie them.

This is in fact rather similar to Benson's idea of multi-levelled policy sectors (Benson, 1982), which are interdependent rather than being deterministic. Hence, the 'deep rules of structure formation' will influence the definition of an issue, which will in turn influence the response of actors on the surface level of a domain. The actions of these 'surface level actors', and their interfaces with user groups, will return to influence the definition of an issue itself. Thus, movements at the surface level of a policy domain will be constrained by deeper levels without being determined by them. 'Drift' at the surface level, when left unchallenged, may create a turbulence which allows some escape from the constraints imposed by levels beneath. For instance, biotechnology may be regarded as the land of opportunity for capital, but key interest agencies may have differing interpretations and will seek to impose a different definition of the problem. The resultant conflict and turbulence (for example, Germany) guarantees the issue an almost perpetual and recurring place on the policy agenda. The advantage of this approach is that is goes beyond the rather narrow focus upon surface level arrangements and relationships between identifiable actors to include an examination of underlying dynamics. Thus, it is necessary to examine the prevailing conditions as they apply within specific policy domains. Differing degrees of maturity of 'state' action apply, as do levels of interest group activity, to examples such as agriculture and fisheries on the one hand, and transport and financial services on the other. This can only be explained by an examination of the differing dynamics underlying each domain.

The Principle of Exchange

Although none of the contributors makes explicit use of exchange theories, they all in their own way emphasize that interest groups cannot be studied in isolation, and that interest group stuctures and activities need to be examined in terms of their embeddedness in wider institutional organizational environments. The Single European Act, as the entire project of integration, is deeply concerned with the exchange of resources, both human and material. The exchange of these resources is widely taken to be mutually rewarding to each member state and to its functional and territorial subunits, and to provide the cement for the overall building of the Community.

There are, however, other resources to be exchanged, which have not always found their way into the juridical codification of the common market. There are power resources of various kinds, which influence the extent to which resources such as goods, workers, services and capital either are exchanged on equal terms, or, whether their transfer actually establishes exchange disequilibria, with resulting power differentials among the participants to the deals. Power and exchange are of course analytical currencies at least as abstract as those of integration or of collective action, and their inclusion enables analysis beyond simple description of the range of physical resources exchanged to highlight the underlying logic of transnational collective action.

Despite the extraordinarily high interdependence among European actors which distinguishes the EC from any other type of international regime or system, we maintain that 'power' is the main resource in transactions between interest actors and the EC. Despite the difficulties in conceiving of these actors behaving in completely self interested ways – political actors are not like market consumers exercising simple choices based upon clear rational calculations – the basic idea of certain actions taken by these parties based upon interest identification is difficult to deny. The pursuit of these interests, and whether it is done at the expense of others or whether mutual benefits can be generated and sustained over time by the interorganizational exchanges under investigation, forms one of the crucial aspects of our inquiry. We do not however define power as a property held by single actors, but, rather, as a property of the relation of these actors in itself (Crozier and Friedberg, 1980). In other words, a public institution such as the Commission is not more powerful than a private interest association representing European business simply because it possesses certain resources of a coercive type (regulatory and legislative resources) which the latter is lacking. The relationship is partly one of power dependence, but more precisely it ought to be thought of in terms of the manner in which these resources are spent in a relation of exchange, and on the domain in which they are invested which influences who actually manages to build up a particularly central position (centrality), being hard to substitute for by actors (substitutability). Here, Colebatch rejects notions of 'technical adjustment', where governments are seen as establishing the conditions for market exchange, or 'partisan advantage', where regulation is seen as a tactic to structure advantage. Rather, he conceives of a 'constitution of order', applying organizational questions to economic relations by conceiving of markets as social constructs involving attempts to restructure relationships (Colebatch, 1991).

To summarize the argument, while juridical and economic analyses of the internal market emphasize the exchange of goods, workers, services and capital as well as the necessary regulatory devices needed for guaranteeing stability of these exchanges, we are interested in studying interorganizational power relations which can develop only through exchange among the actors involved in a given relation, that is, negotiation. Power is a relation of exchange and, therefore, of negotiation. It is not so much resources possessed by the parties to a transaction that are negotiated and exchanged, but the possibilities for action connected to these resources (Coleman, 1972). Exchange theory as originally developed by the early writings of Mauss, Lévi-Strauss and Malinowski, modified by scholars of the rational choice tradition like Homans, Blau and Ekeh, and, more recently, by network analysts such as Emerson and Cook, is a vast field. Fortunately, we are able to rely on a number of fresh approaches which justify our choice for this conceptual framework. This applies both to the study of international relations (Keohane, 1986) and of specific systems of transnational integration (Schmitter, 1985) as well as to the tradition of neo-corporatist research (Marin 1990a, b; Parri, 1989, 1990b; Pizzorno, 1977).

The exchange paradigm is a central feature of neo-corporatism. Interdependencies and resource control between organizations are here seen as the essential policy dynamics, rather than unilateral pressure exerted versus a political sovereign responding to such pressure either by benevolent consideration and special interest treatment, or by strictly negative attitudes in the defence of a poorly defined public interest. Similarly, there are also difficulties in distinguishing between 'actors', a difficulty arising as a result of the interdependency of, for instance, government and business (Colebatch, 1991). While the notion of public interest is generally of a quite hybrid nature, as rent seeking theories have taught us, its meaning becomes even more inflated where its expression at the European level is concerned. *Gemeinschaftinteresse* (common interest of the member states of the EC) here concerns the coincidence of certain interests of single nation states, concerning policy domains under rather specific circumstances. The Commission is less an institutionalized expression of *Gemeinschaftinteresse*, but, at most, an agency designing policies and subsequently policing their implementation after agreement has been reached on certain issues by the Council. Within this field the interests of parts of the Commission can be identified, as the DGs pursue their particular domains.

One dimension of interorganizational exchange can be located in the idea of network analysis. Network analysis, if properly used, may indeed be able to point to a whole range of extremely interesting forms of interest intermediation between and across private and public organizations and may show, as Collins argues, that 'there are kinds of repeated transactions which are neither markets nor hierarchies' (Collins, 1988: 447).

However, the notion of network raised to the same level of explicability as market and hierarchy makes little sense, since also markets and hierarchies can be studied in terms of network analysis. There are certainly pure market networks represented by buyers and sellers, which Aldrich and Whetton (1981) call an 'organization set', as well as networks that fall short of hierarchies, i.e. strategic alliances, or, in the terms of these authors, 'action sets'. These arguments are derived from the context of industrial economics, that is, from a framework where associations are normally absent and where firms are the only actors. Yet associations are precisely one of the many possible devices by which single firms try to solve their collective action problems beyond pure market transactions and below the extreme of vertical integration. Associations and, especially, their interorganizational relations and exchanges with public authorities can, of course, also be studied in terms of network analysis. Our conception of network thus refers to different kinds of structure be it markets, clans, associations, clubs, communities or hierarchies.

Such structures correspond to different governance mechanisms and, hence, regimes and may be positioned at first, functional or sectoral, secondly, territorial or regional, and thirdly, transnational levels of complexity. The notion of regime, in any case, is more encompassing than that of network and refers, first of all, to norms and common standards of behaviour rather than to structural properties of governance. Ours is thus an attempt to detect different kinds of regime (between markets and hierarchies, but including both of these also) at the national and transnational levels of the Community but, particularly, the interrelationships between these two levels. Collective action forms are differing forms of interorganizational regimes.

The variety of methods and theoretical backgrounds adopted by the contributors to this volume reflects to a certain extent the almost insurmountable problems in analysing capitalism as some kind of overall 'system'. The introduction of the transnational dimension complicates the picture. We are, accordingly, working with a wide range of theoretical and empirical tools – ranging from regulatory theories (French regulation school, public interest approach, and rent seeking theory), and network analytical methods and philosophy, over population ecology models of organization to more traditional structural types of analysis and policy domain studies. The integration of these differing approaches may be an impossible task, although the idea of an 'exchange paradigm' is at least able to draw together some themes. The idea of exchange and reciprocity is unusual in the application to the study of international relations and integration theory, but the concept is implicitly present in much of what has been written in these fields.

One attempt to integrate these ideas has been made by Schmitter, who, studying two systems of economic integration in South America (CACOM and the ANDEAN pact), merges the tradition of exchange theories with Hirschman's work on exit, voice and loyalty (Schmitter, 1985). Schmitter argues that, principally, there are three modal responses to crisis and organizational change in integrated systems and that actors, in such situations, will have to consider expanding or contracting the existing scope of policy and/or the established level of authority developed upon common institutions. They may either withdraw, object or do nothing. While 'exit' and 'voice' have been thoroughly explored by Hirschman's work, Schmitter focuses on the third option, which he calls 'suffrance'. This concerns acceptance of the present situation either because the actors are relatively indifferent to the costs and benefits involved because they anticipate future benefits to be forthcoming, or, most importantly, because they derive some intrinsic benefit from continued participation. The more actors choose to pool resources – that is, integrate through transnational collectives – the greater the potential for the 'suffrance' option. There are undoubtedly problems presented by transnational collective action as a result of such large aggregation. These are present in some sectors and domains more than in others, as the experiences of this volume and other works relate. Nevertheless, the potential for 'suffrance' may in fact be greater at the transnational level, although there are clearly examples where the voice option is expressed with coherence.

Notions of exchange have the advantage of being able to highlight interorganizational relations, and to suggest an understanding of power which is not based exclusively upon an analysis of the resource endowment of single actors. Rather, it includes an investigation of the ways and mechanisms by which these resources are spent and activated. Our approach seeks to emphasize these relations, that is their creation, their mechanisms and their eventual strengthening or removal respectively. The idea of exchange is thus applicable to the fields of international relations, remains at the heart of the neo-corporatist tradition and might also be applicable in the interrelationship of 'sectoral policy regimes' and 'territorial policy regimes' at different levels involving complex organizations (Grote, 1992b). The contributions which follow provide scope for the examination of these interrelationships, but also enable a number of key questions to be addressed. These are: the extent to which there are different ways of organizing interests across space, domains and affinities (for example, class); the different forms of action and power-dependence relationships and influences which emerge; and why such differences exist.

2

Organized Interests in the European Telecommunications Sector

Volker Schneider

The New European Dynamics and the Boost of Pan-European Associations

The role of European interest groups and their political status in European Community politics has repeatedly arisen as a topic of academic interest. Social scientists were either interested by questions such as 'who has more influence, labour or capital?', or they asked about the functions these groups played in EC politics, or more generally, in the broader process of European integration. Neo-functionalist integration theorists, for instance, believed that the Europeanization of interest associations is not a result of social and economic integration, but a driving force for the political unification of Europe. During the years of 'Europessimism' or 'Eurosclerosis' such ideas became relatively outdated, and, instead, intergovernmental or regime approaches of integration theory gained in credence. During this time only a handful of Europeanists remained true to the pan-European topic. It looks like an ironical 'U-turn' of history that at about the same time when signs of decline and withdrawal of European interest organizations were noticed by social scientists[1], the Commission's White Book initiated the 1992 dynamics and thus a renaissance in the spirit of European unification and European interest group proliferation.

Particularly astounding is the fact that this new dynamic of integration is, to a large degree, also *due to activities of national and pan-European interest groups of the business sector*. Certainly, the most important factors of the new dynamics are, on the one hand, significant shifts in the domestic politics of important member states of the EC (Moravcsik, 1991), and on the other a new strategy employed by the European Commission to achieve further integration (Bieber et al., 1988). However, both domestic and EC politics are not developing in a vacuum. They are influenced to a large degree by national and pan-European interest group activism. While it is well recognized that European multinationals in the electronics sector played a leading role in the launch of different research programmes (Sandholtz and Zysman, 1989; van Tulder and Junne, 1988), it is perhaps regarded as less certain which role national and European peak associations played in the 1992 initiative.

In October 1983 the Union of Industrial and Employers' Confederations of Europe (UNICE), the peak association of European industry, issued a declaration in favour of a 'fresh start for Europe'. In February 1984 it worked out a long list of concrete measures to 'unblock the workings of the European Community'. In this action plan UNICE asked for the 'establishment of an internal market eliminating financial, legal and administrative obstacles', the set up of 'programmes of European research, development and innovation policy' and some institutional changes such as the application of 'majority voting' in the Council of Ministers. Later these topics were the cornerstones of the famous White Paper initiating the internal market programme and the Single European Act.

In October 1984 the French *Conseil National du Patronat Française* (CNPF) and the Chamber of Commerce and Industry in Paris (the most resourceful in the EC) organized a conference on the new dynamics of European integration, in which about 200 prominent representatives of European industry asked for a new 'Eurodynamism' which would break up the 'Eurosclerosis' of national politicians in the EC.

These mobilization actions thus paralleled the new initiatives emerging from certain member states toward European integration. For instance, changes in France, as emphasized by Moravcsik (1991), were key factors for the new European dynamics. Indeed, the failure of the socialist experiment during the first years of left-wing government (1981–2) led to the conclusion that national economic independence was politically no longer practicable (Dyson 1991: 60). Realizing that even the champions of French industry increasingly had difficulties to meet world market challenges, the Socialists' modernization programme therefore progressively switched towards the promotion of European collaboration: 'The grand foreign economic policy aim of asserting "independence" vis-à-vis the Americans and the Japanese could still be achieved by broadening French mercantilism to include a "European" dimension, with France supplying leadership of course' (Humphreys 1990: 208). Such 'domestic politics' explanations, however, should be complemented by supra- and transnational aspects such as the skilful mobilization and alliance formation activities of the EC Commission, which, in a concerted effort with national and pan-European interest groups, lobbied in the different national arenas for a European relaunch. For instance, the French *patronat*, which, after its *automne noire* in 1981 was pushed to the wall (nationalization programme), had been able to regain its footing in 1983 and 1984. The symposium in October 1984 then appeared not only as a demonstration of regained strength but also as a more offensive posture toward European integration in the sense of a 'European entrepreneurship'. The mobilization of the French business community for a new Eurodynamism and the initiative of Mitterand for a relaunch of Europe during his presidency in the Council of Ministers in early 1984 were not just coincidences. If one assumes that domestic politics and policy cannot be explained only by the preferences of heads of state and governing parties, but also by social interests in the wider sense, this interest group activism (especially within the business sector) has to be integrated into the explanation of state policies (Cawson, 1985b; Lehmbruch and Schmitter, 1982; Schmitter and Lehmbruch, 1979).

The new dynamics in European integration stem to a large degree from business offensives. The successful relaunch of a new integration perspective led to a self stimulating process. The new transfer of competencies and the further expansion of policy areas ratified by the Single Act led to additional impulses for national interest groups to invest in the European representation of their interests. In the meantime their number and administrative resources increased rapidly. A recent bulletin of the German Zentralverband der Elektrotechnischen und Elektronischen Industrie (ZVEI) describes this process as follows:

> significant transfers in competencies from national governments and administrations led to a founding wave of representation offices in Brussels of all kinds – from EC member states as well as from third countries. From Germany alone there are more than a hundred new establishments. By this way a dense and complicated network of co-existing and parallel processing institutions and organization emerged. (ZVEI Mitteilung 18/1990)

From a long-term perspective this new boost of Eurogroups is the fourth of several foundation waves in the proliferation of EC interest groups. The first groups had been established when the European Coal and Steel Community had been created (1952). In a second founding wave (1958), immediately after the start of the EC, the different peak associations in the industrial and agricultural sectors were created (for example, COCCE, UNICE, PC, COPA etc.). During the 1960s there was then a long stagnation period which ended with a further boost in the years from 1971 to 1974 when industrial branch and sector committees were established. The transition in the mid-1980s from 'Eurosclerosis' to a new integration dynamism led to a further hoist. At the moment there are more than 600 European interest groups of which the overwhelming majority represent industrial interests (Grote, 1990). In the context of this growing attention toward European interest groups, this chapter aims to investigate the associational structures and practices in a sector which was 'Europeanized' only in recent history. This is the domain of telecommunications, a mixture of a service and a manufacturing sector. A major goal is to understand what type of European interest associations emerged in this area, and how this system interacts with EC policy-making machinery. For this purpose the essential interest groups in this domain are identified and their patterns of interaction with the EC institutions are evaluated. As it is impossible to deal with 12 member states in the same analytical depth, comparative observations at the national and international levels will be restricted to the four largest EC countries.

In order to unfold the specificities of this European system of interest intermediation, in a first step the politico-economic basis of the telecommunications sector is outlined. The subsequent section then traces the central features of interest domains in this sector and their organizational characteristics. A case study of the drafting process of a European programme then tries to evaluate the role of these Euro groups in EC policy-making.

The Political and Economic Basis of European Telecommunications

Although telecommunications has a long tradition in international cooperation, the European Community only recently gained competencies in this sector. The recent progress in integration of the telecommunications sector is related to dramatic changes at the national and international level of telecommunications which have taken place during recent years. Within one decade only a number of advanced industrial countries transformed their specific political institutions and market structures in telecommunications radically (Grande and Schneider, 1991; Ypsilanti and Mansell, 1987). Political strategies of deregulation then cut back state control, and liberalization opened the markets to domestic and foreign entrants. In a series of countries the former public network and service operators were privatized. Prior to this institutional turmoil, the telecommunications sector showed a remarkable stability for half a century. These traditional arrangements may be described as an organizational paradigm which can be outlined by the following structural facets (Schneider, 1991):

1 A core feature of the old model was the *high degree of horizontal integration* of service provision. In almost all countries telegraph or telephone monopolies predominated. But in a number of European nations the range of telecommunications services from the postal service, telegraphy and telephony to the new telecom services were completely integrated into one organizational unit (private or public monopolies). Only earlier (roughly from the 1870s to the First World War) in some countries did competing telephone services exist. At the beginning of this century, however, they all merged into national monopolies which were managed either by private corporations (with or without governmental licences) or by public administrations. Economists explain these processes by pressures resulting from economies of scale and scope, and by the consumption externalities of network technologies (see Table 2.1).

2 An equally important feature of the telecommunications sector was its *high degree of public control*, that is, its guidance and regulation by 'the political sphere'. The emergence of governmental control over telecom monopolies resulted either from the military significance of telecommunications (national security) or from the fact that the institutional structure of telegraphy had often been

Table 2.1   *Size and organizational forms of telecom systems in European Community countries*

Country	Telephone main stations (million), 1990	Employed by telecom operators 1988	Organizational form of telecom operators	
			1970s	1990s
Belgium	3.7	25,800	GA	PubC
Denmark	2.8	18,700	GA, PubC	PubC
France	26.5	159,500	GA	PubC
FR Germany	29.4	216,200	GA	PubC
Greece	3.8	30,300	PubC	PubC
Ireland	0.9	14,300	GA	PubC
Italy	21.3	113,800	GA, PubC	PrivC
Luxemburg	0.2	700	GA	?
Netherlands	6.0	29,100	GA	PubC
Portugal	1.5	23,000	PubC	PrivC
Spain	9.8	66,100	GA, PubC	PrivC
UK	21.7	223,000	GA	PrivC

GA, government administration; PubC, public corporation; PrivC, private corporation.
Sources: Siemens (1991); ITU (1990); Ungerer (1989: 86–7)

historically preceded by a state monopoly in the postal services. The perception of telegraphy as a threat to the postal revenues then motivated governments to integrate this technological system also into the sphere of state prerogatives. In countries in which telecommunication systems were run as private monopolies (in the United States, for example), governmental intervention was essentially triggered by the so-called 'natural monopoly dilemma' formulated by the OECD in 1983 as follows: 'if the industry's output is shared between several firms, then output will be produced at higher than minimum cost; but if output is concentrated in a single firm, then that firm could use its market power to charge monopoly prices' (OECD 1983: 29). Private monopolies thus tended to produce high telephone rates (monopoly pricing) and some discrimination between user groups (for example, under-supply of poorer regions). In most cases these practices were conceived to be politically unacceptable. They were thus prevented (or restricted) by public regulation.

3 A further organizational feature of the old model was a relatively high degree of *vertical integration* in the telecommunications domain and a high concentration (and often cartelization) of the equipment producer market. For telecommunications operators which were organized as state administrations it would have been difficult to achieve complete backward integration like the AT&T in the United States. In state controlled telecommunications systems the dominant pattern was quasi-integration: a market structure where manufacturing is left to a relatively small family of private firms which are linked by long-term contracts to the private or public telecommunications administration. Up to the 1970s and 1980s this 'court-supplier' model could be observed in a number of countries. In Germany, for instance, the market for switching equipment was divided up by four national suppliers; cables were procured from a rationalization cartel. Additionally, the British Post Office based its procurement on a system of long-term contracts based on market-sharing arrangements (Bulk Supply Agreements). A similar system existed in France; in Italy the integration was achieved by a state holding (IRI). Table 2.2 outlines these traditional market structures in Germany, the UK, France and Italy. These market structures implied high entry barriers for possible 'invaders' from foreign telecommunications industries as well as from other domestic sectors. In addition to the informal politico-economic relations within the 'court-complex', entry was also restricted on technical grounds. Each national area applied specific technical design criteria which were largely incompatible with foreign telecommunications technologies.

Table 2.2   *Number of domestic and foreign telecom equipment producers in 1980 (foreigners in brackets)*

	France	Italy	UK	FRG
Telephone				
Switching equipment	4	4	3	4
Transmission equipment	3	7	3	4
Telephone sets	3	3	3	12
PBX	11(2)	6(4)	5(1)	10(1)
Telex and data exchange				
Switching and				
transmission equipment	1(3)	1(1)	2	2(1)
Telex terminal equipment	2(2)	1(2)	1(1)	3(4)
Cable	2*	1*	2*	9*

* and some small manufacturers
Sources: *Siemens-Zeitschrift*, 6 (1981): 7

4 A further facet of the traditional model was the relatively *low integration of national telecom industries* into the world market. Until the 1980s, a world market for telecommunications products existed only for some of the smaller industrial countries possessing no proper telecommunications industries, and for developing countries. Some world market integration also existed for telecommunications equipment in the so-called 'new services' like telex, data exchange and private switching exchange (PBX). In the core business of telecommunications (cable, equipment for telephone transmission and switching), however, the telecommunications markets of large industrial countries like the United States, Japan, Germany, the UK, France and Italy were highly insulated from each other. In the late 1970s and early 1980s telecommunications equipment in countries such as the United States, Japan, Germany, the UK, France and Italy was mainly procured on the domestic market (OECD, 1983: 131). In this context, it should be kept in mind that world telecommunications until the 1980s was highly limited to the industrial capitalist world. In 1980 more than two-thirds of all telephone terminal parks were located in the United States, Japan and the four large European countries. The total of the OECD countries covered 84% of all telephone main stations in the world, and the remaining world market was highly concentrated. In 1980 only four firms accounted for more than 50% of world sales in telecommunications (OECD 1983).[2]

5 Another important feature of the old model of telecommunications was that the overwhelming majority of users came from the

business and professional sectors: indeed, from its outset up to the 1960s telephony was mainly a medium of business communication. In Europe at least (with the exception of some Scandinavian countries), the residential sector was only penetrated by telephony in the 1970s and 1980s. For instance, in 1960 less than 15% of German households were equipped with a telephone connection – and these were essentially households of business men and mangers. Only 5% of worker households owned a telephone at this time (Elias, 1980).

During the 1980s all five facets of the old paradigm in telecommunications began to change: governmental and private monopolies were broken up; markets were liberated; the telecommunication administrations were transformed into more autonomous public, semi-public or private corporations; international trade in telecommunications equipment and enhanced services increased; and the telephone service also became a real mass service. Today, at least in northern Europe, virtually all households have a telephone. Parallel to these developments, an increasing number of new and specialized services emerged.

Most authors regard this 'great transformation' as a result of the revolution in micro electronics during the past 20 years (Grande, 1989; Werle, 1990). The emergence and development of digital technology, for instance, changed the technological basis of telecommunications radically. It opened new technological trajectories, speeded up innovation, curtailed the product cycles and led to the integration of branches which were previously divided on the basis of different technologies (telecoms, computer industry and business machines). As the basic technology for different sectors converged, it became difficult to preserve the old sectoral barriers and the traditional institutional differentiation between telecommunications (highly regulated) and the computer domain (unregulated).

The relationship between technical pressure and institutional change, however, should not be conceived as a direct and one-to-one relation, in that it is intermediated by a number of structural and institutional variables. Comparative studies show that the transformation of national telecommunication sectors varies with respect to 'radicality' and 'speed'. Countries differ with respect to their economic structures making the technological tensions more or less acute, but also with respect to their political structure, leading to different perceptions, strategies and capacities of action (Grande and Schneider, 1991).

In many industrial countries the state monopoly in telecommunications services was broken up, or, at least, reduced to the domain of basic services. In this deregulation process the United States played a vanguard role. Liberalization and deregulation activities in the United States started as early as in the mid-1970s, and the split of AT&T – for a long time the world's largest telecom operator – was only the culmination point of this process. AT&T, now divided up into a number of smaller companies, became liberated from many former restrictions, giving it the ability to diversify into the computing business and to operate in foreign countries. In the early 1980s, Japan also followed the road to institutional change and liberalization. The first European country in the liberalization process was Britain. In a first step (in 1981), it transformed its telecommunications administration, formerly integrated into the Post Office, into an autonomous public corporation, which was then privatized some three years later. Compared to other European countries the institutional reform in Britain had been exceptionally radical, including the introduction of competition in the telephone network through licensing of a second networks provider (Mercury). This radicality is largely explained by the neo-conservative government of this period (Grande, 1989).

In the mid-1980s the European Community joined the telecommunications deregulation game, and became an active proponent and political force for liberalization. With the discovery of the importance of the information and communication industries (especially with respect to industrial competitiveness vis-à-vis the United States and Japan), industrial policy intervention in this high tech area then evolved to a key topic within the EC. This became accelerated by US deregulation and liberalization. When AT&T was unleashed from restrictions to worldwide engagement, it almost immediately entered European markets by joint ventures with Philips and Olivetti. At about the same time IBM diversified into the telecommunications sector. For a number of EC policy-makers, this seemed to be an alarming development. It was feared that US multinationals, after dominating Europe's markets in information technology, would also defeat Europe's telecommunications industry.

At the same time the US government put pressure upon the Europeans to liberalize their telecom markets and to eliminate distortions in world trade. The perceived threat from US firms on the one hand, and the pressure from the US government on the other, created a favourable situation for the Commission of the European Community (CEC) to acquire new competencies in a domain where its member countries were only poorly integrated (Schneider and Werle, 1990). In a relatively short time it worked out a programme for the creation of an internal telecommunications market through national liberalization and deregulation measures. The dominant idea was that liberalized markets would lead to greater economies of scale and a more efficient concentration of R&D capacities. An important argument for a common European telecom market was also the rising costs in the development of switching equipment. It was argued that a world market share of at least 8% would be necessary to recover the necessary R&D costs in this area. At this time, no European company reached a market share of more than 6%. To encourage cooperation between the different European firms, a number of European research and technology programmes were established.

The pace at which the Commission was pressing for liberalization in telecommunications is clearly shown by the short intervals at which recommendations, council decisions, directives and regulations have ensued. Between November 1984 and the early 1990s, the Commission and Council passed more than a dozen decisions, regulations and recommendations for this area. A further indicator for the explosive growth of this new EC policy domain was the sharp increase of specialized EC consulting committees (Grote, 1990: 242-5).

Parallel to this development, the now famous White Paper also contributed to the new integration dynamics, and the Single European Act in 1987 wrote new areas of action into the Treaty of Rome. These new goals included the creation of a European Technology Community, and the R&D framework programme consisted to a large degree of telecommunications activities (FAST, RACE, BRITE). Also in 1987, the Commission formulated a Green Paper which aimed to establish the major policy guidelines for the European telecom sector in view of the 1992 single market.

Organized Interests in the European Telecommunications Sector

The traditional market structures and institutional forms in the telecommunications sector are also reflected in the associational forms in which the different economic and social interests in the telecommunications sector are organized – at the national and European level. Since the old model of telecommunications was based on a territorial segmentation into relatively insulated national telecommunications systems, there was less demand for the coordination and accommodation of international interests in this sector (Genschel and Werle, 1992). This situation changed when the markets for telecommunications were liberalized and when demand for international coordination increased. The transformations which have taken place (and are still in progress) at the European interest group level are clearly related to this increased need.

The structures of interest organization in telecommunications will be outlined in the following sections. The analysis distinguishes between three categories: the interests of telecom operators, of the producer industry and of the users of telecommunications networks and services.

The Telecommunications Operators
The fact that the systems – at least in Europe – had been operated mainly as public monopolies (administered by state departments, agencies or enterprises) led to an incorporation of the operators' interests into the state organization of each member state. While there existed different organizational models implying higher or lower autonomy from governmental and parliamentary control, almost all systems had a public status, being directly controlled by the political domain. At the international and the European level these interests were thus expressed as governmental interests in the form of 'intergovernmental organizations'.

The international organization of telecommunications authorities has a long tradition. As early as 1865 the International Telegraph Union was founded to represent and coordinate the interests of national public telecom operators at the international level (Renaud, 1990). In 1923–4, an International Consultative Committee on Long-Distance Telephony (CCIF) was established with 20 member countries; in 1956, this institution merged with the International Telegraph and Telephone Consultative Committee (CCITT) of the ITU (Genschel and Werle, 1992: 8–9). In 1949, the European Conference of Postal and Telecommunications Administrations (CEPT) developed as the centre of European cooperation in the field of telecommunications – in spite of some early trials to establish a telecommunications union within the European Common Market (EEC) (Schneider and Werle, 1990: 85–6). The members of CEPT are the postal and telecommunications administrations of all 26 countries of Western Europe, including both EC and EFTA countries. Only in some cases where telecommunications operators had been incorporated into state holdings (Italy, for example) were these organizations indirectly represented by non-governmental international organizations such as the European Centre of Public Enterprises (CEEP). This organization is recognized by the EC as a social partner and has a similar status as the Union of Industrial and Employers' Confederations of Europe (UNICE) or the Committee of Agricultural Organizations in the EEC (COPA).

It is almost certain that institutional changes in most of the national European telecommunication systems transforming the public telecommunications administrations into public (or semi-public) enterprises will also lead to significant changes in the European and international organization of telecommunications operators.

The Manufacturing Industry

The quasi-integration or 'court-supplier' model led to a well-ordered network of national interest intermediation between the few telecommunications firms and the state (including the PTT), in which firms and state administrations had continuous and 'cozy' contacts. In this setting national business associations only had complementary importance and not the same intermediary position that business organizations hold in other more privately governed sectors such as, for instance, the chemical industry (Grant et al., 1989). Since the old telecommunications model was only marginally integrated into the world market, the 'court suppliers' had only domestic interests. In the German context, for instance, only Siemens has a longer history of world market orientation.

The structure of organized interests in the telecommunications industry is also shaped and constrained by the general national framework of organized business. In all four major countries the respective branch associations, with their subsector groups, are more or less hierarchically integrated into 'encompassing national peak associations' (Coleman and Grant, 1988). These national peak organizations of industry are in Britain, the Confederation of British Industry (CBI), in France the Conseil National du Patronat Française (CNPF), in Germany the Bundesverband der Deutschen Industrie (BDI) and in Italy the Confederazione Generale dell' Industria Italiana (Confindustria).

In Germany, the BDI is composed of 36 sector-specific associations which, in turn, are composed of 500 product and territorial organizations. A similar structure exists in France where the CNPF is composed of more than 120 sector organizations (in the manufacturing and service industry), which again are composed of about 800 product (or product clusters) associations (Hartmann, 1985: 150–1). The British system differs from the continental system only in the sense that the CBI, the principle comprehensive association of British business, also has direct firm memberships – it is thus rather more an 'umbrella' organization than a peak association (Coleman and Grant, 1988). In other respects the British system has the same hierarchical structure as the continental systems of business association. Here the product (or subsector) groups are the primary associations composing branch associations organizing whole industrial sectors, which in turn are members in a peak organization covering the business of a whole country.

In this structural context the German telecommunications manufacturing industry traditionally was organized and represented by the Zentralverband der Elektrotechnischen Industrie (ZVEI), one of the largest German business associations. The ZVEI covers a total of 30 subsector or product groups which during the 1980s had about 1,200 member firms covering all important electronic producers, and about 90% of the electrotechnical production within the FRG. The technical and product differentiation of the telecommunications industry (cable, transmission, switching and terminal equipment etc.) was 'transposed' by the internal differentiation of the ZVEI. Some of the various telecommunications segments are organized in different subsector groups: the cable industry is represented by the Fachverband Kabel, and the equipment industry was, until the mid-1980s, organized in the Fachverband Fernmeldeindustrie (telecommunications equipment). Both subgroups have a long tradition. The German Feeble Current Cable Association, founded as early as 1876, played an important role as a supplier cartel to the German Reichspost (Wessel, 1982). The Fachverband Fernmeldeindustrie has existed since the beginning of the century. Such differentiation was stable up to the early 1980s. A change in this profile emerged only through the revolution in micro electronics. In 1985 ZVEI's telecom group merged with the data processing section to form a new sector group named 'information and communications technology'.

Until recently the British telecommunications industry was organized and represented by the small Telecommunications Engineering and Manufacturers Association (TEMA) which, in 1986, had 11 member firms (Grande, 1989: 317). In 1990, this group merged with the Association of the Electronics, Telecommunications and Business Equipment Industries (EEA). EEA's 126 members are the major companies in telecommunications, information technology, the capital electronics equipment and defence sector, and the business equipment and office furniture sector.

In France the business organizations representing the national telecommunications industry are the Federation of Electrical and Electronic Industries (FIEE) and in Italy the National Association of the Electrical and Electronic Industry (ANIE). Similar to the differentiation in Germany, FIFE is also subdivided into 25 specialized subsector groups which cover a total of 800 corporate members in the electrical, electronic and computer sector. These 800 firms account for almost all sales in this area. The product or subsector organizations in the telecommunications sector are the French Telecommunications Industry Association (SI3T) and the French Cable Makers' Trade Association (SYCABEL).

At European level all three associational strata have their own representative organizations. Since the 1950s the national peak associations are represented by the Union of Industrial and Employers' Confederations of Europe (UNICE), and the national branch associations in the electrical sector are represented by the Liaison Organization for the European Mechanical, Electrical and Electronic Engineering and Metalworking Industries (ORGA-LIME). Even the different national subsector or product associations have their own representatives at the EC level, the European sectoral federations (FEBIs).

In the general context of the associational growth at EC level, the organization of telecommunication manufacturers is a relatively new development. The federation of the European telecommunications industry was only founded in the late 1970s. Since the different national telecommunication industries were primarily domestically orientated, there was then no need for interest representation or coordination at the European level. Only the boost in world market integration of telecom industries and the Europeanization of telecommunications policy changed this need. In 1977 the European Conference of Associations of Telecommunications Industries (EUCATEL) was founded by the national subsector associations from Germany, the UK, France and Italy, together with their Dutch and Belgian counterparts. Some years later, in the mid 1980s, when the micro electronics revolution eroded the old sectoral boundaries and when the liberalization wave reached Europe, EUCATEL and the European Conference of Radio and Electronic Equipment Associations (ECREEA) merged to form a joint conference known as European Telecommunications and Professional Electronics Industry (ECTEL). This association is actually the single EC representative of the telecommunications equipment sector. The current members of ECTEL are nine national associations representing the telecommunications and professional electronics industries of eight EC countries, and four national associations representing EFTA countries. ECTEL's national member associations cover some 700 companies, which collectively embrace over 90% of the telecommunications and professional electronic producers in the EC and EFTA.

In some countries the erosion of the traditional boundaries either led to the fusion of different sector organizations, or to more competitive structures of interest intermediation. In Germany there are currently two different and partially competing industrial sector organizations representing the information and communications industry. Both are, however, integrated into the same peak organization, the BDI. One is the ZVEI's subsector organization in information and communications technology. The other is a subgroup of the German Machinery and Plant Manufacturers' Association (VDMA, Verband Deutscher Maschinen- und Anlagenbau). The VDMA is the largest sector association in Germany and represents (with around 2,800 members) virtually all major companies in mechanical engineering, plant construction and information technology.

VDMA's subsector association, Business Machines and Information Technology (FG BIT), had about 60 members at the end of the 1980s. These range from national small and medium-size enterprises to foreign-based multinationals such as IBM. While both ZVEI and VDMA have some overlapping memberships, they are quite different in their orientations towards competition and industrial policy. The ZVEI rather defends some aspects of the traditional market structures in telecommunications, whereas the VDMA is a radical supporter of liberalization measures.

At the European level, both VDMA and ZVEI are members of ORGALIME and a large number of other specialized sector (or subsector) groups (FEBIs). According to recent activity reports of both associations, the ZVEI currently participates in 26 and the VDMA in 40 FEBIs. For a number of these Eurogroups VDMA

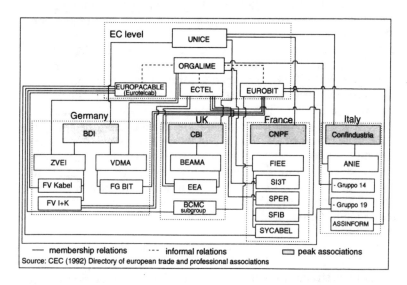

Figure 2.1   *Associations in the European telecommunications industry*

and ZVEI also provide the management and administration facilities. In the broader area of information and communications industries, both VDMA's BIT and ZVEI's IC section are members of the European Association of Manufacturers of Business Machines and Information Industry (EUROBIT); ZVEI's telecom and cable sections are members of ECTEL (European Conference of Associations of Telecommunications) and EUROTELCAB, a business group of the recently founded European Confederation of Associations of Manufacturers of Insulated Wires and Cables (EUROPACABLE).

A special feature of the European architecture of interest organization in the telecommunications manufacturer's domain is that large European (or multinational) firms do not only have the traditional associational links to EC institutions, but also direct channels of interest representation (Wassenberg, 1990). Since the late 1970s and early 1980s several round tables (or groups) of industrialists have been established which provide direct contacts between individual firms and EC institutions. The importance of these new representation structures should not be underestimated. These round tables may even outweigh the position of traditional European business associations in the shaping of EC industrial policy.

The first group of industrialists was established in the late 1970s when the 12 largest European electronics companies formed a

Table 2.3 *Companies most involved in European affairs*

Firms	Round tables and groups				Community R&D programmes			
	G-27	E-RT	SPAG	ECMA	Eu	ES	BR	RA
Philips	●	●	●	●	●	●	●	●
Siemens/Nixd.	●	●	●	●	●	●	●	●
Bull		●	●	●	●	●		
Thomson		●	●	●	●	●		●
ICL		●	●	●	●	●		●
IRI/STET		●	●		●	●	●	●
Olivetti	●	●	●	●	●	●	●	●
GEC/Plessy	●	●						●
CGE/Alcatel		●		●	●	●	●	●
Matra	●	●			●	●		●
Bosch	●	●		●	●	●	●	●
Ericsson				●		●		●
Daimler/AEG		●			●	●	●	●

EU, Eureka; ES, ESPRIT; BR, Brite, RA, Race.
Sources: van Tulder and Junne (1988: 216–29); ECMA MEMENTO (1991)

'round table' group with the European Commissioner for Industry, Viscount Étienne Davignon, to develop proposals for technology programmes and standardization (Thorn–Davignon Commission). The members of this group were GEC, ICL, Plessey, Thomson–Brandt, CIT–Alcatel, Bull, Siemens, AEG, Nixdorf, Olivetti, STET/IRI and Philips. This group played a major role in the establishment of the European Strategic Programme for Research and Development in Information Technology (ESPRIT) in 1983. Eight of these companies also formed the Standard Promotion and Application Group (SPAG) in 1985, aiming at unified European standards in information technology (van Tulder and Junne, 1988). A number of computer firms represented in SPAG are at the same time members of the European Computer Manufacturing Association (ECMA) – already founded in 1960 – which also has a long tradition in the standardization of information technology.

In addition to the ESPRIT round table, another, larger, industrial group was formed in 1983 (Gyllenhammer group). This round table grew from an initial 17 member firms to 27 members (also called G-27). A major function of this group is the provision of a discussion forum and lobbying channels for the largest multinationals in Europe. However, as van Tulder and Junne (1988: 215) convincingly argue, it also works as a reverse lobby in the sense that 'its members act as a strong lobby within their own national context in favour of European initiatives'. The major European firms and their memberships in the different round tables and working groups are listed in Table 2.3. This direct representation of large firms at the EC level also leads to the fact that most of the European multinationals have their own liaison offices in Brussels which are generally more resourceful than the Brussels offices of their branch associations or subsector associations.

The general structure of national and European interest representation in the telecommunications sector is outlined in Figure 2.1, which shows the formal institutional interlocks (formal membership relations, informal relations of cooperation) between the different associations at the different organizational levels. The European business associations and their main characteristics are listed in Table 2.4.

A comparison of national and European associations acting in the European arena shows some interesting aspects. It seems particularly striking that very few of the European subsector federations such as ECTEL, EUROBIT and EUROCABLE etc. have permanent offices in Brussels. Most of them are administered by national associations and their office is periodically shifted between the different member organizations. Although ECTEL's address is the

Table 2.4   *European associations representing the telecommunications manufacturing industry*

Association	Founded in	Types of member	Office in Brussels
Peak associations			
Union of Industrial and Employers' Confederations of Europe (UNICE)	1958	17 nat. assoc.	Yes
Sector associations			
Liaison Organization for the European Mechanical, Electrical and Electronic Engineering and Metalworking Industries (ORGALIME)	1947	23 nat. assoc.	Yes
Subsector associations			
European Telecommunications and Professional Electronics Industry (ECTEL)	1977/ 1985	13 nat. assoc.	c/o Fabrimetal
European Association of Manufacturers of Business Machines and Information Industry (EUROBIT)	1974	9 nat. assoc.	c/o VDMA
European Confederation of Associations of Manufacturers of Insulated Wires and Cables (EUROPACABLE)	1978	6 nat. assoc.	No

same as EEA's, the secretariat of ECTEL is currently provided by FABRIMETAL in Belgium; EUROBIT is administrated by the VDMA FG Bit in Frankfurt; and EUROCABLE by the FV Kabel (ZVEI) in Cologne. These modest administrative facilities indicate that most of the FEBIs are still 'letterhead firms' or 'listening posts' and that national business associations apparently still play a more important role than their collective bodies at EC level. It is perhaps symptomatic that the German VDMA and ZVEI have their own liaison offices in Brussels, whereas the handbooks of EC interest groups list EUROBIT and EUROTELCAB without Brussels addresses.

The users

The users are another important interest category in telecommunications. Here, the traditional institutional arrangements had particular implications for their organization. As has been shown, within the traditional telecommunications system the users were primarily business-men and professionals. Also important is the fact that until the 1970s there existed only a few telecom services: the telegraph, the telephone and, since the 1930s, the telex. All these systems essentially were single-purpose technologies and the usage patterns of these services were rather homogeneous. These user interests thus were often equated with the general interests of business in an efficient communications infrastructure. These interests, by nature, had a strong territorial or regional dimension, and the natural representative of such general business interests historically had been the Chambers of Commerce.[3]

In Germany, the important role of the Chambers of Commerce and their peak association, the German Chamber of Industry and Commerce (DIHT), in the intermediation of infrastructural interests can be traced back to the last century. Especially in telecommunications, the DIHT played an important historical role in the intermediation between the interests of general business users and the German telecommunication administration (Reichspost and later the Bundespost). Currently it is still considered to be an important policy actor and a prominent representative of regional interests in the telecommunications user perspective (Schneider and Werle, 1991). A similar role was held by the Chambers in France. In a study of the early development of telephony in France, Holecombe (1911: 282) considered the Chambers of Commerce not only important with respect to their representation function of French industry, but also with respect to their 'private government' capacities (Streeck and Schmitter, 1985): 'The chambers of commerce not only play an important part in the public representation of private, and especially of business interests, but have also been charged by the public authorities with the performance of administrative duties of ever increasing importance.' From a comparative perspective it is interesting that the French Chambers of Commerce are the most resourceful chambers in Europe.

Internationally, the Chambers are represented within the International Chamber of Commerce (ICC), founded in 1919 and with headquarters in Paris. When the EEC was created in 1958, the chambers of the first member countries formed a specialized forum known as the Permanent Conference of Chambers of Commerce and Industry of the EEC. In 1985 this forum adopted the name of Eurochambers (Association des Chambres de Commerce et d'Industrie Européenes). The ICC also has a strong interest in the communications infrastructure and is, with its computing and telecommunications committee, in contact with the major international and European telecommunications policy-makers.

More specialized associations representing particular user interests emerged only during the 1970s and 1980s. Technological progress enabled the growing differentiation of telecommunications networks and services and the transformation of telecommunications systems in a multi-purpose technology. In correspondence and interaction with this development, business users developed special applications and thus interests for highly focused user issues such as the provision of special data services or better access to leased lines etc. The growing specialization and differentiation led to a multiplicity of user groups at the national and international level which are partially overlapping, and sometimes competing. In virtually all European countries new associations emerged representing rather specialized telecommunications users.

In Germany those specialized user needs are represented by Verband der Postbenutzer (VdP) and the Deutsche Telecom e.V.(DTeV). While the VdP primarily represents small and medium-sized business firms,[4] large firms with very pronounced and specialized data communication needs are organized within the DTeV. In Britain the user interests of large business are represented by the Telecommunications Managers Association (TMA)[5] whereas small business is rather organized in the Telecommunications Users Association (TUA). The organizations representing specialized telecommunications user interests in France are the Association Française des Utilisateurs de Téléphones et Télécommunications (AFUTT), the Club Informatique des Grandes Entreprises Françaises (CIGREF), and the associations organizing the users of specialized data communication services UTISAT and UTIPAC (Dang N'guyen, 1988: 134). In 1987, CIGREF represented 14 banks, nine insurance companies, four transport firms and 19 industrial groups which represent about 40% of the installed base of information technology, and about 30% of the telecommunication revenues of the French PTT (DGT) from the business sector. Finally, the Italian platform for advanced user interests is the Forum Telematico Italiano (FTI).

Most of the national user organizations are organized at the European and international level. The most important international users representative is the International Telecommunications User Group (INTUG), representing several thousand businesses and corporations making significant use of international telecommunications. INTUG was founded in 1974 with the aim of promoting the interests of the users of international communications and cooperating with international telecommunications authorities such as ITU, CEPT, OECD and EEC. INTUG has also institutionalized contacts with the ICC and the Business and Industry Advisory Committee to the OECD.

A telecommunications user organization which is comparable to INTUG is the European Conference of Telecommunications User Associations (ECTUA). Although ECTUA is not the single user representative of the communications and information sector, it seems to have a prominent position in this domain. Another

European user association is the European Association of Information Services (EUSIDIC), founded in 1970, which currently has some 200 corporate members in 26 countries. This association was also a founding member of INTUG. Further user representatives at EC level are the Conference of European Computer User Associations (CECUA) and the European Service Industries Forum (ESIF). The different user categories in the information and communications technology domain are thus represented by an array of different organizations. Most of these groups, however, only command insignificant resources – especially when they are compared to national user organizations.

Technical and institutional changes in national telecommunications systems are shaping a new landscape of organized interests in European telecommunications, and the new dynamics of European integration has led to a growing importance of the European level. However, the true importance of this level can only be properly evaluated from a structural perspective. While the institutional structure of organized interests shapes the opportunity space of political influence, it tells less about the actual operation of these actors in EC policy-making. In order to shed some light on this aspect of interest group participation, the following section will present a short case study on interest group consultation in an EC programme formulation process. The policy programme was the Commission's 'Green Paper for a Common Market in Telecommunications'.

The Green Paper on Telecommunications as a European Process of Policy Formation

Only a couple of years after its intervention in European telecommunications policy, the CEC formulated a Green Paper on a common approach in this sector. The paper was formulated by an *ad hoc* group of officials in the Commission and was circulated in June 1987. The paper was addressed to the Council, the European Parliament, the Economic and Social Committee, the telecommunications operators in the member countries, the European information and communications industry, the users of telecommunications services and trade unions and other organizations representing social interests in these areas.

The Green Paper links the liberalization of European telecommunication markets to the '1992 internal market' goal. Its strategic aim apparently was not only 'agenda setting' but also the creation of a pan-European alliance for the liberalization of this sector. The definition of the situation and the policy guidelines proposed in the

Green Paper are thus geared to the broad goal of less regulation and more competition in this sector – although the continued exclusive provision or operation of the network infrastructure and some basic services by the existing telecommunications administrations are still accepted. In the area of enhanced services and terminal equipment, however, the Green Paper fosters complete liberalization. To guarantee fairness in competition, the Green Paper also asked for the separation of regulatory and operational activities of telecom administrations (Ungerer, 1989).

The formulation process of the Green Paper first started in a small circle of CEC officials, which selectively consulted representatives and experts from national telecom administrations. In order to get a maximum of support and to detect the potential areas of resistance, the CEC internal formulation process was combined with consultation with all the relevant national and European associations and other policy actors in this domain. In January 1988, when this discussion and consultation process closed, more than 45 organizations had responded with support and criticism towards the various propositions of the Green Paper. (A list of these consulted policy actors is published in Ungerer, 1989: 261.)

If one tries to classify the consulted organizations on the one hand with respect to different interest categories (operators, manufactures, users), and on the other hand with respect to the national or the European status, the following picture emerges:

- The CEC consulted all the responsible national telecommunications authorities. With respect to the *operators* the list of consulted organizations is obviously incomplete. The European telecommunications administrations – except British Telecom and Swedish Televerket – are not explicitly mentioned although Ungerer referred to the consultation of this group (1989: 260).
- If one treats the Chambers of Commerce as representatives of business user interests, the *manufacturers* were represented by three individual multinational firms, four national peak and sector organizations, but only by two European associations(!) – the peak association UNICE and the subsector association ECTEL. However, a further European 'representative body' of the manufacturing industry on the list is the Round Table of European Industrialists.
- The *user interests* in the consultation process were expressed by three large firms, 11 national and ten European (including transnational) user organizations covering the broad array of usage and application aspects in the communications and information sector.

- About three organizations on the list can be identified to represent the interests of *labour* or personnel of the telecommunications operators – but no organization is listed to represent labour interests in the telecommunications manufacturing sector.
- Other organizations that were listed are standardization bodies, special European organizations like CERN and RARE, the US government, and EFTA.

The structure of consultation in the Green Paper process thus shows that EC interest groups do not have the same (nearly) exclusive position which national associations have in national policy formulation to represent business interests. In all interest domains European associations, national organizations and even single firms were consulted on an equal base.

After the consultation process the CEC published its conclusions from its 'social feedback' and formulated an implementation plan of the action outlined in the Green Paper. This document ('Implementing the Green Paper') contained a detailed list of measures and a strict timetable. In a Council meeting on 30 June 1988 a resolution was passed in which the telecommunications ministers gave strong support to the major policy objectives established by the Green Paper and the subsequent consultation process. These main policy lines were then passed by the European Parliament on 14 December 1988. In the following year, several directives were issued, aiming at an opening of the European telecommunications markets. It is interesting to note that this speedy conquest of a new EEC action domain was only possible in a constellation in which telecommunication was still perceived as a minor policy issue receiving only minor attention within the policy community and the broader public. In this comparative isolation the early directives issued by the Council and the Commission could be formulated in relative 'harmony' and were thus implemented quite swiftly. In the late 1980s, however, the position of telecommunications policy at the European and national policy agendas generally improved and acquired much more national and European attention. The formulation and especially the implementation process of the more recent directives (for instance, the Open Network Provision and the Services directives) were thus more conflict-intensive. The implementation of the first three telecom directives, for instance, encountered difficulties only in Belgium and Spain, whereas the recent ONP and Services directives faced difficulties in up to ten member states. Meanwhile, the Commission has initiated infringement proceedings against such violations of Community decisions (*Communicationsweek International*, 19 August 1991: 3).

**Conclusion: EC Associations as Horizontal Coordination
Systems**

The overview and analysis of organized interests in the European
telecommunications sector has shown that this associational system
is surprisingly differentiated along several interest dimensions and
strata. Although there are numerous associations in the broad area
of telecommunications, the situation is not 'pluralist' in the sense
that competing organizations represent the same (potential) constituencies. The relationship between these associations is essentially
non-competitive. At each level, from encompassing organizations
like UNICE, through associations covering whole industrial branches down to the European representatives of product- or subsec-
tor-specific associations, there is a single representative for a given
domain or segment. This structure may be influenced by the way in
which business (and other) interests are organized in the different
member countries. However, an additional shaping force was the
consultation policy of the CEC. As Sargent (1985: 236) points out,

> the Commission [is] selective in its consultants with European interest
> organizations. The Commission has instituted a policy of 'recognizing'
> certain European Interest Organizations (EIOs) to which it gives
> preferential treatment during EEC policy formation and implementa-
> tion. A European interest group is said to be 'recognized' by the CEC if
> its name appears on the Commission's list, if it is invited to nominate
> members to advisory committees, or if it is regularly consulted by
> appropriate divisions or services within the Commission.

The effect of this policy was that the European interest groups
system gained features similar to the associational systems within
member states. At the national level, as Coleman and Grant (1988)
have shown, the top of the organizational pyramid is usually formed
by encompassing organizations (peak associations) which are
composed of sub-associations representing whole business branches. The branch associations, in turn, are either made up directly
of firms or of subsector groups representing firms producing the
same product or the same cluster of products. In some countries
there are several associational hierarchies which are differentiated
not only along sector and product lines, but also along territorial
criteria. At the top, however, such 'multiplex' systems are integrated into one or two hierarchical peaks which balance the
different criteria of functional and territorial differentiation institutionally. The relationships between these peaks are complementary
and not competitive – even if there are several hierarchical peaks in
a country. In Germany, for instance, employers' interests in
business firms are represented by the BDA, sector-related indust-

rial interests by the BDI and territorial interests by the DIHT. Complementary interests do not mean that there are not conflicts between these organizations. However, such conflicts rather represent cleavage lines between *different interest categories* (or *dimensions*) and not within a single interest dimension. Competition emerges only in contexts when, for instance, formerly clear-cut sector boundaries get blurred, as is the case with the ZVEI and the VDMA.

The associational system at EC level is thus as similarly functionally differentiated as the systems in the member states. However, there is no formal hierarchical integration of the different strata of the associational system. Against this argument it could be said that the existence of formal hierarchies does not say much about the factual strength of integration. In some countries peak associations are, despite their monopolistic position, organizationally too weak to be uncontested representatives of a societal subdomain. An important feature of the British and the French system is that, despite their formal hierarchical architectures, the relevant policy-makers do not see the associations as single voices for the business community. For some authors this lack of exclusive representativeness explains the growth of numerous direct interconnections between firms and state policy-makers in these countries (Schlencker, 1987; Willis and Grant, 1987).

At EC level even a merely formal integration into an associational hierarchy is missing. The peak organization of business in the EEC, the Union of Industrial and Employers' Confederations of Europe (UNICE), representing both employers and industrial interests, is not composed by EC branch associations *but by national peak associations at the same level of vertical differentiation.* The members of UNICE are national peak associations of business, whereas the members of EC sector associations are national sector associations as well. Finally, the European representatives of subsectors or product clusters are not directly composed by individual firms, as is the case at the national level. The members of EC subsector associations like EUROBIT or ECTEL are also subsector associations at the national level. This system is thus not a hierarchy in which upper levels *represent and control* lower levels, but a more horizontal and network-like system (which, nevertheless, is stratified), in which the different European levels of the organizational systems are institutionally integrated only indirectly through the membership relations of national associations.

Within this structural and institutional context, and only backed by a relatively slim basis of administrative resources, European interest groups are thus not able to play a similar role in policy-making to their national counterparts. Although these groups grow numerically and participate in an expanding array of EC expert committees, their functional performance seems to be limited to information provision for the CEC, that is, to produce a representative picture of the diversity of national and sectoral interests in the European business community. These associations, however, are not yet able to speak for, and to enter into, binding commitments for their members. The goals of European associations are thus still very modest. At the current stage they are glad when they contribute to a more coordinated expression of national and sectoral business interests. 'Many voices but one message' was the title of a recent information bulletin of UNICE (No. 1, 1991) which commented:

> The number of organizations which speak for business and industry at EC level has increased significantly over the last years. On the one hand, this is a positive development: it reflects the growing awareness of companies that the centres of power are shifting and that business has to strengthen its participation in the public policy debate at Community level. On the other hand, the European legislators are likely to receive so many diverging messages from so many different interest groups that they could end up either very confused or able to divide and rule. This cannot be in the interest of European companies. UNICE thinks that EC-Representations of business and industry must be more aware of each other and fully informed of what the other is doing. They should support each other whenever possible. Their messages need not be identical but should at least be on parallel tracks. If and when they feel it necessary to contradict the views expressed by other bodies, they should do this only after fullest consultation and genuine attempts to reconcile the differences prior to going public.

Despite their rapid proliferation and growing importance, the business associations at the European Community level are thus still far away from displaying in policy-making arrangements the features characterized in the debates on neo-corporatism or private interest governance (Cawson, 1985b; Lehmbruch and Schmitter, 1982; Streeck and Schmitter, 1985). A key feature of corporatist arrangements is the ability of associations to enter into bargaining commitments for their national or sectoral constituencies with the state or other important policy-makers. These capacities are still lacking in EC associations. The fact that European interest groups do not yet form an integrated associational hierarchy, but rather a system of horizontal, interorganizational coordination, suggests that the concept of 'policy networks' (Marin and Mayntz, 1991) seems to be more appropriate for the description of associational realities at the EC level than 'Eurocorporatism'.

Notes

1. An example is given by Kirchner in 1985 (published in 1986b: 161) who wrote: 'Instead of improving their capability for problem solving, European interest groups have taken a step back to the role of listening posts, and flirting with the idea of alliances.'

2. Figures from Siemens show a different picture where in 1980 nine firms accounted for 44% of telecom world sales.

3. Cf. Coleman and Grant (1988). The historical role of the Chambers of Industry and Commerce in this sector in Europe is well documented in Holecombe (1911).

4. The VdP in 1986 had almost 3,300 members (about 850 in 1976) (cf. Grande, 1989: 316).

5. In the literature (Cawson et al., 1990: 92–3; Grande, 1989: 336) the TMA with its 550 members in 1987 has the reputation of being well organized and influential in public policy-making.

3
Established and Emergent Sectors: Organized Interests at the European Level in the Pharmaceutical Industry and the New Biotechnologies

Justin Greenwood and Karsten Ronit

Introduction

Both before and after the arrival of proposals for the internal market, studies investigating the impact of organized interests on EC policy-making and implementation have concluded that interest intermediation was more pluralist than corporatist in character (Grant, 1989, 1990; Sargent, 1987; Schmitter and Streeck, 1990). On closer examination, it would appear difficult to sustain this contention given the emergence of responses both to the development of proposals within certain sectors for the internal market, and through the creation of political responses in certain areas of new economic activities for whom the European level provides the first experience of exchanges with bureaucratic authority. Our task is thus to examine political action by one established yet 'sunrise' industry – pharmaceuticals – with that by a new and emerging 'sunrise' economic activity as yet unable to be described as an industry in its own right – biotechnology. The intention is thus to examine how business interests have been organized and politically recognized, and whether they interact reciprocally with EC institutions, particularly the Commission. The purpose of comparing an established with an emergent sector at the European level is to see whether the drive towards integration and the more distinct ambitions to create a single European market have had an immediate impact on arrangements irrespective of the degree of establishment.

Economic internationalization has created a number of dynamics influencing the development of the pharmaceutical industry, and the emergence of the new biotechnologies. In turn, this has issued a number of challenges to the political representation of these concerns. The aim of this chapter is thus to examine the extent to which interest group activity within these domains has been able to address the 'Euro challenge', and the influence which such a challenge has exerted upon the rationality of collective action at the European level. From this exercise might therefore emerge a clearer picture of the dynamics influencing the character of different types of interest group activity at the transnational level; its interface with transnational authority; and the sorts of outputs that might be expected from such inter-relationships.

Both the pharmaceutical and biotechnology business domains belong to a category of industrial activities carrying the somewhat trivialized label of 'sunrise' industries. One recent study has claimed that the role of interest groups in high technology sectors is negligible (Hilpert, 1991). Here, the role of the state has been postulated to be of such importance that the traditional part played by interest groups in interest intermediation is regarded as largely unfound in high technology. Such activity is seen as occurring mainly in declining sectors on the brink of collapse. In such a thesis, the state level is generally supposed to provide the basic structure for innovation, while firms are attributed responsibility in the market dimension. Our intention is to analyse whether interest groups, in whatever form, have entirely lost their role in the pharmaceutical and biotechnology industrial domains; whether they display some variations; and if so, how these can be explained.

One theme which frequently emerges amongst commentators of interest group activity at the European level is the contention that while associations have considerably grown in number, they are, as 'federations of federations', weak and fragmented (Grant, 1990; see, for instance Sargent, 1987). Grant takes this one step further, and asserts that they have little significance beyond a channel of fraternal contact for members (Grant, 1990). One reason for this concerns the posed inability of interests aggregated from member states ('super federations') to act collectively, and particularly beyond the 'lowest common denominator' position (Averyt, 1977; Kirchner and Schwaiger, 1981; Streeck, 1989b). It may well be true that super federations will often experience such difficulties. Nevertheless, our examination of arrangements for political action by the pharmaceutical industry, and even the rather dispersed biotechnology 'industries', provides a challenge to such a thesis. In part, the 'pluralism at the EC' thesis has been informed by a view of associations as the prerequisite organizational format for neo-corporatist structures to emerge. This is a view with which we would take issue, but nevertheless, even on these terms our examples show the possibility of neo-corporatist type structures emerging. From this, it would seem unhelpful to make premature statements about interest intermediation at the EC being of one format or another, in that no single model can hope to take account of arrangements in all sectors.

A variety of similarities has been noted across national boundaries in the regulation of the pharmaceutical industry in Western Europe (Greenwood and Ronit, 1991a, b; Hancher, 1990). Here, the regulatory style is a preference for negotiated settlement between government and industry, and is characterized by delegation of regulatory authority to the pharmaceutical industry in return for compliance-seeking amongst members. Organized interests play a considerable and important role in styling relationships between the industry and the state, and, in the case of the pharmaceutical industry, sector associations have long histories of establishment in countries across Europe. They provide one of the earliest modern examples of not just a symbiotic relationship between interests and the state for information, expertise and cooperation, but of neo-corporatist policy partnerships with state authority. Interestingly, a number of these also significantly predate the idea of the 'overloaded state'. In turn, this suggests a real preference for such a type of arrangement which goes beyond simple pragmatic concerns of trying to reduce the amount of bureaucratic activity.

One expression of organized interests is the existence of private interest governments, and a number of conditions for the establishment of these have previously been conceptualized and identified at national levels. They include: the strength of the association of organized interests; near complete associational membership and the existence of self discipline by such members in pursuit of coherence in wider associational level goals; a strong associational capability for the articulation and representation of interests; a confidence by government in the capacity of the association to secure compliance among its members and to implement negotiated agreements effectively; and a compatibility with public goals (Streeck and Schmitter, 1985). Two examples of this in Western Europe include the Danish Drug Advertising Board (NMI) and the Code of Practice Committee of the Association of the British Pharmaceutical Industry (ABPI). Both these agencies exist against a background of formal legislation on the provision of information about medicines, but act by industry initiative in controlling such information and applying self imposed sanctions without recourse to the law. We intend to uncover the possible existence of such arrangements and other types of relationships normally associated with neo-corporatism. Elsewhere, an impressive array of marketing tactics has been shown to be the key by which the industry achieves its volume sales, largely by personal sales representatives calling on a small captive audience of doctors (Greenwood, 1988, 1991). Throughout Western Europe governments have preferred to let pharmaceutical firms supply the majority of information on medicines to doctors (Greenwood, 1988). In turn, this forms part of the 'rules of the game' between the two partners in a series of neo-corporatist regulatory agreements.

Private interest government has, to date, mainly been considered as a concept at the national level. In an earlier paper, we were concerned to discover the extent to which these arrangements either prevailed, or were developing, at the European level, and the impact this would have upon the operation of organized interests at the national level. In Grant's terms (Grant, 1989), would it be the case that organized interests would intensify at the national level as interests lobbied governments to represent their interests in policy formulation, and in reshaping the implementation of directives; or would it be that national interests would assume less importance given the transnational stage; or would it be that both levels would assume importance?

As long ago as 1977 Averyt outlined the 'orthodox strategy', which was for the formation of Euro groups for political action at the Euro level. These were seen by Averyt as an insufficient basis for the Commission to reciprocate with, needing to be supplemented by contact with national interests. Similarly, other authors have contended that the weakness of Euro groups has meant that effective influence in Brussels is largely sought by interests working through national governments (Jordan, 1991a, b). We do not wish to challenge the assumption that both routes are indispensable; rather, our claim is that the generalization of Euro groups being weak and fragmented, and of little significance, cannot be sustained. In the case of the pharmaceutical industry, for instance, a number of features which characterize relations between government and the pharmaceutical industry in Denmark and the UK, and indeed throughout Western Europe, were found by us to exist, or to be emerging, at the transnational (European) level of interest representation (Greenwood and Ronit, 1991a, b). Interestingly, there is also evidence of the transnational interest association in the sector having a direct impact upon national arrangements between organized business and national governments.

Reformulating interest representation to the transnational level cannot be wholly predicted by a comparative examination of arrangements at the national level. For instance, national private interest government works partly through supervisory competition, with firms eager to report on transgressions by competitors. Such a mechanism may be less reliable at the transnational level because of the introduction of a greater element of diversity, both in size of firms and nature of operations. Similarly, benefits which may accrue to consumers (for example, doctors, patients) from the flexibility and relative speed of self regulatory arrangements (Birkinshaw et al., 1990) may be lost in the remoteness of a transnational agency. A further complicating factor is that the problems of agreement- and compliance-seeking are multiplied at the transnational level, which has led some authors to regard the problem of political aggregation at the European level to be extremely difficult (Grant, 1990; Jordan, 1991). There is no doubt that examples of these problems can be found, and indeed Kirchner and Schwaiger cite the disintegration of COCCEE in 1978, the European organization for the distributive trades (in Jordan, 1991a). What follows, however, is an illustration of the danger of generalizing from such experiences, particularly from an example which significantly predates the demands upon interests imposed by the 1986 Single European Act, and from an example which may be untypical of arrangements elsewhere. Ironically, using just this example, COCCEE was later succeeded and reformulated into another representative Euro outlet.

Transnational Political Action by the Pharmaceutical Industry

The pharmaceutical industry is a genuinely multinational concern, although regionally concentrated in (in order of size) Europe, the United States and Japan. A series of takeovers and mergers has, in recent years, given the appearance of a highly concentrated industry, with a number of very large actors such as Merck and Bristol Squibb (US), Hoechst and Bayer (Germany), Smith Kline Beecham and Glaxo (UK), Ciba Geigy and Roche (Switzerland), Rhone Poulenc (France) and Farmitalia (Italy). Partly because of the multinational nature of the industry, and partly because of the high degree of medicine regulation in each country which it supplies, the multinational pharmaceutical industry is well experienced in acting collectively on the associational level, both nationally and internationally.

The rather similar relationships which exist between pharmaceutical industries and governments in Western Europe (Greenwood, 1988; Greenwood and Ronit, 1991a, b; Hancher, 1990), where private interest governments are rather typical, should not be regarded as coincidental. The pharmaceutical industry is multinational in character and faces almost precisely the same issues wherever it operates. These are a concern on the one hand by national governments for promoting a successful industry and attracting inward investment, while on the other almost identical concerns emerge in relation to medicine prices, information to prescribers and authorization and safety. Regimes from one country can also be replicated elsewhere. For instance, the British Pharmaceutical Price Regulation Scheme (PPRS) (which started life from an industry response to a proposal for state regulation, developed from the Voluntary Price Regulation Scheme of 1957), is taken as the basis for regulating and establishing medicine prices in a number of countries throughout the world. This scheme results from the basis of agreement between the British government and the Association of the British Pharmaceutical Industry (ABPI), and is used by the international pharmaceutical industry as a model in seeking agreement elsewhere. All of these factors have resulted in a commonality of experience for the pharmaceutical industry wherever it operates, resulting in the reproduction of symbiotic neo-corporatist relationships with governments across national boundaries. In turn, it has not been difficult for the industry to reproduce these experiences at transnational levels.

Associational action by the industry at the transnational level reacted to the regulation of medicine safety throughout the world which occurred as a result of the thalidomide tragedy. This was most certainly the impetus behind the very first piece of transnational regulation, Directive 65 of 1965 from the European Community, whereby the Community assumed the role of regulator of the pharmaceutical industry (which was later to flower into a second role as sponsor, repeating this dichotomy from national member states across Western Europe). Because medicine safety action at the European level prompted a flurry of national level regulation, the industry, wary of further transnational action, took the step of creating an association at the international level, the International Federation of Pharmaceutical Manufacturers Associations (IFPMA) in 1968. This responded to a perceived threat to the industry as the near monopolistic supplier of medicine information, its key operational strategy, by the creation of a self regulatory code of pharmaceutical marketing practice, accessible to doctors, patients and regulatory authorities (IFPMA, 1984). This represented one of the very first international business associations with such a role. As such, arrangements at national levels, where private interest government abounds in the field of information regulation, became mirrored at the transnational level. The code itself has not been of particular importance, largely because the perceived threat of regulation prompted by the activities of the World Health Organization (WHO) never materialized. In part, this also reflects political action taken by the industry to meet this challenge (Greenwood, 1989; Greenwood and Ronit, 1991a, b). The important point is, however, that the story demonstrated the ability of the industry to act politically at a transnational level, and provided it with valuable experience in doing so.

Other forums for associability by the international pharmaceutical industry have been the World Pharmaceutical Industry Group (GIIP), which organized the pharmaceutical industry of the EC, and the Pharmaceutical Industry Association (PIA), with pharmaceutical associations from EFTA countries. They were merged to form the European Federation of Pharmaceutical Industry Associations in 1978, and the distinction between associations from EC and EFTA countries is of no significance within EFPIA today. Brussels-based and with a relatively large permanent secretariat of 20 staff, EFPIA was formed specifically in response to the threat and opportunities posed to its interests by the EC. In its short life, influence upon European policy-making in the pharmaceutical sector has been considerable, turning the threat of transnational regulation expressed in EC proposals into agreement for the use of itself as a self regulatory agency to implement policy on drug information, in the creation of Commission proposals for patent law harmonization, and in using the EC to challenge previously established national pricing agreements in the European Court (Greenwood and Ronit, 1991a, b). While the future impact of EFPIA remains partly in the realm of speculation, it is clear that problems of the reformulation of interests from national to transnational levels are not insurmountable, and that a key component of conceptualizing the dynamics of EC arrangements must be to examine the actions of the targets of regulation.

EFPIA records its aim as to ensure that 'the conditions relating to the supply of medicines are appropriate to the production and development of medicines' (EFPIA, 1988). These have found expressions in attempts to preserve its role as the major supplier of medicine information by resort to self regulation, to resist standardized pricing arrangements, to strengthen public confidence in it by yielding to safety regulation, and through concerted action to restore patent life erosion. EFPIA records that

> the ten years of EFPIA have demonstrated the ability of a highly competitive industrial sector, with widely differing types and sizes of national industries and companies, to operate in a coherent manner on matters of common concern. The great achievement of EFPIA has been to catalyse discussions, coordinate views, assure contacts, and create conditions for consensus and common positions in the sector in Europe. This achievement demonstrates the spirit of collaboration, cooperation

and pragmatic compromise of the pharmaceutical industry within EFPIA. It is to be saluted, and its reinforcement over the next ten years is not to be doubted, since it springs from a common conviction of the worth of the pharmaceutical industry in Europe. (EFPIA, 1988)

EFPIA sees itself as a 'unique interface between one of Europe's most dynamic industries, and the broader processes of European policy determination' (EFPIA, 1988).

Although there might be a danger of taking these self-perceptions at face value, a close examination of interest intermediation in the European pharmaceutical industry appears to confirm these views.

European Regulation of the Pharmaceutical Industry

A key feature of regulation of the European pharmaceutical industry is a consideration of its contribution to the economies of Western Europe. Some 2,145 firms employ approaching half a million people, with production totals of 50,700 million ECU (30% of world production) and a collective trade surplus of 5,700 million ECU (EFPIA, 1990b). It exports three times as much as the US pharmaceutical industry, and 15 times as much as Japan's (EFPIA, 1988). Its positive trade balance is equivalent to 12% of total production, which compares with a negative trade balance in Europe for all sectors of −0.67%. The European trade deficit currently stands at −21 billion ECU (EFPIA, 1988).

The European pharmaceutical industry remains a high technology 'sunrise' industry. Of all new chemical entities launched worldwide over the past 25 years, 58% have come from the European pharmaceutical industry, with some 10% of turnover devoted to research and development (EFPIA, 1988). Despite these impressive performance indicators, however, it should be borne in mind that the term 'sunrise' in this context is not without its difficulties. Unlike many other industries to which this term can apply, the European pharmaceutical industry has been well established for decades, and indeed the only new players in the past 20 years have been Japanese firms. Besides witnessing a high level of takeovers and mergers in recent years, there exists a considerable over-capacity for many firms in Europe, not least because of national policies which traded price increases for inward investment. This has enabled firms from non-EC countries, particularly the United States, to gain a firm footing in European markets, but also to secure access to political action through national associations, which in turn affords access to EFPIA. However, these political considerations once again qualify use of the term 'sunrise industry', in that some commentators consider that the industry will continue to face rationalization, particularly with the application of EC rules restricting discriminatory trade practices (Burstall, 1990). In another sense, caution should also be exercised about the application of the term 'sunrise' when the industry may be regarded as intersectoral with chemicals and the newly emerging applications of biotechnology.

Although many partnerships between government and the industry have been built upon a recognition of economic contributions (Greenwood, 1988; Hancher, 1990), tensions have arisen as a result of the need to secure economies in public health spending. Pharmaceuticals now represent an average of 14% of health care spending across Europe (EFPIA, 1988). Taking the point that 'deregulation' inevitably results in a form of 'reregulation' (Cerny, 1991), it is clear that both of these partners have turned to Europe with a mixture of aspirations, without in any sense seeking to disturb the basis of neo-corporatist arrangements at the national level. This does not, however, mean that either party has sought to maintain intact the details of these arrangements, and what has happened at the European level has been a diverse mixture of events. These are best considered by giving attention to the areas of medicine pricing and patents, information and selling, and medicine authorization and safety.

Medicine Pricing in Europe

Until 1984/5, the pharmaceutical industry faced the possibility of a restricting European pricing directive. It complained bitterly that, far from attempting to remove barriers to an internal market, the Commission was creating them by attempting to harmonize pricing schemes (EFPIA, 1990b) (and thus illustrating Cerny's point about the difficulty of sustaining the concept of 'deregulation'). In particular, the German pharmaceutical industry, familiar with a domestic scheme where price controls were largely absent, was horrified at the idea of the proposed directive; by contrast, associations from countries with an established price control scheme (such as the UK) were less perturbed, although still concerned. Partly in response to these differences, EFPIA proposed an alternative scheme, directed against national price schemes it regarded as unfair under the provisions of the EC Treaty. This involved member states which imposed price or profit controls being required to publish detailed criteria for them and to provide reasons for decisions reached, to restrict the length of price freezes and to justify them, to make explicit the bases upon which calculations such as transfer prices had been arrived at and to reach deliberations within 90 days (CEC, 1989c). What became known as the 'transparency directive' had started life for the industry as a regulatory threat and ended, following associational action, as a 'deregulatory' aid for the industry in that the Commission had set clear parameters within which price/profit control schemes could act, making these available to the industry for scrutiny and challenge. Further liberalizing measures are promised at the present time. More than this, however, the industry successfully persuaded the Commission to take the governments of Italy and Belgium to the Court of Justice for infringements of Community rules in pricing schemes to which the industries in both countries had been a party. Similar action is planned against the governments of Spain and Portugal.

Where court action has not occurred, EFPIA claims a success in a recent publication in securing price rises in a number of countries. What is clear, and perhaps a little unexpected, is that a transnational interest group has had a direct impact upon national arrangements. This is a far cry from the suggestion that transnational interest groups are largely ineffective and only used by business for fraternal contact (Grant, 1990), or that interests invariably take the national route to the Commission through their host government (Sargent, 1987). Until any consequences of this emerge, it would appear that the Commission has been used as a 'deregulatory' aid for the multinational industry, and without completely undermining the symbiotic relationship between these governments and the industry.

One further example is also illustrative of the efficacy of associative action. In 1984, the Commission regarded any update of the European Patents Convention as too difficult to consider. Following a concerted campaign by EFPIA to force the issue on to the political agenda, the Commission backtracked and has now produced an imaginative set of proposals aimed at restoring patent erosion and at European harmonization (Burstall, 1990).

The capacity for associative action by the industry at both transnational and national levels is clearly remarkable. Nevertheless, it would also be remarkable, given its relatively concentrated nature, if instances of action by individual firms or by collectives of larger firms were absent outside the associational level. There is a cleavage within the pharmaceutical industry supplying European markets between research-based, innovative firms, and smaller generic or non-innovative producers. Burstall found only some 33 firms in the former category, while 1,450 were found to be in the latter (Burstall, 1985). In discussions concerning patent and pricing arrangements, DG III has consistently favoured in its policy decisions the research-based industry. For instance, an explanatory memorandum to a Commission proposal for a Council Directive on medicine pricing and reimbursement records that

> the single minded pursuit of short term financial economies will effectively undermine the research capacity of the pharmaceutical industry . . . the maintenance of a high level of public health within the Community will to a large extent depend on the activities of the Community's own pharmaceutical industry. It will not be in the interests of the European patient to become dependent on research conducted in third countries. (EFPIA, 1988)

It would appear from the above that a fundamental decision has been taken by the Commission to approach the industry from the perspective of research-based producers. This may represent either the strength of large, research-based firms within EFPIA, or the existence of individual firm lobbying and/or collective but non-associational business political activity. It would not appear to be action taken by national associations through national governments in that the proposal was itself drafted by the Commission (and not later inserted by the Council), and because of the cleavages within member states concerning attitudes towards cheaper, generic-based producers.

Medicine Information and Selling Control

Commission proposals for advertising are still at the draft stage at the time of writing, and the details are only partly settled following a rapidly arranged recent round of consultations by the industry. Here, we understand that the industry may have some difficulty in agreeing a package of proposals, in that considerable differences have emerged in EFPIA's advertising committee between member associations. For the moment, these remain partly buried while waiting for the full range of proposals to emerge. Indications are, however, that the industry may have lost the battle over proposals for mandatory pre-publication approval of advertisements, although it may respond by attempting to settle for a mixed pre- and post-approval system if it is able to resolve differences between national associations. Although this emphasizes the difficulties of maintaining European-wide cohesion, elsewhere industry unity has successfully headed off a Commission proposal for commercial information regulation by achieving agreement over the use of self regulation through EFPIA. The Council decision to proceed in this way (111/8118/90 – EC) in fact follows very closely the UK government's stated position on self regulation, while EFPIA's newly created self regulatory 'European Code of Practice for the Promotion of Medicines' (EFPIA, 1990a) follows very closely the UK ABPI's own code, which, we understand, formed the basis for agreement between the industry and the Commission. Each member association of the Federation (which includes EFTA as well as EC countries) 'is required to establish procedures for ensuring that its member companies comply with the requirements of the Code and for dealing with any complaints as to non compliance which may be made' (EFPIA, 1990a).

For this purpose, the Federation has established a Committee to oversee the working and development of the Code. This is a very clear example of reproducing arrangements at the transnational level which prevail throughout most member states, and, as such, provides one of the clearest examples there could be of a private interest government at the transnational level. It also establishes the superiority of a neo-corporatist agreement established at the European level over such agreements previously made at the national level, following EFPIA's offer for the standardization of self regulatory codes to meet EC objectives. In this sense, the Euro interest group has been directly used as a vehicle of European integration. This is some way from the argument that Euro associations are weak, fragmented and of little importance in the dynamics of Euro policy processes, or that interests prefer instead to work through national governments to secure representation in Brussels. Also of interest is that the strategy mirrors very closely the response of the industry in acting on the international level in 1968, in the shape of the IFPMA and its self regulatory code which was designed to meet the regulatory threat posed by the World Health Organization. Once again, the ability of the industry to act cohesively and collectively at the associational level and beyond national boundaries is emphasized.

The example suggests that the industry has been able to act beyond the 'lowest common denominator' position. While the agreement secured in respect of advertising (as opposed to other forms of promotion) did not meet with the industry's complete approval – for instance, in the UK the industry will have to severely curtail its use of samples – such differences have been overcome through the recognized importance of securing wider agreement to meet the threat of regulation through Council Directives. Of importance here was the ability of EFPIA to be able to deliver the promise to the Commission of securing the compliance of its members over the negotiated settlement, and in the proposal to act as an agent of policy implementation, either through itself or through national associations acting within the agreement.

The effort invested by the industry to secure such an outcome illustrates the importance it attaches to its own control of marketing activities. Just as important to it is the need to ensure recognition of its right to perform the major role in informing doctors about its products, particularly through the use of medical representatives, which has elsewhere been demonstrated to be the key to the success of the industry (Avorn, 1982; Greenwood, 1988; Strickland-Hodge, 1979). While Commission proposals concerning the promotion of rational use of medicines by member states are currently awaited, the draft proposal on pharmaceutical marketing no doubt reflects EFPIA input in recording that 'medical sales representatives have an important role in the promotion of medicinal products' (CEC, 1989c).

This represents an important achievement for the industry, in that its most important selling strategy is thus legitimized at the highest level. In the UK, for instance, the 'rules of the game' operate to delegate the responsibility for drug information to the industry, which spends some £50 for every £1 spent by government on this task. Half of this industry spending is devoted to the representative. It is likely that this method of informing doctors about products is likely to continue to take precedence in that the directive simply records that member states should take 'all necessary measures' to ensure that prescribers have access to 'neutral objective sources of information about products' (CEC, 1989c). The interpretation of this is left open to member states, and it appears unlikely that the position of the medical sales representative as the main agent in securing business for his or her employers will be open to challenge initiated from European sources. In this, associational action has been important in offering self regulation and compliance, and has achieved its basic demands at the expense of conceding less important issues, such as the demand to publish retail prices in advertisements, a curtailment upon the use of samples and mandatory pre-publication scrutiny of advertisements (EFPIA, 1990b, CEC, 1989b).

Marketing Authorization

Associational action is also in evidence over schemes for the authorization of marketing (that is, recognition) of medicines across member states. Directive 65/65 required that marketing authorization, where granted, should be on the grounds of safety, therapeutic efficacy and quality. The 'second directive' of 1975 (73/319) extended the provision of this to establish a partial mutual recognition of a licensing authorization granted by one member state to some or all other member states, assisted by an EC committee, the Committee for Proprietary Medicinal Products (CPMP). The scheme was the best agreement which could be reached at the time, and attracted industry support on the grounds that it would be preferable to an all-powerful centralized agency. However, it proved cumbersome, slow and unreliable, and, following EFPIA representations, a number of detailed changes were made to speed the system up. This included direct company representation on the CPMP, and the introduction of an accelerated scheme for high technology products. At present, EFPIA has let it be known that it favours a European Medicines Agency to handle authorizations, and this forms the basis of Commission proposals which are currently under consideration. It is interesting that the European pharmaceutical industry has resisted a role for itself in authorization and safety fields, preferring instead for European regulatory authorities to develop schemes for which it will bear ultimate responsibility in the event of a safety crisis.

These events are revealing because they display a number of interesting features which challenge some of the orthodoxies which have emerged concerning interest intermediation at the European level, and the supposed weakness in particular of Euro associations as a result of the difficulties of acting beyond the 'lowest common denominator' position (see, for instance, Streeck, 1989). In the case of the pharmaceutical industry, agreement has been possible within the industry on rather more than the 'lowest common denominator' position. This is because of the familiarity and uniformity with which the industry has responded to regulatory threats from national governments across Western Europe, and in this sense issues like proposing itself as the agent of (self) regulation did not come unnaturally to the industry.

Although EFPIA has not had its own way in every instance, it has clearly had a considerable impact upon the regulatory flavour of EC action in the sector, to the extent that its major demands have been incorporated. Of interest is that there are remarkable similarities between what we have described at the transnational levels, and events at national levels in this sector. Another similarity is in replicating strategies adopted at the international level, for the transnational level. The key factors in the ability of the industry to act effectively through the 'super federated' format at the European level appear to be its multinationalization; its common experiences across national boundaries; and its experiences of having engaged in international political action.

Throughout, the role of associational action in influencing

regulatory outcomes has been decisive, particularly in acting as an agency for negotiation, compliance-seeking and as an agent of policy implementation. It would appear that the thesis of Euro groups being weak and unimportant, and secondary in importance to the use by national governments of national interests for EC representation, cannot be generalized in the way in which it has been. This is an important finding, not least because those who have advocated this idea have come not just from the neo-pluralist camp but also from those whose ideas have previously been associated with neo-corporatism (Grant, 1989, 1990; Sargent, 1985, 1987; Schmitter and Streeck, 1990; Streeck, 1989a). In providing our case study, we have not sought to generalize our findings elsewhere. Rather, the emphasis has been upon challenging other generalizations which now appear to be unsustainable. In this sense, we are mindful of the point made by Bonnett (1985), namely that no single model can describe arrangements in all sectors.

Another contribution of our research has been to apply the idea of private interest government to the transnational level, whereas previously its use has been restricted to the national level. However, much of our contribution here has been centred upon the role of the sector association. Interest intermediation takes a number of forms, including action by large firms and collective but non-associational action, and should not be thought of as confined to traditional sector activity. This diversity is best witnessed by examining political action in another area, namely the application of biotechnologies.

Emergent Areas: The Case of Biotechnology

An immediate difficulty which presents itself is the idea that biotechnology cannot be described either as a sector or as an industry within its own right. More accurately, it is concerned with the application of biotechnologies across other industries, whose potential impact is enormous in that some 40% of manufactured output worldwide is biological in origin (Sharp, 1985a). One helpful definition which is often used by other authors is that employed by the 1980 British Spinks Committee report (see, for instance, Orsenigo, 1989; Sharp, 1985a, 1991a, 1991b), namely that it is 'the application of biological organisms, systems and processes to manufacturing and service industries' (ACARD, 1980).

Three stages in the development of biotechnology need to be identified to provide clarity about definitions (Sharp, 1985a; 1991a). One is centuries old – the use of yeast in the production of bread and alcohol, of rennin in cheese, and the cross-breeding of plants and animals for stronger and more domesticated species. The second emerged from developments in understanding the role of micro-organisms, which found expression in the discovery of penicillin and in attempts to use natural and cultured micro-organisms in therapeutic and other environments. This stage was characterized by observation of occurrences without explanation and thereby the means to decisively intervene (Orsenigo, 1989). The third stage – sometimes termed the 'new biotechnologies' – originates from the discovery in the 1970s of the means to cut and splice genes, thereby 'intervening with nature' (Sharp, 1991a). The term applied to this – 'genetic engineering' – enabled biotechnology to be conceived of separately from the traditional pharmaceutical sciences, and it is this conception with which we are concerned. Despite a whole series of false dawns, it is most certainly a 'sunrise activity' which is newly emerging, and as such provides an interesting contrast with the established pharmaceutical sector from which it has partly emerged. It cannot, however, be regarded as an industry in its own right, for three main reasons. One is that the 'new biotechnologies' emerged not from the search for industrial application but from the scientific laboratories of the United States (Orsenigo, 1989). Another is that it has been developed not by the large firm dominated pharmaceutical and chemical industries where commercial uncertainties and long-term investment needs made it unsuitable, but in the public sector and from small firms developing from public sector support. While it is true that firms such as Wellcome and ICI have been involved since the early days of the search for new biotechnology applications, they have, along with other large firms, also played the role of bystanders waiting to see if the results of research in small firms would make them worthwhile candidates for takeovers. A third reason is that its potential for applications makes biotechnology more a cross-sectoral activity encompassing the chemical, pharmaceutical, agricultural, food and energy industries.

These factors combine to influence political action within this domain. The interest community surrounding biotechnology was heavily dominated by scientists and by the public sector in the first instance. Political events surrounding the fledgling technologies thus involved exchanges between scientists, who could count upon the emotional appeal of public support for new technology (Orsenigo, 1989) and the public sector, anxious not to be left behind other countries in embracing the opportunities presented by a new industry which promised to become as economically significant as the micro processor industry. During the initial stages of the development of the new biotechnologies, industry was little more than an interested bystander. It is only in recent years with the transfer of responsibility away from the public sector to the private sector for developing the new biotechnologies, and with the formation of a new 'industry university complex' (Kenney, in Orsenigo, 1989) that any recognizable pattern of political action has emerged. Because of the cross-sectoral nature of these industrial interests, political action represents a complex variety of forms involving associational action within the biotechnology areas and related sectors, cross-sectoral but non-associational action, and individual firm-level lobbying. Another key feature is that the relatively recent transfer of development to the private sector from national public sectors has meant that the important level of political authority has at once been the European one, rather than a previously existing heritage of individual national exchanges between industry and governments. This new scenario creates a very different picture for the political scientist in examining the dynamics of political action at the European level, and as such provides a valuable contrast with research based upon adapting political action in sectors from the national to the European level. In practice, it means that the European structure of political exchange has developed in some cases before the national level. Before examining this, however, it is necessary to go back a stage to chart the development of the new biotechnologies within Europe.

Development of the New Biotechnologies

The development of the new biotechnologies has been led by the United States, followed by Japan and only thirdly Europe as a collective entity. The strength of the United States in this field can be attributed to a number of factors. One is the general lead provided by science to the United States. Another is the extent of public support, which exceeds that of all other countries in the world taken together (Orsenigo, 1989). This public support was directed mainly into academic research, which later partly blossomed into the proliferation of small companies, often created by scientists from academic institutions. A third reason concerns the entrepreneurial culture of the United States. Sharp comments that

> the very large sums of money poured into academic research in the life sciences in the US help to explain the early and continuing dominance of the US in this new technology, and the small new biotechnology firms were par excellence an American institution – in many respects an extension of the academic research laboratory, where American scientists, brought up in an entrepreneurial culture, were prepared to gamble on their skills and knowledge to make themselves millionaires.

They were in part also a copy cat phenomenon – after the success of the semi conductor firms in Silicon Valley, the venture capitalists were only too anxious to branch out into new pastures. (Sharp, 1991b)

In the fields of pharmaceutical medicine and chemistry, very close linkages between industry and academics have been the norm. This does not apply to biology and industry, where new links had to be forged. This centred upon the need to exploit the findings of research scientists in the laboratory. Thus 'industrial development of biotechnology required the establishment of new institutional linkages between industry, technology and science and between agents and forms of knowlege which had never interacted before' (Orsenigo, 1989).

These linkages developed very rapidly in the United States, and to a lesser extent in the UK. Such links generally, however, proved very slow in developing in most of Europe. However, one spur was provided by the fear of losing leading scientists amongst the universities, which proliferated the formation of small companies. In almost all cases, this was given public assistance by national governments, although marked differences arise across EC countries as to the way in which such assistance emerged. Some of this will come as no surprise to the political scientist. French governments, for instance, have played a leading and direct role in generating and organizing innovative activities. Others, after an indifferent and uncertain start caused by ideological reticence about public intervention (the UK, for example), or by a failure to foresee the potential until relatively late (as in Italy), became actively involved through a mixture of earmarked funds for scientific research and assistance grants for small firm start-up. Some of this resulted in the formation of non-profit institutions which made a high contribution to patenting activities (France, UK), such as through the creation of Celltech in Britain in 1981 following the Spinks report (ACARD, 1980). In others (for example, Germany), public support was given at a stage too early to reap benefits, leading to a string of notorious failures and false starts. Here, conversely, countries with a relatively late entry were not hampered in that some of the euphoria surrounding the new biotechnologies had evaporated and nobody expected quick and easy windfalls.

Space here does not permit a full examination of the way in which the new biotechnologies developed in member countries of the EC (for a fuller discussion of this see Orsenigo, 1989; Sharp, 1985a, 1991a, 1991b). Despite some important differences in the ways in which this occurred, the reasons for public involvement in the development of biotechnology are relatively uniform. They include the lack of links between biologists and industry; the lobbying capacity and public appeal of scientists; unwillingness of large commercial firms in other sectors to take long-term and very uncertain risks; the associated suitability of the public sector to start initiatives which might affect the long-term performance of many powerful and important related industries; the lobbying power of these large concerns; the implications for public health associated with biotechnology, both positive and negative; the possibility of providing alternative and almost limitless supplies of energy and food; the anxiety amongst individual countries and the EC not to 'miss the boat', particularly when other countries were taking initiatives; the opportunities provided by new technology at a time of recession; and the need to turn some good basic research in the laboratory into industrial application.

Partly as a result of these shared influences, the dominant pattern across Europe became established by the mid-1980s. This relied upon fostering collaboration and links between researchers, and the creation of small (mainly non-profit) firms from public sector initiatives through which significant contributions could be made to industrial applications, with the possibility of larger industries entering at a later stage (Orsenigo, 1989). The major difference between US and European development was that smaller firms in the commercial sector did not develop in the same way as in the United States (Sharp, 1991b). In Europe, once the infrastructure had developed, the larger concerns took an active interest. Sharp comments that

> Until they were clear that this new technology was 'going places', it was much easier for the large firms to buy themselves into the technology by placing contracts with, or buying an equity stake in, one of these small firms. On all sides it was a marriage of convenience – for the pharmaceutical and chemical companies it was a quick and reasonably risk-free way of gaining access to the technology; for the venture capitalists, a new and potentially fertile field of development; for the academics, an easy source of funding with which to pursue leading edge research. (Sharp, 1991b)

In fact it is difficult to talk of a single 'European' pattern emerging. What is clear, however, is that in Europe the development of the new biotechnologies has been less small firm dominated than was the case in the United States.

The 'marriage of convenience' has seen many recent takeovers, invariably initiated by pharmaceutical firms. This includes Glaxo's takeover of Biogen's European laboratory in 1987, Bayer's acquisition of Molecular Therapeutics and Molecular Diagnostics, the 1989 takeover of the Canadian firm Connaught Biosciences by Rhone

Poulenc and Hoffmann La Roche's takeover of Genentech in 1990. The pattern appears to be small firms supplying the technology, large firms supplying the means. Another feature concerns the massive investment in biotechnology research by pharmaceutical firms (Sharp, 1991a; 1991b). In this sense, Orsenigo sees biotechnology as a 'powerful factor changing the conventional boundaries of individual industries, the sectoral and technological interdependencies and the pattern of firms technological diversification' (Orsenigo, 1989).

Although this may currently be something of an overstatement for the variety of sectors upon which biotechnology touches, it is clear that all of the major industries concerned contain significant interests in the application of biotechnologies, particularly in the case of pharmaceuticals. It follows from this that political action contains a diverse mixture of associational, individual firm and cross-sectoral political activity.

Political Action Surrounding the Application of Biotechnologies

The responsibility shouldered by the scientific community and the public sector for the development of the new biotechnologies partly accounts for the relatively low level of political activity surrounding it at the national level. During the early to mid 1980s, scientists and industries unprepared to take on activities themselves provided encouragement to governments to become involved. In some EC member states, a national association for biotechnology has never developed, either because of the lack of an 'industry' (Greece, Portugal, Luxemburg) or because the presence of one is regarded as too sensitive. One example of this latter phenomenon is Germany, where the politicization of the 'biotechnology issue' has meant that the political channels of the chemical industry (VCI) are used. This provides another explanation for the low level of political activity surrounding biotechnologies at the national level, in that, for the large firms, the politicization of biotechnology provided a deterrent for joining national biotechnology associations, and hence it is typical for membership of these associations to be dominated by small and medium-sized enterprises. In most (but not all) other member states a federation (of scientists, industrialists and small firms) emerged. Only in France had a fully developed association, Organibio, emerged by the mid 1980s, and it was this agency which sought to replicate the associational model in other EC member states which had taken initiatives with the new biotechnologies. The latest 'conversion' to such a structure has been that of the Spanish in spring 1991. In a wider European context, national associations are seldom found, and even in countries with notable interests in biotechnology – such as Switzerland and Sweden – no genuine biotechnology associations exist. This perhaps emphasizes the lead given to the development of the new biotechnologies by scientists, who had created their own own Euro organization as early as 1978.

It is the industrial associational model which now predominates in the seven EC member states with formal agencies concerned with the new biotechnologies, not least because, as one national association director told us, 'corporate members can pay for an interest group – scientists can't'. In Britain, for instance, the Association for the Advancement of British Biotechnology ('A2B2') started life as a federated structure in 1985, and it was not until the protest and subsequent departure of ICI from the federation that a fully fledged industrial association was formed in 1989, the Bio Industry Association (BIA). This contains two membership categories – corporate and associate, although it is only the former that has representation on the board. Membership comprises some 18 firms, representing a number of large firms in other sectors (although still excluding ICI), and some single entity bio firms. Policy is made through seven working parties reporting to the board, comprising of members and coopted individuals. Although it only has a full time secretariat of four staff, it is in fact one of the largest of the seven national associations in Europe for biotechnology (France, Belgium, Denmark, UK, Spain, Italy, Netherlands). The lack of resources has meant that these have been largely reactive agencies – another factor contributing to the low degree of political activity at the national level. A final factor concerns the full time secretariat of these agencies, which tend to be led by scientists who make up for their lack of political lobbying experience with their enthusiasm as scientists for the industry.

There is a tendency across these member states for national biotechnology associations not to be formal members of pharmaceutical associations, although there is an informal network created through firms holding membership of both associations. This is not unusual for the Scandinavian associations, but might be in the case of the UK, where non-membership may be related to political differences, which found expression in the choice of a federated structure, and through a 1989 UK Green Paper on regulation of medicines, to which A2B2 responded without consulting other associations, and whose position was considerably out of line with the ABPI – indicating the presence of both cleavages and differentiation between the two 'industries'. In this respect, biotechnology has not been as reliant, at least in member states, upon other single sectors (such as pharmaceuticals) for political action as might be imagined, except in the unusual case of Germany. For reasons which are rather unclear, in the wider European context, there does however appear to be a tendency for political action surrounding biotechnology to be initiated by chemicals sector associations, such as is the case in Sweden and Switzerland.

National associations meet approximately every two months in Brussels. Until recently they have not possessed collective premises, a secretariat or even a name, and when they choose to act on a 'European' issue themselves they do so by choosing the national association with most experience in the particular area (a recent example is provided by the choice of Organibio to lobby on a patents issue). Collective political action through the work of the national associations is thus limited, no doubt partly by their own lack of resources. As a result of this weakness, small and medium-sized enterprises have been left, at least until the present, without an effective Euro voice.

As might be expected for an activity only recently emerged from the public sector, the UK Bio Industry Association has only just begun to engage in lobbying activities itself. As a small single actor, its influence is limited, however, and for Euro representation the work of the Association is supplemented by a working arrangement with the Confederation of British Industry (CBI) Working Party on Biotechnology (comprising representatives from the agrochemicals, chemicals, food and drink, soap and detergents, pharmaceuticals and brewing industries). This arrangement is confusingly known as the UK National Biotechnology Association (UK NBA), and seeks to influence Euro interest representation for biotechnology (Mazey and Richardson, 1991). The strengthening of the BIA appears to have emerged from the perceived failures of A2B2, and the recognition by associated sectors of the need to influence the EC not by working through the UK national government, but by going direct to the Euro interest group, the European Biotechnology Co-ordinating Group (EBCG).

The EBCG was formed in June 1985 at the request of DG XII (Science, Research and Development), anxious to have a single collective entity with which to reciprocate. It consists of the seven national associations (since April 1989 – emphasizing how Euro organization predated the national level), and sector membership from other industries concerned with the application of biotech-nologies (BIOFUTUR, 1989). This in itself may be part of the problem, in that a glance at these related 'industries' demonstrates the diversity of the interests involved. They are: CEFIC (chemicals); EFPIA (pharmaceuticals); AMFEP (food/enzymes); CIAA (food and drink); GIFAP (pesticides); EBPG (patents); ECRAB (agrochemicals); and, since 1989, COMASSO (vegetable growers); FEDESA (veterinary products) and GIBIP (Green Industry Biotechnology Platform). However, the EBCG too lacks premises and a secretariat, meeting instead by rotation quarterly at the premises of one of the Euro sector members. Herein lies an indicator of the weakness of the EBCG, in that for one important meeting, whether by accident or intent, the Euro chemicals association, CEFIC, was not invited. Most commentators have regarded EBCG as largely ineffective (Mazey and Richardson, 1991); and indeed, by mid 1991, it was on the point of collapse. The Commission, in summer 1991, was itself openly expressing dissatisfaction with the inability of the EBCG to act as a representative outlet for biotechnology (EBIS, 1991).

Perhaps unsurprisingly, it is CEFIC which has led the way in attempting to reform the EBCG, although its proposal for direct company representation was defeated. It is CEFIC, rather than EFPIA, which has been most anxious to improve Euro lobbying on biotechnology because it is the chemicals sector which is most affected by activities of the Commission, Council, Parliament and the ECOSOC. These have mostly been concerned with environmental release, and have only affected the pharmaceuticals sector directly in the field of live vaccines. This suggests that those concerned with biotechnology interests have been largely reactive at the European level, not least because of the problems of representation.

The concern of CEFIC to establish effective representation at the European level has found expression through the formation in 1989 of the Senior Advisory Group Biotechnology (SAGB). Located until recently within CEFIC premises and sharing CEFIC resources, SAGB began life as seven major firms including ICI, Monsanto (US owned), Unilever, Rhone Poulenc, Sandoz, Ferruzzi and Hoechst. Seven key individuals from these firms employed its Director, Brian Ager, a former employee of the UK Health and Safety Executive, the Commission and the OECD (Mazey and Richardson, 1991). It has until recently been a partial representative of biotechnology interests by virtue of its large firm orientation, although with so few members to represent, it has proved intense and effective lobbyist in Brussels – to the point that the Commission regards it as over-aggressive. It is however an effective response to the problems of representation with a group involving a large number of sectors, and its influence is suggested by a recent DG III paper to the Council which uses statistics and information produced by the

SAGB (Shankley, 1991). Since June of 1991, its status has changed from that of an internal group within CEFIC to an independent association affiliated to CEFIC. The plan to expand the SAGB beyond its stronghold in the chemicals industry to an initial target membership of 20 firms has now been exceeded. The principle of direct firm membership is to be maintained, albeit from a wider membership base of 30, and which is now more freely open to those electing to join.

One of the successes of the SAGB has been to persuade the Commission to create a high level coordination group for Biotechnology policy, the biotechnology Coordination Committee (BCC). This consists of DG III (Internal Market and Industrial Affairs), DG VI (Agriculture), DG XI (Environment and Consumer Protection) and DG XXII (Science, Research and Development). This latter Directorate is regarded as extremely friendly to industry, not least because of the existence of CUBE (Concertation Unit for Biotechnology in Europe) within DG XXII. This plays the role of an information secretariat within the Commission, to which the SAGB has provided considerable assistance. The coordination group has been concerned with the development of biotechnologies, which have partly found expression in programmes such as EUREKA, FAST, SPRINT, VALUE, SCIENCE, ECLAIR, FLAIR, HUG, COMMETT, BAP and BRIDGE. The Commission has also been concerned with the regulation of biotechnologies, and in this the role of the SAGB in encouraging the formation of the BCC has been significant. In turn, the BCC has sought to involve biotechnology interests through the development of round table forums – itself an impetus in the form of a challenge to these interests as to who should represent biotechnology concerns. The advantage of the SAGB is that, as a relatively small direct membership forum, it is able to be of much greater assistance to the Commission through its ability to respond quickly and with an assured voice.

The success of the BCC coordination group has been to outnumber DG XI, regarded by the industry as hostile. Thus, the SAGB successfully persuaded the group, through its contacts with DG III and DG XII, to oppose a proposal from the European Parliament, supported by DG XI, for the introduction of the 'fourth hurdle', whereby socio-economic need would be added to other criteria of safety, quality and efficacy in biotechnology regulation. Ironically, some of the best contacts of the seven national associations collective exist within DG XI, which invited them and the SAGB to a meeting on environmental release, which SAGB subsequently refused to attend – highlighting the cleavages between these two agencies, and the difficulty of speaking with one voice for biotechnologies. We are given to understand that the planned development of the SAGB does not include extending an invitation to the national associations for membership although the two parties have most recently shown a greater willingness to enter into mutual dialogue.

The structure of the SAGB is an interesting one in the development of a Euro representational forum, not least to those who have pointed out the difficulty of a 'federation of federations' in producing meaningful responses. The SAGB is one of the first direct membership forums. It may well be that those domains where difficulties are experienced with the 'super federated' structure may increasingly develop direct membership Euro forums. Nevertheless, in line with our own argument that Euro super federations can themselves be successful, we would point to the role of one such agency, CEFIC, in the establishment of the alternative format SAGB.

Of interest is the possibility of an emerging private interest government in the field of biotechnology. A para industry agency, the Comite Europeen de Normalisation (CEN), has been working for some time to establish safety standards within the industry at the European level. Four of its groups working under Technical Committee 233, which is concerned with biotechnologies, have been developing an expert code on safety in recent months, and, with the support of DGs III and XII, have proposed that it should be delegated responsibility for the formation of a code, and to make recommendations for arrangements to implement the code by interests concerned with the application of biotechnology (BIA, 1991). Whether this will be fully agreed by the Commission and Council (and in particular by representatives of Denmark and Germany where biotechnology, and especially gene splicing, remains a highly politicized issue) remains to be seen, although the provisional support given by DGs III and XII in mid 1991 provide important backing.

Where an interest relates specifically to a particular sector, it is relatively easy for the concern to be taken up by the sector association involved. Hence EFPIA has influenced the Commission's decision to implement an accelerated procedure for the mutual recognition of biotechnology products across member states when introduced in one, through the deliberation of the EC's Committee on Proprietary Medicinal Products (CPMP), designed to facilitate recognition across member states (EFPIA, 1988). This provides one of the few examples of effective cross-sector collaboration, with EFPIA promoting a biotechnology concern in a way in which the EBCG envisaged would secure the political interests of biotechnologies. As we have argued, this model provides the exception rather than the rule, in that, although cross-sectoral linkages have promoted associability, the most important channel of influence has been the SAGB, which permits direct firm membership rather than being a federation of federations at the European level. This may suggest the direction in which the most effective political action can be taken by interests at the European level.

The SAGB provides an extremely important and influential example of large firm cooperation at the European level. One director of a national association for biotechnology described its achievements to us at the Euro level as 'little short of miraculous'. It is, however, difficult to know whether to classify it as an association given its relatively small size, although it at least possesses premises from which to operate and a full time secretariat, which is more than the other two aggregations of interests in the field have at the European level. The SAGB provides the only effective form of action for large firms involved with biotechnology, in that other action is prevented by the disorganization of other agencies and the difficulty of working through the Council via the national level because of the politicization of the 'biotechnology issue' in Denmark and Germany. In the latter country, this is so intense that first Bayer decided to abandon its biotechnology operations in Germany in favour of a base in the United States (Fishlock, in Sharpe, 1991b), shortly followed by Hoechst. It remains to be seen whether the rather loose collection of national associations will eventually disintegrate in favour of the SAGB, a fate which now seems to have befallen the EBCG. This may be unlikely, given that large firms cannot apparently see their biotechnology interests to be coincidental with those of small and medium sized enterprises. What is clear, however, is that the European level is of far greater importance than the national level in representing interests to the EC. Emerging from public sector hands in the member states, the creation of a commercial stake in biotechnology followed the passing of the Single European Act, which has meant that the important level of political authority has at once been the European one. For this reason, the European level of interest organization is considerably more important, and displays a greater level of development, than the national level. Although on the face of it the case of EBCG supports the thesis of the relative weakness of Euro groups, the importance of the SAGB is a challenge to the idea that effective interest representation can only occur through the national level.

The infancy of the new biotechnology applications may seem to some a plausible explanation for the events which we have described. Indeed, its infancy makes it all the more interesting to study at the European level in the sense of suggesting futuristic patterns which may emerge elsewhere. What is also clear is that events are unfolding rapidly. However, we want to counsel against a sort of 'temporal determinism', which suggests that, given time, a more certain and known form of political representation will emerge in this domain. Evidence from elsewhere suggests that different arrangements prevail in differing domains, with rather differing outcomes. Indeed, this is one of the points with which this contribution has sought to take issue, namely the rather premature generalization of 'pluralism at the EC'. Evidence from this book suggests that such a thesis is unsustainable in a blanket form.

Conclusions

Our case studies here lend themselves to a number of conclusions. One is that the thesis of Euro groups being weak and of little importance cannot be sustained as a generalization. Another is an important finding of as clear an example of meso corporatism at the EC level as one could wish to see, and as such provides a challenge to the 'pluralism at the EC thesis', and an extension of the concept of private interest government, which until now had only been applied at the national level. Another conclusion is that the European level is itself important, and appears to exceed the importance of the national route via domestic governments for European representation in the cases we have outlined – hence challenging Averyt's 'orthodox strategy' (Averyt, 1977). Here, we have demonstrated the important role performed by Euro associations in European integration by applying the distinctive ideas of interest intermediation.

The comparison between the two fields of pharmaceuticals and biotechnology is an interesting one. In the former, which we have characterized as a 'sunrise' but established industry, the story has been one of 'mirror images', that is of regulatory arrangements and patterns of collective action from the national (and international) level being reproduced at the transnational level. This is remarkable, not least because of the greater problems of collective action through a greater level of aggregation from the national level, and because the pharmaceutical industry has proved capable of acting beyond the 'lowest common denominator' position. Almost throughout, there is a clear preference for associational action, even in an industry which has become increasingly concentrated over the past 20 years. The key to the success of the pharmaceutical industry in acting coherently through the 'super federated' format at the European level appears to be as a result of a number of factors. Key amongst these are its multinationalism, its common experiences across member states and its experience in international political action.

Interest intermediation can take a number of forms. In contrast to the pharmaceutical industry, where a clear preference exists for political action through the associational level, the field of biotechnology displays a variety of patterns for such action. Most successful is that taken by a collective of large firms, who, in contrast to other aggregations, at least possess a base and a secretariat. More than this, however, is that collections of national biotechnology associations have achieved little, and attempts to solve the problem through the creation of a cross-sector forum have proved unsuccessful. Small and medium-sized enterprises are thus left without an effective Euro voice, although one interesting question remains why large companies remain members of the national associations. One explanation may well be their interest in developing contacts and finding information useful for takeovers.

It is the large firms involved in biotechnology who have the most options. Another one is through membership of a related individual sector Euro association (such as EFPIA). Where these have restricted their efforts to biotechnology issues of direct concern to them, some success appears evident. This would suggest that there are real difficulties in acting collectively on the European level, particularly when working together with sectors which have little experience of cooperation. Time may ease this problem, although one suspects that the outcome will be a structure of individual firm membership of Euro associations in biotechnology, in the shape of the Senior Advisory Group Biotechnology. Such a forum – direct firm membership of Euro associations – may be a pattern which is replicated in other fields in the future; indeed, it may be that the pattern presented by the pharmaceutical industry is unusual, and that rather than providing influence through a 'federation of federations' at the Euro level, interest group activity might develop effective strategies at the Euro level through direct firm membership. However, although it may appear on first sight that the pattern evident in biotechnology confirms the view of those authors who have highlighted the difficulties presented by the 'super federated' Euro association, it ought also to be recorded that the effective biotechnology forum, the SAGB, was itself created by such a 'super federation'

A final key issue concerns the observation that the European level has always been the most important level of aggregation for those concerned with the application of biotechnologies, as a function of the relative newness of its arrival on the commercial sector, which in any event postdates the passing of the Single European Act. Perhaps it is this, more than anything, which points the way to the future development of interest group structures, which may well consign the national level to secondary importance, but which may also display the ability to create neo-corporatist type arrangements at the transnational level.

The pharmaceuticals and biotechnology domains share certain common features as well as displaying some differences. Both can be classified as high technology 'sunrise' concerns. Both have been considered of major importance by the EC (and member states) and have become objects of regulatory measures or programmes. Large corporations exist in both domains. Both are forming part of a transnational-global industry and their outlook is firmly trans-national. On the other hand, one sector may be characterized as established whereas the other is new and emergent. One is reasonably coherent whereas the other is more fragmented and complex. One is an industry whereas the other is a technique. One has been relatively stable whereas the other has recently experi-enced turbulent development. These fundamental differences need to be taken into account when drawing comparisons as to representative structures at the EC. The important point is that it would be foolish to expect all sectors or domains to act uniformly, and that different models surely apply in different domains. Nevertheless, we have identified processes in both of these areas that can reasonably be termed as characteristic of neo-corporatism. It may well be the case, for instance, that fragmentation allows for a more pluralist pattern in the case of biotechnology than in the closely knit pharmaceuticals sector. What we do not claim is that policy processes at the EC are characteristically neo-corporatist in character, just as we have also demonstrated the unsustainability of claims about processes at the EC being more pluralist in character.

An investigation of these two 'sunrise' domains shows that interests have performed a vital role in EC processes. The 'state' (however embryonic it may be at the European level), has been most active, but this does not imply that private actors have been correspondingly weak or inactive. Indeed, political efforts are very much conditioned by cooperation with interest groups. This includes legitimizing and sharing political initiatives, and sometimes shouldering responsibility through the ability to act as agencies of self regulation. The Commission has encouraged the formation of representative outlets by industry, a process which can be witnessed at the present time in the case of biotechnology. All observers have noted the enthusiasm shown by the Commission since the 1950s for the formation of reciprocating structures. In addition to fostering a cooperative spirit, involving experts and providing the Commission with policy-relevant information, there is also evidence that where coherent representative outlets (such as EFPIA) emerge, they can provide a solution to bureaucratic overload. More provocatively, we might end by suggesting that the Commission may find the advantages of these more distinctive forms of interest group structures highly attractive.

4
Interests, Groups and Public Policy-Making: the Case of the European Consumer Electronics Industry

Alan Cawson

Introduction: the 'Europeanization' of Interest Representation?

As chapter 1 has suggested, casual observation of the increase of representational activity at the European level shows a secular trend towards the proliferation of interest groups stalking the corridors of the European Commission in Brussels. The political momentum of the process of completing the Single Market has brought with it a steady growth of organized lobbying activities as a variety of different groups seek to protect their interests in line with their perception of the spreading of European tentacles into policy domains hitherto reserved to national governments. Most observers seem to agree that the vast majority of the many hundreds of new organizations are politically weak, and that the sheer weight of numbers is indicative of pluralistic patterns of politics. Indeed the leading exponent of modern corporatist theory has declared that the political universe of Brussels has tended to replicate the pluralism of policy-making in Washington, where the dispersion of policy-making institutions into multiple channels of influence is matched by the fragmentation of interest organizations (Schmitter, 1990). The corporatistic patterns of state–group relations in many of the nations of the 12 has not been translated into a supranational corporatism of the EC.

While Schmitter is careful not to foreclose the outcome of what is plainly a process subject to maturation and change, we should perhaps be more cautious than he is in assuming that the proliferation of interest groups is itself evidence of a pluralistic process. Schmitter's initial conclusion is based on a grand view of the limitations of the process of state formation (for without a state, one cannot have corporatism) in the context of multiple, conflicting and chaotic interest organizations. In the sense that the relationship between interest organizations and state institutions at the European level does not fit the prevailing (but not uncontested) concept of corporatism, Schmitter is clearly right. But there are several problems in stressing the pluralistic appearance of European interest group politics without examining in greater depth than Schmitter does the actual processes through which policies are formulated. We know very well from case studies at the meso level within nation states (Cawson, 1985b) that there is considerable variation by sector in policy systems, and that pluralism in one sector can quite happily coexist with corporatism in another sector within the same national policy space.

⇒ Several recent studies of industrial policy-making at the sectoral level have analysed the complex interactions between sectoral influences (such as the degree of concentration in a sector, the density of interest representation, the organizational capacity of interest associations, the composition of final demand, amongst others) and national influences (such as the organization of the state system, the prevailing national ideologies, the different systems of public law, and so on) (Cawson et al., 1990; Grant et al., 1989). Given this variation between sectors and between countries, it would be surprising if the movement towards interest organization and the development of policy domains at the supranational level in Europe showed a uniform trend, whether towards or away from 'corporatism'. Indeed the decade of the 1980s demonstrated the decomposition of many of the national corporatisms within Europe, not into pluralism, but into varieties of meso level corporatism. If there is to be a trend of any kind towards a European-level corporatism in the next century, we should expect that it will be an uneven process with considerable sectoral differences. If we are to map this trend, we will have to do so through the careful aggregation of empirical studies at the sectoral level, rather than by extrapolating from observations of contextless supranational phenomena.

As Theodore Lowi once observed, 'policies make politics'. Lowi (1964) was concerned to show that the type of policy under consideration affected the political process which underlay it: for example, the struggle to influence distributional issues was quite different from that around regulation. Lowi's observation is equally relevant to the issues discussed in this book, in that we cannot divorce the interpretation of interest group politics from the policy-making institutions and domains at which they are targeted. 'Who governs?' is a more critical question for the study of EC policy-making than 'who speaks?'.

The suggestion in this chapter is that the logic of influence (in the sense of how to organize to affect outcomes) is dependent upon the logic of policy, and that this varies according to the policy at stake. In the case of the European consumer electronics industry, I will argue that the logic of policy can only be grasped by examining in some detail the characteristics and recent history of the sector. The account of interest organization in the sector will reveal considerable associational weakness, yet at the same time the account of policy formation will reveal the strength of private interests in formulating public goals. This apparent paradox is quite simply explained: the crucial organizational actors which wield considerable power in setting the policy agenda for European electronics are not formal intermediary associations, but are large firms. These firms have monopolized representation, although sometimes under cover of an associational fig leaf to conceal the naked exercise of power, and have bargained successfully for, amongst other things, public subsidies. On the other hand, the officials in the European Commission have recognized that public policy cannot be framed by denying a role to the large firms, and have sought to implement their policy objectives by securing commitments from the firms. I will argue that the pattern of policy-making conforms closely to the prevalent conceptual definition of corporatism, and is indeed 'Euro corporatism', albeit within a single sector.

The next section of this chapter is given to an overview of the trajectory of the industrial politics of the sector from the 1970s, which shows how policy-making shifted decisively to the European level. Following that, I look at the institutions of representation, and trace a parallel (but subsequent) shift towards a European associational structure. The development of collaborative public/ private programmes is then discussed, and the weight of influence of the big firms is analysed. Finally, I offer some conclusions as to what lesson might be drawn from this sector for the general question of *Whither corporatism?* at the European level.

The Europeanization of an Industrial Sector: Consumer Electronics 1970–90

In the 1970s there was no 'European' consumer electronics industry except in the aggregates of the statisticians. In each country nationally based firms were producing largely for national markets, with very little intra-European trade in its principal products – television sets and, less important, audio products (Chrisaffis, 1988). The one significant multinational firm, Philips, maintained manufacturing plants in several countries, and in reality behaved as a loose confederation of national 'mini-Philipses' with considerable autonomy from the Dutch headquarters. The national markets were divided both by different technical standards (especially in television), in the case of France and Italy by pre-Treaty import quotas, and by considerable variations in taste and preference. Each country's firms were organized into national trade associations (in the case of Germany, a division of the electrical engineering association) which played an important part in fostering a collective view within the industry and moderating competition (Cawson et al., 1990). In the larger countries and markets the industry was relatively concentrated (in Britain, for example, the three biggest television manufacturers accounted for 62% of sales).

What changed all this in the 1970s and early 1980s was the impact of Japanese competition, at first through imports and subsequently from the products of Japanese factories located in Europe. The European firms had used their control of transmission technology patents (PAL and SECAM) to restrict imports to small-screen sets (14-inch and below), believing that this was an insignificant segment of the market. But they had failed to anticipate the trend towards the purchase of second sets, and when home computers and video recorders appeared at the end of the decade the Japanese firms profited from the spurt in multiple ownership of TV sets. Moreover, as Japanese firms set up production lines in Europe, at first in Britain, later in Germany, France, Spain and Portugal, they were able to build market share in larger screen sizes at the expense of the European-owned firms.

The Japanese turned out to be far more efficient producers of quality products than were the European firms, not simply because they profited from very large production runs (double the average of the Europeans), but because they had made important innovations in set designs, reducing the number of discrete components and increasing the extent to which these components were inserted automatically, thus reducing the labour content of the sets. The response of European firms to intensified competition varied in different countries. In Britain the industry negotiated bilateral import restraint with the Japanese industry (through a series of industry-to-industry negotiations over several years), while at the same time the British government encouraged inward investment by the Japanese firms. One by one the British firms left the industry, and by 1987 not one British-owned firm made colour TV sets in Britain. In France the impact of Japanese competition was at first moderated by a protectionist trade regime, with quotas placed on imported sets, and inward investment was prohibited to secure the position of the 'national champion' domestic producer, Thomson. In Germany the position was very similar to that in Britain, with domestic firms struggling against imports and sets produced by foreign-owned plants. The major difference in Germany was that the indigenous firms were absorbed, not by the Japanese, but by other European firms, especially Thomson, but also by Philips and later by the Finnish firm Nokia.

A crucial push to these twin processes of 'Europeanization' and 'Japanization' (namely, cross-border takeovers and inward investment) was given by the spectacular success of a new domestic consumer electronics technology, the video cassette recorder (VCR). Apart from Philips and Grundig (the latter at first independent, but later controlled by Philips), none of the other European TV producers had tried to develop its own VCR. The Japanese firms Sony and JVC (the latter a subsidiary of Matsushita) had developed, respectively, the Betamax and VHS formats for the domestic VCR which were smaller, more reliable and technically superior to the early Philips N1500 machines. Sony chose to go it alone, but JVC licensed its VHS system to Philips's major competitors in each of the major European markets, and succeeded in developing a strong market position in advance of the later V2000 machine developed by Philips and Grundig.

The outcome of this format battle lost Philips and Grundig a great deal of money, but, more importantly for the purposes of this chapter, resulted in a decisive shift in public policy-making for the sector away from national capitals to Brussels. Unlike TV, where trade restrictions preceded the Treaty of Rome, VCR was a new product, and the provision of the Treaty whereby external trade was reserved to the Community was uncluttered by such hangovers. The French attempt in 1982 to cure its burgeoning balance of payments deficit in electronics by funnelling all VCR imports into France through an obscure customs post in Poitiers, combined with the action taken by Philips and Grundig in making a formal complaint of dumping against Japanese VCR producers, spurred the Commission into action. The EC Industry Commissioner, Viscount Davignon, negotiated in great haste a bilateral agreement between the EC and the Japanese external trade ministry MITI by which the Japanese agreed to moderate their exports of VCRs to the EC, and set a floor price related to the costs of production of Philips–Grundig VCRs. The Voluntary Export Restraint agreement (VER) was to last for three years (to give the European firms a 'breathing space') and thereafter VCRs would be subject to a tariff of 14% (compared to the average EC tariff for industrial products of 8%).

The VER had several consequences, mostly to the detriment of the very producers whose interests it was intended to serve! It failed to save the European VCR technology, abandoned by Philips in favour of the now universal VHS system. Secondly, its floor price allowed the Japanese firms to make super-profits in the European market at the expense of European consumers. Thirdly, and most important, the protectionist policy accelerated the flow of inward investment into Europe, and even into France whose government realized that it was better for France to have at least some of the plants located there rather than in Britain or Germany.

During this same period the concentrated industries of the separate European countries begin to coalesce into three major transnational European-owned firms, and eight European sub-sidiaries of the largest Japanese firms. The French national champion, Thomson, which had been nationalized in one of the first acts of the Mitterrand government in 1981, began to make a series of acquisitions (including Telefunken and Nordmende in Germany) which culminated in the purchase of Ferguson in Britain and RCA in the United States in 1987, thus turning a national champion into an international champion. Philips began to reign in its sprawling empire of autonomous national missions and turned to a product division structure controlled from Eindhoven in Holland. Finally the Finnish conglomerate Nokia, having bought control of the Swedish industry, moved into France and Germany, buying the ex-ITT subsidiaries in those countries which included Europe's largest CTV factory based in Germany.

At the end of the 1980s the transformation of the industry from a mosaic of national segments to a European industry dominated by European-owned multinational companies was almost complete. It should be emphasized that this process predated the Single European Act; indeed a good deal of the political lobbying by industry which precipitated passage of the Act came from firms in industries which were subject to increasingly global competition from the USA and Japan who saw the creation of a single market as a necessary condition for coping with that competition. The SEA has, however, had an important influence on the operation of the Japanese firms in Europe. In 1985 they were manufacturing subsidiaries organized and controlled entirely from the headquar-ters in Japan with almost no communication between the different subsidiaries. By 1990 most of these firms had established European headquarters with some devolution of corporate policy-making (Sony's concept is 'global localization') through horizontal co-ordination of plants in different EC countries.

The transformation of the industry can be attributed principally to the intrasectoral factors I have so far examined, namely increasing international trade, intensifying competition and the impact of technological development. The economic weaknesses of the European firms, which were acutely visible as balance of trade deficits across the Community deepened, led them to insist on political solutions in the form of different kinds of protection. European politicians and bureaucrats were also becoming increasingly alarmed at the apparent ease with which the Japanese were able to dominate consumer electronics markets, and were more and more ready to accede to the demands of the firms led by Philips and Thomson. Protection can take very different forms, however, and its different forms give rise to different kinds of politics.

Rule-based policies, such as tariffs, foster classic modes of pressure group politics which target public authorities. The latter determine the rules, which are then administered through bureaucratic procedures. Elsewhere (Cawson, 1982) I have stressed how allocative policies of this kind (which distribute benefits and/or obligations according to strictly defined criteria) are linked to pluralistic input politics and bureaucratic output procedures. We can see the decision by the EC in 1983 to establish a special 19% tariff on compact disc players as such a response to pressure from Philips (which operated the only EC factory producing such players).

Voluntary export restraint agreements are more complex in terms of both formulation and implementation. Quotas have to be agreed (and policed), floor prices have to be set (and price-setting monitored), and disputes have to be settled (for example, on the apportionment of the quota). In the case of the 1983 VER for video recorders, the agreement was negotiated at intergovernmental level, but on the basis of industry definitions of the damage that was being done to firms, and industry estimates of what would constitute adequate protection. Moreover the VER itself was implemented through an *ad hoc* committee consisting of EC bureaucrats and representatives of the major European firms.

A third kind of protection is anti-dumping procedures, where a complaint is filed by an injured party that it has suffered 'material damage' as a consequence of firms selling products on the EC market at prices lower than those which prevail in the country of origin. In such cases, after an initial investigation, the EC may decide on provisional duties to be levied on the offending exporters pending a full investigation, after which the duties may be made definitive. There have been several complaints of dumping of products such as CTVs, VCRs, microwave ovens and CD players over the past few years, and several Japanese and Korean firms have been fined by the EC. The pressure on the EC from the major European firms to find against importers has been considerable. In this case the firms are involved in supplying the initial evidence required to prompt the Commission to act, but are not directly involved in the implementation of the policy, which is carried out by EC officials. But since in anti-dumping cases what constitutes prices set 'in the ordinary course of trade' in receiving as well as originating countries (that is, what exceptional conditions are discounted), and how average prices are calculated is open to a good deal of interpretation, the administration of the policy is conditioned by the weight of political pressure exercised by the complainants.

A final form of protection to be considered here is the determination of rules governing the operation of local subsidiaries of foreign companies. The EC has developed a *de facto* policy of requiring specific levels of 'local content' (that is, EC content) to be achieved by inward investors in order that their products be deemed of EC origin and thus freely tradable within the Community. The precise legal status of these rules, and of agreements signed by incoming firms and host governments, is open to question, but such has been the clamour of the European industry against 'screwdriver plants' that foreign firms have tended to treat such rules as legally binding and have acceded to pre-specified levels of local content in negotiations over such matters as investment grants and regional aid. Beyond calculations of local content have been undertakings about the 'quality' of investment, including commitments to transfer technology and establish Research and Development as well as manufacturing activities. Such bargaining between firms and governments has tended to take place at the national level, although the Commission has attempted to reduce the extent to which national governments bid against each other by increasing state aid in order to attract inward investment to their countries. The European firms have been unable to block such investments completely, but have had some success in influencing the conditions attached to them during negotiations.

The form of protection which most directly involved corporatist patterns of negotiation over policy formation and implementation was the VER, and it is unlikely that the 1983-6 agreement will be repeated. As we shall see later, however, there are other forms of policy response to the problems of the industry besides restrictions on trade, and these show much more obviously the embeddedness of industry interests in public policy-making.

Interest Organization in the European Consumer Electronics Sector

Broadly speaking, the pattern of associationalism in the sector has followed the changes in the structure of the industry: trade associations at the national level have become less significant as national industry boundaries have blurred, and the various national organizations have federated at the European level. Moreover, the presence of inward investing firms, especially the Japanese, but more recently Korean firms, has led to a structure of parallel representation. But the most important characteristic of these associations is that they are legitimating devices for the big firms rather than powerful bodies in their own right. This leads to the caveat that we should not mistake associational weakness for a lack of influence on policy of the industry itself.

In Britain the trade association for the consumer electronics industry is the British Radio and Electronic Equipment Manufacturers' Association (BREMA). The association has in membership almost all manufacturing (but not importing) firms within the product category of audiovisual consumer equipment (Amstrad has been the major British-owned firm which has declined to join). Its membership over the period 1975–90 has remained relatively constant at between 12 and 15 firms, but whereas in 1975 almost all were British-owned, in 1990 none is. Initially there was considerable opposition to allowing the Japanese to join, but after Sony was admitted to the Confederation of British Industry in 1975 (as the first Japanese member), this died away – fortunately for BREMA because without the Japanese it would cease to exist. BREMA is a relatively small organization with few permanent staff. For the Japanese, membership had more symbolic than pragmatic significance; it was a token of the firms' desire to be seen as good corporate citizens of British industry. In practice the Japanese maintained a very low profile, and did nothing to disturb the delicate situation whereby the organization demanded protection from the British government against the effects of Japanese competition spearheaded by the parent companies of its own members! In recognition of the sensitivities of the situation, the Japanese firms sent their British rather than their Japanese managers to BREMA council meetings. The policy stance of BREMA was dictated by the interests of the largest and long-established firms, which by 1985, as one by one they left the industry, was reduced to Thorn EMI and Philips.

In Germany the composition of the association, and its rules of membership, are rather different. Consumer electronics firms are organized as a subassociation of the ZVEI, the central organization of the electrical engineering and electronics industry. Full membership (with voting rights) is restricted to German-owned firms, but Japanese firms have been admitted as 'extraordinary members'. Firms suggest that an important reason for joining the subassociation is the opportunity to participate in the work of its technical commission, which is an important interlocutor with government over standards issues. Decisions made by the subassociation reflect the market power of the firms, and Philips in particular (Cawson et al., 1990: 290-1). In France consumer electronics firms belong to a trade association, SYMAVELEC, which is consulted by government on technical and trade issues, but as in Britain and Germany, is a relatively weak actor in negotiations which tend to take place directly between the major firms (especially Thomson and Philips) and the individual ministries (especially Industry and Finance) (Cawson et al., 1990: 274).

In 1983 nine national trade associations[1] formed a European Association of Consumer Electronics Manufacturers (EACEM). For its first seven years EACEM had no permanent officials and no headquarters. The secretariat shifted every two years to the offices of a different national association, and it functioned largely as a letterhead organization under whose auspices the interests of the major firms were represented. The organization was deemed appropriate because the issues of trade policy which increasingly exercised the firms, especially over VCRs, were being determined in Brussels; the organization was possible because Philips and Thomson were dominant players in the three most important national trade associations, those of Britain, France and Germany. Philips was a leading member of all nine associations, and Thomson of five.

The first major initiative of EACEM was the preparation in 1984 (by Philips and Thomson) of a document entitled 'Meeting the Challenge – European Response to Japanese Monopolization of World Home Electronics Markets'. The document proposed that tariffs on video recorders, hi-fis and all new products be increased to 20% for a period of three years, after which they would be set at the then prevailing rate for TVs of 14%. The then current rate for VCRs and hi-fis was 8%. The demands were pressed at meetings between officials of the European Commission and representatives of Philips, Thomson, Grundig and BREMA, at which the BREMA representative dissociated himself from the 'anti-Japanese sentiments' expressed in the paper, and pointed out that the most severe problems came not from the Japanese but from Korea and other Pacific basin producers.[2]

Although the demands for 20% tariffs were rejected, and the 19% rate for CD players has not been repeated, a uniform rate of 14% was established, which represented a significant increase for VCRs. Commission officials were aware that the 'EACEM position' did not fully reflect the views of all members of all the national associations, and in the absence of permanent officials, the case had to be argued by the representatives of the firms themselves – truly a transparent fig leaf! Subsequent policy documents were submitted to the Commission by EACEM in 1986 (on local content) and 1988 (on the need for strategic action to safeguard the industry), again drawn up largely by Philips and Thomson. EACEM also became the vehicle through which anti-dumping complaints were filed, but again Japanese membership of some of the constituent associations created some difficulties. A resolution adopted in 1986 cited two small Japanese VCR producers and three Korean firms as guilty of injurious dumping against European producers of VCRs (including Japanese producers with factories in Europe). While purporting to speak on behalf of all member firms, the document listed Japanese firms separately with the inscrutable rider that 'These producers are supposed to support the complaint, but have not expressed that the complaint has been lodged on their behalf.'[3] Evidence for the complaint was collected mainly by Philips and Thomson, and the document was prepared by Philips although it was presented to the Commission over the signature of the Secretary of EACEM, Angelo Teli.[4]

Compared to the limited resources of EACEM's revolving secretariat, Philips maintains a formidable lobbying organization in Brussels. Its head, commonly referred to inside Philips as 'our Ambassador to Brussels', is in constant contact with Commission officials. Philips organizes training seminars for EC officials to acquaint them with the problems of the electronics industry, and presents its own position papers on current issues. In addition to these contacts at all levels of the Commission, Philips lobbies through national governments and its former President, Wisse Dekker, was a founder member of the Round Table of European Industrialists. It is not at all surprising that the resources of a fledgling European trade association cannot match those of the major electronics producing firm; what needs explanation is why major firms like Philips consider it necessary or advantageous to work through such weak organizations.

In 1990 EACEM established a permanent secretariat in Brussels, and appointed its first full time Secretary-General, Gerard Nauwelaerts. The Chairman of the EACEM Council, Richard Norman, is also Chairman of the BREMA Council and for many years represented Thorn EMI Ferguson. Philips and Thomson each provide a Vice Chairman. The Council meets three time a year in different European locations. EACEM has three committees on technical, statistical and after-sales service, and its permanent staff are beginning to undertake the detailed research on trade matters previously carried out for EACEM by Philips and Thomson. The organization holds an annual meeting, alternately in Japan and Europe, with the Electronic Industries Association of Japan. One of its main preoccupations in 1990 was the development of a common position on satellite broadcasting, and it is not at all surprising that EACEM's demands for EC legislation in support of common standards and orderly market behaviour matched the public positions taken by Philips and Thomson, the major partners in the Eureka programme for the development of high definition television (HDTV) considered in the next section.

The advantage for Philips and Thomson of a strengthened EACEM lies in the public cloak of legitimacy through which their interests can be credibly argued to be representative of the industry as a whole. While there appears to be no danger of bilateral contact between large firms and the European Commission diminishing in significance, the addition of an EACEM voice is especially important for the public rhetoric of policy-making. It is also helpful that the Japanese members of constituent trade associations can be put in the awkward position of being seen formally to endorse the protectionist sentiments of the European producers. As long as the arguments about trade policy are conducted within the now conventional terms of the need for a 'level playing field', in which access for Europeans to the Japanese market is as easy (or as difficult) as access for the Japanese to the European market, then so long will the Japanese firms find it difficult publicly to dissent from EACEM positions. It has fallen recently to well-known figures such as Akio Morita, the President of Sony, to make the argument on behalf of the Japanese firms that inward investing firms like his own have found the unreliability of European components suppliers the most important brake on increasing levels of local content.

Sony is the most innovative of the Japanese consumer electronics firms, and it tends to do first what other Japanese manufacturers do after a brief interval. In 1973 Sony was the first Japanese electronics firm to build a factory in Europe, just as it had been the first to do so in the United States a short time before. Sony is a relatively small player in the Japanese market, making two-thirds of its sales abroad. Its ambition in Europe is to be treated as an 'insider' firm – in the same way that the Philips subsidiaries were for years treated as 'insider' firms in the national industries of the countries in which the factories were based.[5] By 1989 Sony employed 8,300 people in Europe, only 300 of them Japanese. Its decisions to expand and intensify local production in Europe are based partly on commercial motives – the desire to be closer to a major market – and partly on political considerations reflected in local content rules and anti-dumping actions.

In 1987 Sony created Sony Europa, with headquarters in Cologne, and installed a Swiss-born Chairman, Jack Schmuckli, as head of European Keiei Kaigi – a half-European, half-Japanese Executive Committee, charged with responsibility for coordination of strategy amongst Sony's eight plants in six European countries. Schmuckli and his American counterpart, the Chairman of Sony America, Mike Schulhof, have been appointed to Sony's main board in Japan. The company is aiming to expand its recently established R&D facilities in Europe, but admits that economic considerations alone would not justify decentralizing R&D to Europe. Sony wants to get access to some of the protected telecommunications and professional electronics markets in Europe, and a commitment to R&D is seen by the firm as the price of admission, just as local manufacturing in the 1970s was seen as the price of admission to European consumer markets. In 1991 Sony announced a further £100 million investment in Wales to create a European manufacturing headquarters, which will increase CTV production by 50% to 1.5 million sets a year, and increase employment in Wales from 2,000 to 4,000.

Sony's reorganization of its European operations has one eye on the Single Market, and the other on the European Commission. With European firms like Philips and Thomson still speaking publicly of 'trojan horse' investments, and the new French Prime Minister Edith Cresson taking a hard line in public over Japanese trade policy, the Japanese firms continue to consider themselves politically, although not economically vulnerable. Ironically the European firms have created a series of bilateral partnerships and joint ventures with Japanese firms which have made the continued presence of the Japanese in Europe important to their own survival. Thomson's and Bosch's VCR production is carried out through joint ventures with JVC and Matsushita respectively, and there is a raft of cross-licensing and technology transfer agreements, the most important of which has been Philips's collaboration with Sony on the CD audio standard, and its continued collaboration with Sony and Matsushita over the development of new interactive multimedia technologies based on CD.

Thus while membership of national trade associations and, through them, of EACEM is useful politically to the Japanese firms, it is insufficient as an effective channel of influence. The Electronic Industries Association of Japan (EIAJ), which established a European presence in Dusseldorf in 1962 – 12 years before the first local factory was built – remains a crucial resource for the Japanese firms in Europe. It does not enjoy the same privileged access in Brussels that Philips and Thomson do, but its role was critical in building up the Japanese presence in Europe through negotiations with national governments.[6] A more important prize for these firms would be admission to the various collaborative R&D programmes supported by the Commission, but up to now this has been strenuously opposed by the European-owned firms. I now turn to an examination of such programmes to assess the extent to which they offer 'structural privileges' to the European firms.

Collaborative R&D programmes

An important feature of European technology policy in recent years, as a consequence of the perception of heightened competition and a 'technology gap' between Europe and the United States and Japan, has been the promotion by the Commission of several very large-scale collaborative R&D projects, in which substantial subsidies are offered to firms which agree to pool resources with others based in different EC countries. The most important programmes have been ESPRIT (on information technology) and RACE (on telecommunications infrastructure), but there have also been smaller programmes concerning technology in traditional industries (BRITE) and in education (DELTA). In addition, the EC has become deeply involved in steering a number of the Eureka projects established after 1985 when at the behest of France Europe launched its civilian equivalent of the US Star Wars defence programme. Support for these programmes is channelled largely through DG XIII (Telecommunications, Information Industries and Innovation), which is now responsible for the second largest item of EC expenditure after the Common Agricultural Policy. These areas of Commission activity have been strongly influenced by French industrial policy thinking (Sharp and Shearman, 1987: 45). The Commissioner responsible for DG III (Industrial Affairs), Viscount Davignon (who had negotiated the export restraints agreement for VCRs discussed earlier) had initiated in 1979–80 a series of consultations with the heads of the 12 leading electronics and IT firms in Europe (later known as the 'IT Round Table'). The group set up a technical committee, which later became a steering committee (Sharp and Shearman, 1987: 49). Over the next two years the Round Table firms and EC officials reached a consensus that focused R&D programmes (defined as 'pre-competitive' to avoid falling foul of EC competition rules) would be a suitable instrument to strengthen Europe's technological base. This alliance of major firms and European officials was able to bring pressure to bear on national governments to back the emerging initiatives within the Council of Ministers. A pilot phase of ESPRIT was agreed in 1983, and a full ten-year programme (1984–93) was finally agreed in 1984 with a budget of 1.5 billion ECUs. ESPRIT was administered initially by a special IT Task Force consisting of permanent officials and a large number of 'experts' seconded from industry. The Task Force was absorbed into DG XIII in 1987.

Thus in its creation and implementation, ESPRIT involved the major electronics firms in a process of interest intermediation which conforms rather closely to the idea of corporatism. In this case there was no pre-existing association to act as interlocutor, but an *ad hoc* grouping was fashioned specifically for that purpose. It was neither necessary nor would it have been manageable to have worked through existing interest associations, and we can see the subsequent 'Europeanization' of producer organizations such as EACEM and the European Electronic Component Association (EECA) as fitting in to an already corporatized policy network.

In terms of consumer electronics, rather than the broader field of Information Technology, the most important initiative was the formation in 1986 of Eureka 95 to develop a HDTV system for Europe. If present investment commitments are realized, EU95 will be the largest single investment project in Europe after the Channel Tunnel. In the remainder of this section I will look at its formation and progress in some detail as a case study of the incorporation of major firms into industrial policy-making at the European level.

In 1986 the Japanese government proposed to the international broadcasting standards body (the CCIR) that a revolutionary high definition television technology[7] be adopted as a world standard for advanced television. The MUSE standard had been developed collaboratively from 1970 in a £100 million programme by the Japanese state broadcasting corporation (NHK) and several major firms led by Sony. Had the CCIR decided to adopt MUSE, then European firms would have been forced to license Japanese technology and cope with a 15-year lead in the development of HDTV, on top of the other difficulties we have seen that they faced in competing in conventional TV and video. The European firms had been very slow to grasp the significance of the Japanese strategy of working through the US broadcasters and a US consumer electronics industry already dominated by Japanese manufacturers. In 1985 the EC's IT Task Force had used the Round Table of IT firms to alert them to the significance of the Japanese moves in the United States, and jointly they succeeded in persuading European governments to block the Japanese proposals at the 1986 CCIR meeting.

In July 1986 EU95 was formally initiated, with the specific objective of developing a working HDTV proposal to present to the 1990 CCIR meeting as an alternative to the Japanese standard. The project leader was Philips, and the other three core firms were Thomson, Thorn EMI and Bosch, which reduced to three when Thomson bought out Thorn EMI's consumer electronics division in 1987. The companies decided to base their technology around a new transmission system, MAC, which had been pioneered by the IBA in Britain as providing a technically better solution for satellite broadcasting than the existing PAL and SECAM systems. In consultation with the Commission, the Eureka firms proposed a two-step route to HDTV in which MAC would be used for Direct Broadcast Satellites (DBS), and would later be upgraded to full high definition (HD–MAC) on a compatible path so that the early MAC equipment would not be rendered obsolete by the high definition system. In 1987 the Council of Ministers issued a directive that all DBS services be broadcast in MAC.

Unfortunately for the Commission and the Eureka partners the directive was framed to apply only to the new high-power DBS satellites. The private SES consortium based in Luxemburg had launched a medium-power Astra satellite, which Rupert Murdoch intended to use for a new English language multichannel DBS service called Sky. The licence for the 'official' British DBS service had been won by a consortium called British Satellite Broadcasting (BSB), which was obliged to use MAC – a technology for which the required receiving equipment (including the decoder microchips) had not yet been developed. The delays in designing and producing MAC chips allowed Murdoch to launch Sky ahead of BSB because the loophole in the MAC directive permitted the use of existing PAL technology for satellites designated as 'telecoms' rather than 'television'. In partnership with Amstrad, Sky was able to launch its service in February 1989, more than a year earlier than BSB. The latter, after serious problems in raising its initial capital of over £700 million, lasted less than a year before merging into a new company BSkyB in October 1990. The new company announced its intention of discontinuing MAC transmissions from the high-power Marco Polo satellite, but was forced by the IBA to promise to continue parallel broadcasting in PAL and MAC for two years.

The BSB débâcle posed a serious threat to the European HDTV strategy, which depended on an orderly transition to MAC ahead of the move to HD–MAC. The EU95 project had succeeded in demonstrating a working system in 1990, and the CCIR meeting once again deferred any decision on a single world HDTV standard. From October 1990 until June 1991 Philips and Thomson mounted a sustained campaign of lobbying EC officials, including the IT Commissioner Filippo Pandolfi, orchestrated at all levels including pressure from EACEM as well as efforts to press national governments into support for MAC. The French government was the most insistent advocate of MAC, both in terms of public support and public subsidies to firms. The French government announced £400 million state aids to the loss-making Thomson group, including £100 million specifically earmarked for HD-MAC development. President Mitterrand had personally intervened to help persuade Chancellor Kohl to put pressure on the German broadcasters to use MAC for their DBS channels.

Equipment manufacturers such as Philips and Thomson had a clear interest in securing the maximum commitment to MAC, and were pressing the Commission to recommend to the Council of Ministers that the MAC directive, due to expire in December 1991, be replaced by a tougher version which would also apply to medium-power satellites such as Astra. For the Commission to have accepted such demands would have meant that most of the 2 million or so dish owners in Europe would have had to buy new equipment. A series of meetings between Pandolfi and satellite broadcasters in the first half of 1991 failed to reach agreement on a new MAC directive, although the most likely outcome is that the Commission will spend over £350 million subsidizing satellite broadcasters to transmit programmes in both PAL and MAC over a ten-year period. The equipment makers have agreed as part of this bargain to introduce dual-standard PAL/MAC decoders and sets priced competitively with single-standard equipment.

The outcome of this conflict of interests reflects in no uncertain way the power exerted by the major producers, and the policy momentum established by their incorporation into the public/ private HDTV partnership between the Commission and the industry. The outcome is especially interesting in the light of technical developments in HDTV in the United States, where the same major firms, Philips and Thomson, have a major stake in TV manufacturing. In the United States the regulatory body for broadcasting, the Federal Communications Commission (FCC), has declined to rule on satellite HDTV standards, but has concentrated its efforts on an upgrade path to HDTV via terrestrial broadcasting, insisting that new HDTV programmes are also broadcast on existing standards. Four of the six contenders for the technology to be chosen by the FCC are fully digital systems; the Japanese MUSE systems and the European MAC are both hybrid analogue/digital systems. Philips and Thomson are arguing in front of the FCC that they can deliver a working all-digital HDTV system in the United States by 1995, whereas the very same firms are insisting to the European Commission that all-digital TV is a very long way off, and that the EC should back the MAC system for the foreseeable future.

The cosy and closed relationships forged in Europe between the TV manufacturers and the EC, and justified by the argument that Europe must have its own stake in new television technologies, threatens to be eroded, not by the countervailing pressure of consumers, or even the muscle of broadcasters, but by technological uncertainty arising from the transition from analogue to digital technology. It is tempting to conclude – at least as a working hypothesis – that the greater independence of the FCC and the refusal of the US government to adopt a corporatist industrial policy solution for HDTV development indicates a degree of pluralism in policy-making in the United States which contrasts with the greater propensity towards corporatism in EC policy-making.

The situation is complicated, however, by the fragmentation within the European Commission between different directorates. The development of French-style collaborative industrial policies in the electronics sector spearheaded by DG XIII contrasts sharply with the pro-liberal stance of DG IV (Competition Policy). DG III (Industrial Affairs and Internal Market) seems to have moved from its interventionist stance of the early 1980s under Commissioner Davignon to a more liberal position adopted with its responsibility for overseeing the Single European Act. DG IV is investigating the legality of the state aids given to Thomson, and has expressed public concern about EU95 moving from R&D collaboration towards a cartel-like coalition of firms producing HDTV equipment.

Even if we can detect outposts of corporatism in many of the industry-related activities of the Commission, there is no guarantee that this tendency will continue unchecked in the future as long as the turf fights and policy differences between different sections of the Brussels bureaucracy continue. Corporatism, as has often been observed, requires the partners to deliver on the agreements made. In the case of the HDTV strategy, the larger part of the £2 billion investment required is promised by two firms in financial difficulties. It remains to be seen whether those firms can deliver, whatever their intentions.

Conclusions

I stressed in the introduction to this chapter that the issue of Whither corporatism? in Europe cannot be addressed except through detailed analyses of the different sectoral domains. The case of the consumer electronics sector suggests a trend towards a form of micro-corporatism where policy is determined and implemented through bargained agreements between the EC and major firms.[8] As yet formal associations play a relatively insignificant role in policy-making, although they have proved useful to the large firms as a legitimating device. Collective action involving more than one firm has been carried out through *ad hoc* groupings (like the IT Round Table) or through formal collaborative programmes negotiated with the Commission. The recognition of policy problems and the insistent search for solutions has produced its own pattern of interest politics in this sector, which has excluded from participation firms defined as outsiders (most importantly, the Japanese firms). I also suggested in the case of the HDTV strategy that technological and financial uncertainties were likely to undermine the firms' role, and intra-Commission conflicts threaten to subvert the interventionist stance of the 'sponsoring' directorate, DG XIII.

Such a picture, whilst confined to one sector, does not allow any straightforward assertion of a supranational pro-corporatist dynamic. But neither does it resemble a Washington-like mosaic of multiple points of pressure in a pluralistic political process. Existing political practices in many settings have tended to exhibit a dualism between corporatism for the powerful and pluralism for the powerless, and it would be surprising if the totality of interest group politics in the new Europe turned out to be much different.

Notes

1. From all EC-12 countries except Ireland, Greece and Luxemburg. The Greek association joined later.

2. DG III, memo F. Braun to E. Davignon, 28 May 1984.

3. Enclosure 2 to Complaint made by the European Association of Consumer Electronics Manufacturers (EACEM) against Imports of Video Cassette Recorders from Korea and Japan (n.d., 1986).

4. Interview with senior manager of Philips UK, September 1987.

5. Information in this section comes mainly from the *Financial Times*, 2, 4 and 6 October 1989.

6. See Cawson (1991) for a detailed analysis of the role of the EIAJ in Europe in the 1970s and 1980s.

7. HDTV offers roughly twice as many horizontal lines as current television

standards (1,125 for MUSE, 1,250 for HD–MAC) and will be shown in wide-screen aspect ratio (16x9) 'letterbox' format compared to today's (4x3) pictures.

8. The distinction between macro-, meso- and micro-corporatism is discussed in Cawson (1985b; chapter 1).

5
Small Firms in the European Community: Modes of Production, Governance and Territorial Interest Representation in Italy and Germany

Jürgen R. Grote

Introduction

Given the bias in favour of large multinational corporations (MNCs) in the European Community's recent and most relevant programmes on joint R&D and high technology, it seems that those developments of the 1960s which led to 'merger mania' and industrial giantism in many leading Western European countries to fend off the American challenge, are now being reproduced on a wider, namely transnational scale. Most schemes of the Community's Technology Framework Programme favour the big 12 European MNCs (Grote, 1992a; Mytelka and Delapierre, 1987: 245; Peterson, 1991; Sharp and Shearman, 1987) and, more significantly, large enterprises participating in ESPRIT, Eureka and other initiatives of a similar character, are explicitly exempt from EC competition rules. Although Japan's economy is highly diversified and possesses a considerable share of small and medium-sized subcontracting firms and networks (Koshiro, 1990), the Commission seems to attribute the success of Japanese industry mainly to the sponsorship of large firms. Small and medium-sized enterprises (SMEs) account for 95% of companies within the Community and provide more than 60% of employment in industry and in excess of 75% in services (Revue Internationale PME 1988: 32). Yet, SMEs, 'despite apparent European Commission provisions to the contrary, are gradually squeezed out of the markets' (Shearman, 1989: 6) of high tech products and of those with a strong R&D content.

While preoccupations of this kind help explain the relatively negligent portion of the Framework Programme's funds actually paid out to SMEs,[1] it is also true that small firms benefit from a whole range of other Community initiatives which, although forming part of different policy domains, such as, for example, structural interventions and regional policy, aim at increasing their potential to cooperate and to adopt both new strategies and innovative technologies.

This chapter looks at the capacities of small firms in Germany and Italy to respond to the internationalization of markets and to overcome the disadvantage of size, either by acting collectively through their associations or by relying on alternative institutional arrangements being able to advance their interests. Since the notion of small firm, because of the incompatible definitions being used for it across the EC member states, hardly lends itself as a coherent unit for statistical analysis, special attention is being paid to the craft fraction of this category, that is, *l'artigianato* in Italy and *Handwerk* in Germany. Craft is easier to identify and, important in the present context, is also better organized. Artisan firms account for a relevant part of economic activity, with 46.1 and 38.7% in Germany and Italy respectively. Since about 1985, the EC Commission has shown an increasing interest in the small firm and craft domain and has recently established its Directorate General XXIII to deal specifically with the concerns of SMEs.

The decision to highlight here this particular domain is determined by two considerations. First, as outlined by Schmitter (1990), that capitalism can no longer be studied as a whole, but must be broken down into subsystems, such as, for example, sectors, interest domains and other autonomous or self regulating contexts and levels. By looking at the economic and organizational performance of the SME domain in Germany and Italy, Schmitter's claim will be tested that 'the practices of capitalism are becoming more, not less, diverse within national economies, at the same time that they are becoming more similar across national economies' (1990: 12). Secondly, with regard to the European dimension, it has become increasingly difficult to speak of a coherent Community strategy to respond to demands by the private sector or to incorporate interest organizations into transnational decision-making (Schmitter and Streeck, 1981). The Community is neither more nor less corporatist than its members – it is simply organized in a different manner, namely in a highly fragmented way that follows sectoral and domain-specific lines without always being able to manage the required degree of internal coordination (Grote, 1990). The EC 'commands resources, distributes benefits, allocates markets and market shares, adjudicates between different interests, and rules upon the actions of its member governments – all . . . within limited sectors, but nevertheless taking [it] into significant and sensitive areas of domestic politics' (Wallace et al., 1983: 405). To what extent do these sectoral activities eventually manage to modify the small firm domain, and to what extent are organized interests prepared to take advantage of the Commission's recent initiatives or, more likely representing an organizational goal, to defend established national sectoral regimes in the light of impending liberalization?

Organized collective action by small entrepreneurs and artisans – although representing probably the most efficient way of defending the category's interests and mastering the required organizational adaptations a firm has to undertake in order to remain competitive on international markets – is but one of many different means to improve the performance of the domain. Recent literature (Schmitter, 1990) has demonstrated that the availability of resources needed by smaller firms to stay in business is dependent on the supply of capacities which are unlikely to be provided by market forces alone.[2] These capacities may be generated by the general provisions of an *externally enforced* SME policy granting firms special treatment in the form of tax allowances, exemptions from competition rules or of public procurement contracts. External enforcement may, of course, also imply the public regulation of associational systems for the representation of SME interests. Public policies or hierarchically imposed economic solutions, such as buyouts and mergers, may be supplemented by a variety of modes of collective action and other *self enforcing* mechanisms chosen by the industry itself. These span from more economic types of cooperation and alliance, such as joint ventures or less formalized interfirm agreements, to socially generated structures, such as corporate networks, which might be either of an informal ('clubs') or of a formal nature ('business interest associations' and 'private interest governments'). Most research on the comparative industrial performance of SMEs, however, has adopted a kind of 'industrial archaeology' (Loinger and Peyrache, 1988: 130) approach thus underlining the crucial importance of a third means for enforcing cooperation. Flexible specialization of small firms, for example, is supposed to function in a *spontaneously equilibrating* fashion, based on the existence of regionally and subregionally structured 'communities' and other socially determined clusters of localized production.[3]

Needless to say, each of these mechanisms for the creation, enforcement and maintenance of inter-firm cooperation and flexible production is embedded in the more general context of national regulatory frameworks and the prevailing industrial cultures of different countries. Yet, complementing the latter, modes of production and sectoral governance are, of course, also anchored in particular regional or otherwise subnational arrangements. In this

context, 'community' figures only as the most conspicuous arrangement for the creation of territorial cohesion among local entrepreneurs, without necessarily representing the only and, as shall be
demonstrated, most efficient and enduring avenue to this end.
Regional variations in the performance of SMEs depend on the
structure of the nation state and on the policies operated by
different layers of government. These may be either of a federal–
decentralized or of a unitarian–centralized nature, with important
consequences for territorial and functional exchanges between
public authorities and private interests as Parri (1989, 1990a, b) has
demonstrated. Secondly, they depend on different mechanisms to
combat fragmentation and achieve cohesion within the domain as
well as on the way in which the category defines itself, that is,
creates a corporate or domain-specific identity among its members.
Both the definition of the interest domain and the mechanisms
being operated to defend it, can either be chosen autonomously by
the industry concerned, or be authoritatively imposed by the state.
Neither of these will be a concern of national authorities and
domestic interest associations alone, although both of them are
more than marginal to the stability of regulatory frameworks at any
other level of economic and political complexity. Territory,
therefore, comes in almost by default if one looks at the responses
of small business to state intervention and the regulation of their
markets and competitive conditions. It matters as well, however,
with regard to Community policies. Most of the assistance measures
being adopted since the European Parliament declared 1983 the
'European Year of Small and Medium Sized Enterprises and the
Artisanat', are territorially diversified and form part of regional and
structural fund allocations with an increasing involvement of
regional authorities and regionally organized interest associations
(Bianchi and Grote, 1991).

As demonstrated by Cawson in this volume for the case of large
firms, it is apparent that size of enterprises is a decisive criterion for
the organization of business interests. The same also applies to the
territorial location of firms. The neo-corporatist tradition has taken
account of this but has either focused on large firms (Grant and
Streeck, 1985) or emphasized the territorial logic of collective action
without simultaneously studying both categories comparatively.
Also, this literature has more often focused on interest associations
alone, thus omitting regional politics and especially government as a
key actor in subnational forms of interest intermediation. As
claimed by Allen (1989: 163), for corporatist theory to retain
validity or explanatory power, 'it needs to be tested more
thoroughly by looking at the specifics of economic policy within

regional governments in industrialized nations'. The volume on regionalism and business interests by Coleman and Jacek (1989a), for instance, uses a rather unspecified notion of region[4] to highlight all possible forms of collective action at various levels below that of the central state. Given the emerging relevance of a proper regional level of public policy-making and private interest accommodation, and taking account of Community initiatives being envisaged by increasingly popular scenarios in terms of a 'Europe of the Regions', this chapter emphasizes German '*Länder*' and Italian '*regioni*' as an increasingly important layer for interest intermediation. Although the principal aim of the arguments forwarded here is to highlight the shape of a future policy of the Community in the small firm domain, ample space will be given to a comparative description of small firm performance in both countries. Germany and Italy have not been chosen by accident for this comparison. The discrepancies in the way the small firm domain in the two countries is structured are of such a magnitude that it is possible to speak of two more or less distinct modes of production and governance in which organized interests come to perform very different functions. A transnational regulatory policy for SMEs elaborated by the services of DG XXIII of the EC Commission will have to choose between the options offered by these two cases. Neither of these, however, can be generalized to represent the predominant pattern of post-Fordist mass production as is being claimed by the proponents of the most influential model, namely the participants in the Italian debate on industrial districts (Pyke et al., 1990) and the advocates of 'flexible specialization' (Piore and Sabel, 1984). Nor can 'diversified quality production' of the German type (Sorge and Streeck, 1988) claim to be immediately applicable to other regulatory environments, despite the appeal it possesses in comparison to American 'macho-Fordism' or Japanese 'Sony-paternalism' (Streeck, 1989a). The question of to what extent an eventually emerging European enterprise policy (CEC, 1988a) will ultimately include essential parts of the German variety of organizing the small firm domain to become a 'specific European accumulation model' (Streeck, 1990b), crucially depends on several factors which will be outlined in the concluding section.

National Level Regulation as an Input into Small Firm Performance

One of the early students of the traditional sector has underlined the fact that it would hardly be possible to pursue the role of small firms without specifying the history of the actors, the action and the national context, 'or else fall into circular arguments about survival and functionality' (Berger, 1980: 100). It is precisely this kind of circularity which makes up much of the work on industrial districts and small firms both in Italy and Germany. The mainstream arguments either emphasize community forms of localized production or stress the relevance of technological developments in the districts, thus neglecting other factors which might determine growth and survival of the domain at least to similar extents. Among the most important of these are organized collective action by small firm owners and different forms of intervention and assistance by public authorities. Both are fairly distinct in Italy and Germany, possess different historical roots and have developed according to different logics. This section highlights the second factor, namely the role of the state as a sponsoring agency and external enforcement mechanism for small firm development.

One of the most conspicuous paradigm shifts in the analysis of industrial society over the past 30 years has been linked to the attention being given to the issue of enterprise size. In the 1950s and 1960s, small capital was conceptualized at best as an anachronism in a situation where 'the technology and specialization of the industrial society are necessarily and distinctively associated with large-scale organizations' (Kerr et al., 1960: 39). Fordist production patterns and the political modes of regulation corresponding to them as, for example, central wage bargaining, incomes policies and other demand-led forms of state intervention, have intrinsically been associated with corporatist policy-making. Partly as a result of the turmoil of the 1970s, the analytical bias towards large-scale enterprises has been increasingly substituted by dualist approaches, with authors focusing on the functional role small firms would posssess for capitalist development. Yet, in most cases, dualist authors continued to regard big business as the general rule since modern forms of 'industrial citizenship' could hardly be expected to emerge in a system which was based on non-unionized wage labour, temporary and often 'black' work, below-average wages, deficient health and safety regulations and lack of other types of labour legislation. The existence of an extended small firm domain and policies designed to further its development was not judged as something positive in itself but, rather, as being based on 'a fundamental division and effective depoliticization of the working class, with the concomitant disappearance of any organized challenge to the capitalist order in the name of economic democracy and social equality' (Goldthorpe, 1984: 340). Since Fordism's capacity to fill economic space is limited, small firms step in and occupy the vacant market niches at the peripheries of economic uncertainty.

While in countries with corporatist wage bargaining the unions take the central role, in dualism it is employers and their management who take the lead in tapping new sources of labour supply and in developing new methods of organizing production and new forms of employment. Views of this kind, albeit less evident and more sophisticated than presented here, have remained recurrent themes of corporatist writers until today (Schmitter and Streeck, 1991).

This rigid contraposition between two patterns of industrial society in which corporatism alone is attributed the label of a state-induced form of socio-economic organization that would maintain and extend existing levels of welfare, has recently been modified by Weiss (1988). She sees small firms as playing a proper and autonomous rather than merely a functional role in capitalist development. Her argument is of interest for two reasons. First, it emphasizes the positive role played by the Italian state in the creation of a class of small entrepreneurs and, secondly, in doing that, it underlines the importance of external enforcement mechanisms for the governance of the small firm domain. Elements introduced by functionalist authors as lying behind the strange growth of the Italian small firm domain, for example, the containment of employment thesis (Berger, 1980) or the argument that governmental promotion of small firms mainly serves the clientelistic control of the labour force (Pizzorno, 1975), are at best ranked second in this explanation. Weiss's main argument is that Italy's small business economy expanded and prospered because it had something its European counterparts lacked – a highly sympathetic state: 'While governments elsewhere celebrated its contraction or encouraged its elimination, the Italians created a distinctive category of small capital and set about populating and replenishing it' (Weiss, 1988: 9). While Italy is indeed a national case departing significantly from the big business norm, the question remains, however, whether the two elements of Italian industrial development, that is, the simultaneous existence of a large public enterprise sector and that of a dense web of small and very small firms, has exclusively to be conceived in positive terms or whether there are also pathological ingredients to it. Weiss's answer is very affirmative and almost replicates the ideological assumptions of the Democrazia Cristiana (DC), the Italian Christian-Democratic party which, definitely, has been mainly responsible for the country's present economic structure.

Small entrepreneurship was viewed by the DC as an end in itself and not just as a means to decrease unemployment figures and to develop peripheral parts of the national territory. Weiss suggests that primarily two themes had dominated the post-war debate on small enterprises in Italy. While the first was the original economic contribution of the domain, the second lay in its socially cohesive role in transcending capital–labour antagonism (1988: 83). The first theme can easily be verified by looking at economic statistics concerning small firm growth and employment shares of small establishments throughout the past 40 years or so. More important appears to be the argument which highlights the role of the '*ceti medi*' (middle classes) in the strategy of the DC. It also demonstrates that, unlike the German case, the creation of a traditional class of small owners and artisans has, from the beginning, been a political project pursued by the governing party without much interference by the interests concerned, namely organized groups of small entrepreneurs. The slogan accompanying this strategy, '*non tutti proletari, ma tutti proprietari*' (not everyone proletarians, but everyone property owners) accentuates the fact that the creation of a new entrepreneurial middle class has been at least as important as the objective to 'deproletarianize the worker' and come to grips with unemployment. Already by the end of the 1950s the strategy showed its first desired effects as noted with great satisfaction at the DC's seventh National Congress in 1959: 'the Italian social structure is progressively freeing (*sic*) many citizens, because the number of people who can live by independent or semi-independent labour, or at least organized in small firms, is increasing . . . the Italian social structure is moving in a direction that refutes the Marxist hypothesis, that is, in an entirely opposite direction' (Democrazia Cristiana, 1961: 321). A conception as that of the DC of the 1950s and 1960s which views dependent wage labour as contradicting free citizenship is of course interesting in itself. Yet, more interesting is the fact that many of these catholic thoughts of the 1950s and 1960s frequently recur in the writings of more leftist proponents of the industrial districts of the 1980s. We shall come back to that argument in a later section.

In any case, relevant parts of the governing party developed a kind of anti-monopolist stance in their industrial policy in the light of growing discontent on the part of the labour movement. This attitude, which can also be found in some of the early policy deliberations of the German Christian Democrats,[5] was, in part, also explained by the extraordinarily rigid position of the Italian employers association Confindustria which blocked any attempt to recognize union demands even where these were of relatively modest character. The main challenge to post-war democracy, according to the view of Italy's governing party, was of an internal nature and related to class unrest and growing support for the Communist Party. This makes the Italian case different from that of other countries where the principle of restructuring was to cope with external challenges. The other great European powers had all suffered a dramatic slide in international position either as a result of occupation or defeat. Italy was 'the only belligerent nation to emerge as it had entered the war: as "the least of the Great Powers"' (Weiss, 1988: 171) and, accordingly, had less problems with re-establishing a level of competitiveness that it had never possessed before, while Germany had to pay considerably more attention to the external pressures of international rivalry in the economic field. That put internal social cohesion and the principle of collaboration into the heart of the demo-christian project in Italy.

The most striking difference between the two countries is, perhaps, between the almost exclusively policy-led establishment and legal definition of a category of small enterprises in Italy and the self enforced regulation of the domain in Germany where the state, although certainly of importance for the granting of public status to the chambers of artisans, had been much less concerned with problems of maintenance and enlargement of the governing's party electoral base.[6] A purely structured system for the representation of small enterprise and artisan interests, together with major preoccupations of the DC with its declining electorate as a result of dramatically increasing unemployment figures makes the Italian government action on behalf of small enterprise deducible 'not from the interests, needs or demands of particular socio-economic groupings but from the independent goals, ideals and interests of the ruling party' (Weiss, 1988: 125). Although to some this will appear somewhat exaggerated, there is something to the argument that the domain in Italy has, so to speak, been created from above and not, as in Germany, from below, that is, from the 'acquired position' of an already well-established category of interests. Ample evidence for this is provided by the artisan law of 1956 and by its successor amendment of 1985.[7] The centrepiece of the legal definition of what artisanat is meant to be[8] was the specification of a maximum number of people employed – a fact which should have marked consequences for the consecutive mushrooming of small and very small firms. Article 2 of Law 860 specifies the maximum number for enterprises falling into the category of craft enterprises as ten employees including the owner and his family members for those firms which are not engaged in batch production, and five employees for the rest, that is, firms working in arts articles, tailoring and transport and enterprises with, though limited, serial production.

The amendments to the 1985 law which, in theory, would have provided an occasion to induce product diversification and a more efficient application of new technologies by either raising the size limit substantially or completely abandoning it, continued with a quantification in the definition of craft enterprises (Article 4 of Law 443), setting a margin of between eight and 18 employees. The only exception were so-called traditional product manufacturers and firms operating in the fashion sector which are allowed a maximum workforce of 32. The state, hence, had created an extremely decentralized system of very small productive units. Most of the activities of the chambers and of single-interest associations representing small entrepreneurs and artisans in Italy, are located at the provincial level. The formal acknowledgement of the amended text of the law of 1985 (Article 9), that it is up to the regions to provide for more precise clauses regarding the management of the category, has not much changed this fragmentation. In essence, in Italy the national regulatory framework for craft enterprises, represented by Laws 860 and 443, has encouraged the specific form of parochial interest representation which is so typical of the country.

The laws, however, not only inhibited forms of medium- to large-scale production of customized craft products, they also preempted the very concept of artisan production from any characteristic distinguishing it from other forms of economic activity (Ridolfi, 1985: 161). An entire range of industrial firms, provided their workforce did not exceed the established upper roof, now formally qualified for craft treatment and for the transfer of benefits deriving from this recognition. The law, therefore, reflects the idea that it is impossible to establish a qualitative definition of craft enterprises based, for instance, on some degree of testified professional qualification or other possible criteria. Ridolfi maintains that this enabled a substantial sector of the country's industrial population (roughly 40%) to escape the economic policy regulations imposed by central government in order to end up, ultimately, in circuits of political exchange at subnational level being controlled and managed by the local councillors responsible for the craft sector. In general, it can be said that the Italian artisan laws have at least been co-responsible for a further promotion of the black economy, for the sustained existence of structural dualism, for a professional de-qualification of artisans themselves, for the difficulties craft interests have in Italy to identify and establish themselves as a specific category and, not least, for a perpetuation of the pathological fragmentation of supply structures which characterizes large parts of the economic system. The unwillingness of government to invest into the creation of interfirm networks and the continued practice of individual transfer payments to single enterprises is not only apparent in the craft sector but concerns the entire range of small and medium-sized enterprises (Bianchi, 1990). Assistance measures for small enterprise remained rather underdeveloped,[9] at least until the approval of the Law on Small Enterprises (DDL Battaglia-Righi) by the Chamber of Deputies in autumn 1991.[10] The main objective of governmental policy has been and remains the multiplication of enterprise and not its expansion, or other measures encouraging small firms to grow. A report by the Christian Democrats to the Chamber of Deputies, presented in the course of debating the first artisan law, underlined that 'there would be no justification in a policy which facilitated the development of artisan enterprise into an industrial one . . . the latter would be a policy encouraging the death of the artisan. It would not defend the artisanat, but would promote the expansion of firms so that they become medium, if not large.'[11]

Returning to Weiss's argument that it was neither the containment of employment, as suggested by dualist authors, nor the clientelistic control of the labour force and the *petit bourgeoisie*, as suggested by Pizzorno, which explain the ruling party's interest in small entrepreneurship but, rather, the original economic contribution of the sector and the 'social project' of the Democrazia Cristiana to promote social cohesion, the rigid dichotomy posed between the two views now appears to be somewhat artificial. In reality, it is a question of emphasis whether the bolstering of craft concerns is interpreted as a contribution to decreasing unemployment rates or whether the ideological spirit lying behind that motive, namely assurance and extension of hegemony, are made responsible for the phenomenon. Moreover, Pizzorno's celebrated revelation which opened a vast discussion on forms of political exchange in Italy and elsewhere, that 'economic credits correspond to political debts' (Pizzorno, 1975), and that it is precisely patterns of individualistic exchange which explain the bizarre forms of territorialized political mediation in Italy, has the advantage not just of highlighting conservative techniques for the creation of party support but applies equally to leftist parties, the latter having to react to the successes of the small firm policy of the DC, were they not to lose ground in a terrain of potentially reactionary character. As Berger (1980: 112) notes, 'the Left . . . vies with the Christian Democrats in presenting itself as a protector of small, independent property and has gone along with most of the protectionist legislation of the postwar period'. That it did so according to patterns which were not very different from those characterizing the national political system as a whole, namely by following the logics of territorial political exchange especially at provincial and communal level, is convincingly demonstrated by a number of authors who point to forms of neo-localist parochialism even in the heartland of flexible specialization and industrial districts which is predominantly ruled by Communist or Communist coalition government.[12] Protectionist measures such as the 1972 law regulating the opening of new supermarkets and virtually halting the modernization of commerce, are by no means alien to the Communists either. The PCI called for a rapid implementation of this legislation 'in order to block the expansion of monopolistic supermarkets and the proliferation of licences' (*L'Unitá*, 18 September 1971). The party, in reacting to the increasing strength of the DC-operated artisan interest association Confederazione Generale Italiana dell'Artigianato (Confartigianato or CGIA) which, in a sense, represented the direct outcome of the state-corporatist associational system working under fascism, meanwhile had created its own association, CNA (Confederazione Nazionale dell'Artigianato) and, hence, had to satisfy the demands of its own clientele. Although the devices the PCI had at its disposal to build up consensus and establish networks of political exchange in the regions where it was involved in government were, by far, less comprehensive than those in the possession of the Democrazia Cristiana,[13] the simple capacity of permitting and licensing the exertion of certain economic activities is a powerful tool for regulating the market.

To summarize the points explaining the extraordinarily high share of small enterprises in Italy, it is now possible to say, first, that the small firm domain in that country is a result of a deliberate project of a political party and, secondly, that the mechanisms enforcing governance of the domain are politically 'over-determined' to such an extent that the notions of 'communitarian self management' and of 'regional external economies' as the main sources of a superior small firm performance lose at least the primary importance being ascribed to them in recent writings on the 'Third Italy'. Some argue that the prominent role in small firm development being accredited to the state is somewhat exaggerated. Bagnasco (1988: 58–9), for example, rightfully mentions the strong market element guiding the development of small firms in Italy. Political interventions, in his view, have only followed and accompanied the spontaneous growth of the small firm domain rather than having given it a direction or regulating it. Yet, it is important to note that this applies only to a second phase, so to speak, of potential political intervention in favour of the domain, where the state has exclusively left it to the market to decide over the fortune of small enterprises. The relevance of public authorities appears to be decisive, however, during the initial phase of the domain's creation and definition, where government has set the framework conditions for the growth and multiplication of small firms. Once having been set up, the domain developed essentially by way of *'laissez-faire'*. Finally, and most importantly in the present context, it also appears that business interest associations, if at all, had only marginal impacts on the development of the domain.

Despite the existence of an even higher share of craft enterprises in the overall number of firms, the German case clearly exhibits different features. Although granting especially the artisan sector a set of special rights which are exceptional in Europe, the German state did not appear to be particularly interested in the quantitative growth of the domain. Ideological motives such as the maintenance of a 'healthy *Mittelstand*'[14] certainly have also played a role in the deliberations of the fathers of the Social Market Economy.[15] Yet, contrary to the Italian case, a class of small owners did not have to be created from scratch but was already well established in the immediate post-war period. It enjoyed a high degree of associational power and autonomy that made it less vulnerable to any kind of disturbance from either the state or the allied forces. With regard to the craft sector, Streeck (1989a: 66) has noted that the types of political exchange which initiated the legal institutionalization of *Handwerk* in Germany, go as far back as the 1870s and 1880s.[16] While still characterizing many of the mechanisms at work in the Italy of today, exchanges of this type are far less relevant in the German case, not least because of a higher turnover in government than in Italy where Christian Democrats have always held hegemonic positions in government.[17]

The objective of the German government, hence, was not the uncontrolled multiplication of the domain as in Italy but, rather, the achievement of a reasonable equilibrium between large and small firms. This is in part explained by the competition principle of the German economic policy guidelines which sought to remove, modify or to prevent the harmful consequences of legislation if it resulted in SMEs as the victims. If this was impossible, 'the federal government intervenes in favour of SMEs and restores the balance through special measures of assistance' (Denton, 1968: 63). In general, however, German economic policy of the immediate post-war period appears to be characterized by an emphasis on the growth and enlargement of already medium to large enterprises deemed to be absolutely indispensable for the achievement of competitiveness on international markets. Contrary to the Italians, who perceived their weaknesses as being predominantly political and of a domestic nature and who, accordingly, opted for investments into internal social cohesion which, as has been demonstrated, prompted a vast economic and territorial dispersion, the German situation was characterized by a concentration on the re-establishment of an economic system which had been seriously decimated. The objective was to maintain at least to some extent the competitiveness which had characterized the country's economy before 1939. Given the widely accepted superiority of large-scale enterprise characterizing the economic thought of the period, and considering the Fordist organization of the US economy which figured as a blueprint for German restructuring (Berghahn, 1984), it is not surprising that together this resulted in an industrial policy which was largely inclined towards fostering concentration. The cartel law had been so watered down by the amendments of the Federation of German Industry (BDI) that it became virtually useless. Yet, considering this and the practice of German legislation to 'encourage concentration by granting tax benefits to firms that merged their subsidiaries' (Braunthal, 1965: 252) at precisely the same period that the *Mittelstandspolitik* was launched, does not in itself compromise the latter's seriousness altogether.

That small business policy in Germany has always been a special policy area has become especially apparent during the most recent change of mood which has led to an euphoric rediscovery of the small firm. Whatever the reasons for this rediscovery – contribution of SMEs to employment levels, their higher flexibility and innovative potential, or the change of political climate after the election of a new government in 1982 – the Federal government has adopted an impressive number of individual measures, special programmes and amendments to laws aimed explicitly at the small business constituency. As noted by Weimer (1990: 136), Germany is one of the few countries to have an overall research and technology plan for small and medium-sized firms, a fact which led to about 25–30% of total federal expenditure on civil R&D being channelled to SMEs.[18] Other support measures concern assistance to newly founded companies where, according to experts, prospective entrepreneurs are able to shop around for assistance from about 100 different support programmes. Fiscal measures and exemptions from regulations complete the picture. The Federation of German Manufacturing Industries (BDI) has estimated that more than half of the company-related tax relief granted between 1983 and 1985 benefited small and medium-sized firms and as regards the Employment Protection Law of 1985, a substantial number of special provisions for small firms have been included.[19] However, as much as these measures seem to reflect real changes in government attitude towards the small firm domain, they are nothing more than a consequence 'of the country's long-standing small business policy' (Weimer, 1990: 140) which, in reality, has not undergone any dramatic changes in emphasis since the immediate post-war period.

The special concern and attention given to a healthy base of small enterprises in Germany becomes more apparent where not merely transfers of financial resources and other types of assistance are concerned, but state intervention into the associational interest domain of the category. With regard to the way this manifests in the case of *Handwerk*, Streeck has characterized the formation of public–private arrangements which are so typical of Germany, as 'a perfect example of a private interest government' (Streeck, 1989a: 89). This can most convincingly be demonstrated by the craft associations' attempts to defend their sectoral interests in the turmoil of allied military occupation. With a background of an exceptionally long and successful corporate tradition, German artisans were able to achieve considerably more after the end of the war than any other category of economic interests. By the end of the 1940s, most of what had characterized the craft sector during the Weimar Republic had been re-installed. The national peak association of the category, the Zentralverband des deutschen Handwerks (ZdH), was established in 1949 and by that time all craft enterprises in West Germany, apart from those falling under the jurisdiction of the US military authorities, were obliged to register in one of the local chambers of artisans and pay their membership fees. There were, indeed, marked differences in handling the concerns of the interest domain across the different territorial sectors of allied military occupation (Kübler et al., 1982). Ullmann (1988: 256), for example, reports a masterpiece of persuasion accomplished by the officials of the different regional guild associations belonging to the British sector where hostility to corporatist forms of associationalism was less accentuated than in the territories under US authority. Promising to re-establish the artisan law of the pre-fascist period, the craft associations managed to get a draft law accepted by the military authorities which included all the essentials of Nazi legislation, apart from the clearly discredited ones such as coercive membership,[20] the Fuhrer principle and the (honorary) tribunal (*Ehrengerichtsbarkeit*).

Most of the associational activity of organized *Handwerk* until 1953, when the artisan law (*Handwerksordnung*) was passed by a great majority in the Federal parliament, was dedicated to convincing the allied forces of the fact that the achievement of the long-demanded organizational structure during the Third Reich did not reflect ideas of National Socialist origin[21] but, rather, those of a long tradition within the category, going far back into history. This demanded a great deal of combined persuasion both by the governing party and the chambers of artisans and guild associations. The main obstacle to the passing of an artisan law which would be binding for the entire territory of West Germany were the US military authorities who deeply disagreed with compulsory chamber membership and with certain licensing practices which enabled the chambers to operate a system of entry barriers to the sector unmatched in Europe. The centrepiece of a *Handwerk* licence was the master certificate (*Meisterbrief*) which required a total of about seven years of permanent upgrading of one's professional qualification.[22] Today, it carries exactly the same entitlement to run an artisan business as the prestigious university degree of Diplom-Ingenieur (graduated engineer). For the Americans, this clearly contradicted their own principles and this form of state-corporatist arrangement must have looked 'like one giant conspiracy to restraint of trade' (Streeck, 1989a: 66). The last step which had to be mastered before the *Handwerksordnung* (HWO) could be approved by parliament on 17 September 1953,[23] was, hence, the massive critique brought forward by the US military government, itself representing the influential views of leading American economists which had their stronghold in the US Treasury Department (Berghahn, 1984: 187). Although the craft sector had at its disposal an impressive organizational structure, the state had to assist its attempts to achieve the desired organizational cohesion and the inclusiveness of artisan associationalism. This was done by making use of an exceptional tool, namely the personal intervention of the then Federal Chancellor Konrad Adenauer who had to write twice to the High Commissioners of the United States, John McCloy and J.B. Conant, in order to accelerate the legal procedure.[24]

When the *Gesetz zur Ordnung des deutschen Handwerks* had passed through parliament, *Handwerk* had finally achieved the aims it had strived for for decades, while the state was now in a position to mandate most of the concerns of the sector to the chambers which themselves had acquired the status of a public law body. The last 40 years or so show extensive evidence of the fact that everything concerning the professional needs of the category such as the qualification of artisans including apprenticeships and vocational training, the selection of firms being in particular need of government aid, the organization of centres of formation and information as well as technology transfer centres, was now being run according to para-state principles of 'self governance'. The differences in comparison with the Italian system are obvious. There were no numerical restrictions with regard to a maximum number of employees in order to qualify for the status of a craft firm. Accordingly, the sector was characterized by a relatively stable number of artisan firms throughout the last decades while Italian figures were exploding during the same period. The major entry requirement was rather the accomplishment of the master title which secured the sector an outstandingly high level of professional qualification of labour and management and, subsequently, enabled it to increase its share in customized quality products. Contrary to Italy where investments in training and qualification are dramatically underdeveloped, the institution of the German chambers and associational system has enabled the sector to undertake precisely those investments which single firms and hyper-rational entrepreneurs are unlikely to provide as a result of opportunist behaviour, 'free-riding', low quality-low price competition etc. (Streeck 1989a: 66). As noted by Klinge (1990: 33), this high level of qualification not only provided inputs into the *Handwerk* sector but also benefited industry as a whole,[25] as many who had finished an apprenticeship in the former continued working in the latter.

Following the scheme outlined in the introduction to this chapter, it can be said that state activity has in both countries influenced the organizational forms the sector has adopted. But while in the Italian case the state has created a legal framework (Law 860 of 1956 and Law 443 of 1985) basically guaranteeing a quantitative extension in the number of firms, the German HWO is a masterpiece of persuasion of public authorities by organized craft wishing to defend its corporate interests. More importantly, the Italian authorities, having created the framework conditions for the growth of the sector, failed to provide most of the measures necessary for survival and successful adaptation to changing economic conditions.[26] The state left it, essentially, to the market to arrange for appropriate solutions. In Germany, on the other hand, the passing of the HWO provided an opportunity to delegate the management of the sector almost exclusively to the chambers of artisans and the guild associations who established an encompassing system for regulating the concerns of the entire category. The following sections will show how the small firm domain has developed in both countries and to what extent this development has been shaped by associations representing the category. Attention will be given in particular to the territorial distribution and activities of craft enterprises across the German *Länder* and the Italian *regioni*.

The Quantitative Relevance of Small Firms and Craft Enterprises in Italy and Germany

It is accepted that small and medium-sized firms have provided substantial job-generation all over Europe, in a period when large enterprises have suffered a severe decline in employment rates. In particular, this has applied to small units of up to 100 employees. As demonstrated by Loveman and Sengenberger (1990: 8), the time series behaviour of small unit employment shares has followed a 'V' pattern in which declines through the late 1960s and early 1970s are reversed and small unit employment share increases into the 1980s. This pattern is evident both for enterprises and establishments,[27] and for the total economy and manufacturing. Public authorities have taken account of these developments to various degrees. After decades without any particular measures in favour of SMEs in Italy, the parliament there has recently passed a special law for this category, whose objective is to improve the industrial habitat of small firms.[28] Although paying more attention than before to the role of small firms, German authorities, on the other hand, did not need to change their policies significantly, as an explicit SME strategy has always been an essential part of both federal and *Länder* economic policies (Weimer, 1990). The most obvious change has, rather, occurred at the transnational level of the European Community where the Commission has established a new Directorate General to deal mainly with SME concerns.

Employment share data, although not able to indicate with precision the actual reasons behind the growth of small units in the different sectors (services, manufacturing, etc.), may give an approximate idea of the relevance small firms possess in both countries. If one follows the OECD definition of small firms as those with less than 100 employees,[29] then the share of small enterprises in total employment ranges from roughly 42% in West Germany[30] to nearly 70% in Italy (Table 1).

Table 5.1   *Employment by enterprise size in Italy and Germany (total economy)*

Country	Year	No. employees			
		1–20	21–99	100–499	500+
Germany	1970	17.2	24.3	18.3	40.3
Italy	1981	53.2	16.1	12.2	18.5

Source: Loveman and Sengenberger, 1990: 9

As regards numbers of enterprises, in Germany 98.9% of firms fall into the category of 1–100 employees,[31] while only 1.2% employ more than 100 workers (Weimer, 1990: 99). At this level of aggregation, there appears to be little or no differences between Germany and Italy, since data for the latter demonstrate that only 1.7% of firms possess a workforce of more than 100 (Lanzalaco, 1989: 248). More interesting are the data on number of enterprises and on employment shares in the 'small' and 'medium' classes. These show that, contrary to the expectation that Italy would have an outstandingly greater number of small and very small firms, the relative figures for both countries rather almost equal each other. For example, 88.5% of non-agricultural enterprises in Germany do not employ more than nine employees and 97.8% not more than 49. Figures for Italy are 98.3 and 99.2% respectively. Therefore, differences do not occur in the relative number of small and very small firms in overall economic activity but, rather, in their degree of concentration, measured in terms of employment share of the remaining 1.2 and 1.7% of enterprises employing more than 100 employees, that is, in firms falling into the 'medium and large' categories. Firms of this type employ 58.6% of the workforce in Germany but only 30.7% in Italy.

As to the share the craft sector obtains in these figures, it appears yet again that differences are not ones of relative share of the artisan sector in the total economy (agriculture excluded) but relate to the absolute numbers of craft enterprises in both cases. Tables 5.2 and 5.3 show both absolute and relative figures for the craft sector in both countries as occurring at the level of German *Länder* and Italian *regioni*.[32] Given an almost equal population of the 'old *Länder*' and the whole of Italy, the results are most astonishing. It turns out that the share of *Handwerk* in the German economy is actually far higher (46.1%) than that of the *artigianato* in the Italian system (38.7%). At the same time, of course, more than twice as many craft firms are registered in Italy (1.4 million) than in Germany (611,000).

This in part reflects what has been argued above, namely that legal restrictions of the Italian type do not apply to the German definition of a craft enterprise. As a result of this, a German firm being operated under the legal umbrella of *Handwerk* may, in exceptional cases, have as many as 500 or more employees, while the mushrooming of Italian figures can only be explained as the corollary of both legal restrictions imposed on the maximum size and incentive structures which make it attractive for non-artisanal business also to register as a craft enterprise. It appears that the total number of German firms in all categories and sectors,

Table 5.2   *Craft enterprises and minor trades as a share of all registered firms in Germany as of 1 January 1991*

Land	IHKs industry total	Craft	Minor trade	HWKs craft total	Craft as % of total
Schleswig Holstein	30,295	19,599	3,288	22,887	43.0
Hamburg	39,154	10,536	2,406	12,942	24.9
Niedersachsen	70,831	55,635	7,459	63,094	47.1
Bremen	10,876	4,068	698	4,766	30.5
Nordrhein Westphalen	192,675	122,559	20,913	143,472	42.7
Hessen	70,636	50,028	6,276	56,304	44.4
Rheinland Pfalz	36,840	35,007	3,598	38,605	51.2
Baden Wurttemberg	102,164	97,462	11,904	109,366	51.7
Bayern	125,842	118,591	16,979	135,570	51.8
Saarland	9,502	7,987	978	8,965	48.5
Berlin/W.	25,840	12,099	3,404	15,503	37.5
Total	714,655	533,571	77,903	611,474	46.1

Source: Author's calculations based on data by Industrie- und Handelstag 1991 (for IHK data) and Zentralverband des deutschen Handwerks (for craft and minor trades)

registering either with the Chambers of Industry and Commerce (IHK) or with the Chambers of Artisans (HWK), almost equals the total of craft enterprises being registered in Italy with the Camera di Commercio, dell'Industria, dell'Artigianato e dell'Agricoltura (approximately 1.3 and 1.4 million respectively). Another important feature is the territorial concentration of craft in both countries which can only in part be explained by the geographic size of the regions in question. The three *Länder* of Nordrhein Westphalen, Baden Wurttemberg and Bayern alone account for 388,408 craft enterprises or 63.5% of the German total. Similarly, 755,839 craft firms or 55.4% of the Italian total are located in just one quarter of the 20 regions of the country, namely in Piemonte, Lombardia, Veneto, Emilia-Romagna and Toscana, that is in the old industrial regions and in the heartland of the 'Third Italy'. As regards the craft share in total activity in the Italian regions, figures would have been more pronounced had we chosen the provincial level of aggregation. Certain clusters emerge around the borders of adjacent regions showing peaks of considerably more than 45% in the border areas of Veneto, Lombardia and Emilia-Romagna. The same applies to the other extreme, exhibiting a share of *artigianato* of less than 25%. These areas are located around the border zones of Lazio and the Marche and around those of Calabria and Puglia.[33] All of the 'Third Italy', except the Trentino-Alto Adige, that is all of the

North–East–Centre (NEC) regions, possess a higher than 40% share of craft firms in the total number of enterprises, agriculture being excluded. In general, differences in this respect between the regions of the Mezzogiorno and those of the North–East–Centre, are far less significant than one might have expected. They are significant, however, with regard to the absolute numbers of firms operating in the two clusters of regions.

It is difficult to calculate the share of the craft sector in the two

Table 5.3 *Craft enterprises as a share of all registered firms in Italy as of 29 August 1991[1]*

Regione	Total firms	Agriculture	Total less agriculture	Craft	%
Valle d'Aosta	9,676	82	9,594	3,621	37.7
Piemonte	305,936	3,643	302,293	124,475	41.2
Liguria	118,445	1,162	117,283	44,083	36.7
Lombardia	660,801	6,107	654,694	251,210	38.4
NORTH	1,094,858	10,994	1,083,864	423,389	38.5
Trentino-AA	60,466	649	59,817	21,958	36.7
Friuli-VG	81,349	1,719	79,630	31,929	40.1
Vento	322,597	7,011	315,586	133,240	42.2
Emilia-Romagna	316,664	7,799	308,865	134,106	43.3
Toscana	285,505	4,787	280,718	112,808	40.2
Marche	115,294	3,221	112,073	50,840	45.4
Umbria	54,321	1,461	52,860	23,582	44.6
NEC	1,236,196	26,647	1,209,549	508,463	41.8
Lazio	268,260	4,373	263,887	84,291	31.9
Campania	306,090	4,925	301,165	78,183	26.0
Abruzzo	86,234	2,310	83,924	33,472	39.9
Molise	18,879	866	18,013	7,423	41.2
Puglia	215,041	4,290	210,751	77,457	36.8
Basilicata	32,472	962	31,510	14,572	46.2
Calabria	105,088	2,769	102,319	32,511	31.8
Sicilia	237,884	5,087	232,797	69,493	29.9
Sardegna	93,625	1,280	92,345	36,620	39.7
SOUTH	1,363,573	26,862	1,336,711	434,022	35.9
Total	3,694,627	64,503	3,630,124	1,364,874	38.7

[1] Due to inconsistencies of the regional data, row values do not always correspond to column values. For all mean values, only the columns have been considered.

Source: Author's calculations of data provided by the data bank CERVED (Societa Nazionale di Informatica delle Camere di Commercio, Industria, Artigianato, Agricoltura) in August 1991, by CERVED (ed.), *Movimprese, Movimento anagrafico delle imprese italiane, primo semestre,* 1991, and by CERVED, 1989.

countries in the overall category of small firms, that is, those with less than 100 employees. Rather outdated figures (1970) are available only for manufacturing in Germany where the number of craft enterprises reached 77% of small firms, with an employment share of about 54% (Weimer, 1990: 98). What clearly emerges from the figures presented above, is the extraordinary importance of small firms, and especially of those belonging to the craft sector, in both Italy and Germany. Italy, moreover, provides an extreme example even when being compared to other OECD countries. While Hungary and the UK exhibit the lowest employment shares in small establishments as a percentage of the total economy (18.3 and 26.2%) of all OECD countries investigated in the ILO study (Loveman and Sengenberger, 1990), Japan's figures are 56.0% and Italy's 59.3%.[34] As to the employment share of large establishments (more than 500 employees), the country with probably one of the highest degrees of economic concentration of all Western industrialized nations, that is, the United Kingdom, scores highest with 46.8%, while Italy closes the list with 19.6%. It represents an extreme case both in the classes of small and very large establishments.

Given that it is possible to speak of a disadvantage of size, the question arises as to how this disadvantage is actually surmounted, and how growth and employment shares of small units can be explained in the general context of an industrial policy which aimed to sponsor small firms and enabled them to grow. Possible answers to this question essentially converge around two motives. One interpretation highlights economic, technological and efficiency elements as those underlying the move into smaller units. The shift is explained by an increased turbulence in international markets, by the instability of demand, by more differentiated consumer tastes for customized quality products, as well as by the micro-electronic revolution and subsequent lower capital costs. A second interpretation, stepping out of the narrow efficiency logic, highlights institutional factors as being responsible for small firm performance. The critical role of social and political organization is accentuated in these approaches which are also supposed to represent the 'most pervasive and persuasive' ones (Loveman and Sengenberger, 1990: 46) available on the menu of possible readings. Interpretations of this kind are based on the conviction of a crisis in the institutional structure which accompanied mass production and of a movement toward an alternative based on 'flexible specialization'. The term 'flexible specialization' is commonly associated, in this context, with work undertaken in the tradition of Piore and Sabel's discovery of a 'second industrial divide' and, in particular, with research on 'industrial districts' in parts of the 'Third Italy' by scholars such as Becattini, Brusco, Bagnasco and others.

As regards this second interpretation, however, two of the most conspicuous devices providing for high quality production of small units are frequently left off the research agendas of Italian '*distrettisti*' and their American interpreters. The first is regulatory intervention and provision of protective measures by the state, the second the contribution of organized interest to social order in localized economic systems. The uneven distribution of mechanisms of this kind in Italy and Germany and their relevance both for the creation and the upgrading of the craft sector have been outlined in the preceding section. In what follows, emphasis is put on 'communitarian' institutions being built around localized markets and areas of production which, especially in the view of many Italian regional economists and sociologists, represent the cornerstone for the success of industrial districts in the Third Italy. They are also supposed to be easily applicable to other economic and institutional environments thus ultimately leading to a generalized and new pattern of production which would progressively replace Keynesian models of macro-regulation. Charles Sabel, at least, maintains that there would be nothing utopian about such a prospect (Sabel, 1989: 58). Comments on regional economies and their embeddedness in non-economic institutions in Germany are reduced to a necessary minimum in the following sections, not only because the discussion of spatial systems of small enterprises (SSSE) and of industrial districts is, basically, an Italian one, but also because a very detailed analysis of German *Handwerk* and its associational formats at the various territorial levels of the Federal Republic exists already (Streeck, 1989a).

Trust and Solidarity: an Alternative to Self-governance by Associations and to Publicly Imposed Norms?

Small firm performance in Italy and Germany can be cast in terms of two generalized concepts which dominate the current debate on the institutional structures supposed to be the most appropriate ones for a further consolidation of this sector of economic activity. These are 'flexible specialization', which essentially has grown out of the Italian experience, and, secondly, 'diversified quality production'[35] denoting more particularly the German experience. It is claimed here that these concepts occupy the end points on a continuum of policy options from which transnational actors and, especially, the EC Commission will have to pick up those elements which could ultimately be merged to create something like a

European enterprise policy and, more particularly, a strategy for SMEs. Small firm policies and regulatory institutions of other EC member states which, probably, represent a mix of the two models, are located on this continuum as well, while some countries will not be represented on it at all.[36] The question which can now be addressed is which of the major governance mechanisms outlined in the introduction have to be accredited to either of the two modes of production. A second question relates to the geographical, institutional and administrative levels at which these production patterns materialize and prosper and, moreover, to the problem of the most appropriate tier at which both public policy intervention and organizational activity of private interests are likely to reap the highest benefits for the small firm and craft sectors. A third question, commented on later, is related to the European Community's capacity to influence the behaviour of individual entrepreneurs by going beyond traditional financial incentives, that is by employing alternative mechanisms and empowering regional governments, business interest associations and trade unions with the authority to (self) regulate the interest domain of small firms.

On a purely technological account and from a micro-economic perspective which primarily accentuates the internal organization of firms, the two modes of production could be distinguished in terms of standardized price-competitive and customized quality-competitive production on the one hand and low and high volume production on the other. This has been suggested by Sorge and Streeck (1988: 30) who present a contingency table of four alternative product and manufacturing strategies.[37] While asserting that the low volume production of customized quality-competitive goods and the high volume production of standardized price-competitive goods look quite familiar and are, therefore of less interest, they draw attention to the conditions for the emergence of a new type of production which they call 'diversified quality production'. This pattern, which is characteristic of the German case, has enabled firms to introduce a hitherto unknown degree of variety, as well as quality in large batch production. Two different trajectories lead to this form of industrial restructuring. Either craft producers manage to extend their production volume 'without having to sacrifice their high quality standards and customized product design', or mass producers move 'upmarket by upgrading product design and quality, and by increasing product variety in an attempt to escape from the pressures of price competition and from a market segment which seems to be becoming smaller' (Sorge and Streeck, 1988: 31). The small artisan firms of the 'Third Italy', most of which have not managed to diversify their range of products and continue to produce for the same traditional market they supplied 40 years ago, do not make the leap from traditional craft production to more advanced forms of internal organization, not least as a result of the, partly self-imposed, legal constraints to growth. It is this type of production which is customarily associated with flexible specialization.

The Italian debate on this pattern of production claims that market failure in the provision of such public goods as interfirm and, more general, social cooperation is rectified by communitarian norms which would control opportunistic behaviour and free-riding. Attempts have been made to demonstrate that the German counterpart to 'market' and 'community', as mechanisms enforcing cohesion and governance on the interest domain of small firms, lies somewhere between 'public authorities' and 'interest associations'. In what follows, trust and solidarity as the main ingredients of communitarian production patterns are the subject of a more detailed analysis.

Interestingly, although in principle agreeing with the mainstream arguments of the Italian debate, Weiss is of the opinion that the 'collaborative character of craft production [could be explained] without recourse to prior conceptions of community' (1988: 202). What Weiss does not recognize is that, once 'community' is removed from the agenda, the much celebrated model of a social organization of production in Italy would, ultimately, end up in '*laissez-faire*' and a pathological mixture of political and economic markets. This is, indeed, increasingly acknowledged also by other participants in the debate. However, what authors on flexible specialization frequently tend if not to disguise, then at least to treat only in a remote fashion, is the restricted geographical space in which this mode of production is thriving while, on the other hand, diversified quality production, albeit to different degrees, can claim to be present in the entire territory of the 'old' Federal Republic. Flexible specialization is essentially limited to industrial districts, that is, to areas which, according to Alfred Marshall and his followers,[38] are characterized by localized patterns of production, a relatively self-contained labour market, matrices of localized technical interrelationships, a web of socio-cultural connections, extended family entrepreneurship and, most importantly, productive specialization (Becattini, 1990b: 161). A glance at the spatial mapping of Marshallian Industrial Districts (MIDs) presented by Sforzi (1988, 1990) immediately reveals that their existence is essentially limited to tiny fractions (roughly between 5 and 10%) of a handful of regions as such Toscana, Emilia-Romagna, Veneto, Marche, Piemonte and Lombardia. Sforzi has counted a total of 61

MIDs in Italy which account for a share in total employment of 5.4% (Sforzi, 1990: 80–4). It is useful to underline the fact that the entire discussion of flexible specialization in Italy is restricted to a description of a pattern of production which, at best, can be found in between 2 and 5% of the national territory. As narrow as the evidence for flexible specialization is, as glorious are the claims made by its proponents are, especially as regards its generalization to the level of a new mode of production it represents nothing less than the predominant pattern of post-Fordist mass production.

Since most of this discussion is concerned with smallness in very general terms, different types of enterprise are rarely distinguished from each other. It frequently happens that, while describing the inderdependencies of a group of firms which qualify as craft enterprises, authors use the more flimsy notions of small or small and medium-sized enterprise and vice versa. It was demonstrated above that the legal distinction between firms does make a considerable difference especially in respect to the limits to growth of small units. Also, while community norms of reciprocal trust between a small group of artisan firms whose owners are in daily face-to-face contact may very well have worked in the past – albeit no longer being sufficient at present – entrepreneurs of medium-sized firms with a proper management structure are less likely to be exposed to continuous exchanges with members of their direct environment and, especially, are less likely to adhere to communal obligations if these are not backed up by some form of coercive institutions. Yet, the literature continues to glorify trust and solidarity among competitors as the two main sources of com-munitarian production. It is not important here whether Hannah Arendt's philosophy of work ethics (Sabel, 1990: 62) or the mentality of certain groups of Italian workers who do not like to become a 'dehumanized hand in a large factory' (Becattini, 1990b: 164) are elicited to explain the strange dominance of social values and attitudes over economic efficiency criteria to underline the argument. What is more of an issue, especially with regard to the likely patterns a European small firm economy might assume in the Europe of post-1992, is the insistence with which such institutions are passed off not only to depict the very peculiar features of a 'neo-artisan' or mercantilist fraction of economic activity in Italy but, moreover, are held to represent a blueprint for applications to other and, eventually, more developed economies of the western world (Amin and Robins, 1990: 186). Every time it comes to a definition of the institutional context required for flexible spe-cialization in industrial districts, the debate drifts into cloudy assumptions about a 'thickening of social interdependencies', a strange 'sense of belonging' and, eventually, a form of public policy intervention where neither the actors nor the means of enforcement are ever spelled out in more precise terms. It shall, of course, not be denied that communal, publicly unregulated and spontaneously equilibrating forms of production do exist in many of the 61 districts of the 'Third Italy'. Even where they exist, however, there is now an increasing awareness also among the *'distrettisti'* themselves that cultural traditions and institutionally underdetermined social norms may rapidly lose vitality in the modernizing, internationalizing post-1992 European economy (Streeck and Schmitter, 1991: 154). It is hardly understandable, therefore, in a world being in increasing need of design capacities, prediction and planning, that the very absence of these capacities is perceived in terms of a comparative advantage over more solid forms of economic organization. The almost systematic negligence of interest associations in most of the work on flexible specialization, therefore, reflects the same neo-Darwinian attitude which had already characterized the writings of the forefather of the debate. As noted by Farry and Streeck (1991: 17), organized interests and especially 'trade unions, in Marshall's view, contributed to the success and survival of industrial districts primarily by their absence'.[39] Apart from this, there is a bias in this discussion to re-interpret some of the very weaknesses and pathological elements of parts of Italian socio-political and economic life in purely positive terms. Parochialism, for example, might also come under the cover of a 'sense of belonging', muddling through as a process of permanent adaptation and an 'amoeba-like evolution', *omerta*' and complicity[40] may reappear as 'trust and solidarity', the incapacity to grow as 'flexibility' and so forth. This is not to suggest that most of the small firm domain in Italy is working according to principles of this kind. Yet, it should not be discounted that they are more than just exceptional deviations from the norm, to be found only in some parts of the Mezzogiorno. What makes small appear beautiful, especially in the context of regional economies which are frequently characterized by an institutional vacuum, lacking state assistance, 'black' work and unprotected labour market regimes,[41] must not necessarily be beautiful in itself. More recent work on flexible specialization in Italy makes increasing use of the networking metaphor and substitutes smallness with resource pooling and strategic alliances. If 'small is beautiful may not be forever' (Blim, 1990: 255), it appears equally questionable whether 'networking is beautiful' is able to contribute to the districts' survival in the long term, not least because the proponents of this concept continue to consider exclusively the economic dimension of interfirm networks in industrial districts and industrial '*réseaux*', and tend to neglect all kinds of non-economic production inputs as, for example, domestic and regionally based institutions and forms of collective self organization by industry (Grote, 1991).

As regards these latter, there are, of course, some indications for the fact that the governance of the small firm economy, at least in parts of the 'Third Italy', goes beyond the mechanisms being customarily mentioned, namely beyond trust and solidarity as the main ingredients to communitarian forms of localized production. For the case of Emilia-Romagna, for example, Parri (1991) has tried to apply the same conceptual framework being used in this present chapter and has found out that there are incidents of private interest governments in that region. Each of the major Emilian development agencies and consortia is analysed in terms of specific mixtures occurring between different modes of management, regulatory principles and rules of enforcement. Parri's conclusion is that a substantial part of these can be cast in terms of private interest governments, social networks, alliances and, albeit to a very limited extent, of regulatory intervention by regional public authorities. Interestingly, forms of private interest government, even in as cohesive and entrepreneurial a region as Emilia-Romagna, do not emerge as the result of a particularly well-equipped regional state apparatus with substantial political autonomy and financial and coercive resources, as the example of the German *Länder* would suggest but, quite the opposite, as a consequence of institutional and administrative weakness. A truncated regional administration tries to pool resources with a poorly developed system of regional interest representation in order to achieve both more autonomy from the centre and a self generated provision of the territory with public goods. That willingness and political determination, as important as they are, do not always result in success due to institutional and organizational constraints, should be self evident. At the same time, initiatives of this kind also document that some more advanced regions have recognized the present shortcomings and that the traditional modes of sectoral and territorial governance which were 'spontaneously regulated by a mix of markets and communities have ceased to guarantee that an adequate response is being given to increasing competitive pressures' (Parri, 1991: 77). Today, it is the very structure of the districts themselves which appears to be insufficient and inadequate. The traditional, informal and 'loosely coupled' ties between the enterprises of the district do not reach the critical mass of pooled resources and strategic coordination which is required to adapt to new technologies, to diversify production and provide for a more sophisticated system of professional qualification. On the other hand, the traditional structures having represented the cornerstone for success of the districts in earlier periods, today appear as the main obstacle for their further development (Parri, 1990a, b: 69). As warranted by the leading Italian economics newspaper, this is not only a problem of structure but also one of the dimension of enterprises populating the districts. *Il Sole* writes that 'the myth of the district, meanwhile, is broken and the entire experience is dissolving either versus hierarchies or versus the market'.[42] Even a region such as Emilia-Romagna, therefore, has to be looked at with some caution. While certainly representing a success story from a more narrow Italian perspective, when exposed to a cross-regional comparison in the wider European context, it fares considerably worse and, on most accounts, does not manage to catch up with more advanced regional economies. In an interregional clustering of 24 European regions using ten variables to measure economic performance, the results for Emilia-Romagna kept it in a group of intermediate regions throughout the entire period of 1971–84 (Garmise and Grote, 1990: 63).

The preceding observations have tried to capture the problems of one of the most advanced Italian regions in terms of organizational self help. But what are the obstacles to a more rational and predictable way of organizing production and systems of production in the more general context of the entire Italian economy? If 'community' is either absent or not anymore sufficient in the vast majority of Italian regions, thus leaving most of the country's small enterprises to a hybrid mixture of economic and political markets, where, then, are the reasons to be found for the shortage of supply with either more adequate government policies or with associational forms of territorial self organization? Only few authors have raised this problem so far. Trigilia's work (1986, 1989a, b, 1990a, b) represents an exception to most of the mainstream arguments of the flexible specialization school. His hypothesis converges around what he calls 'the regional paradox' of the Italian social and institutional system. That paradox is characterized by growing exigencies for proper regional government which, for a number of important reasons, do not translate into explicit demands and into a system for interest representation at that level. Note that the way in which regions and proper regional regulatory institutions are perceived in Trigilia's work substantially departs from another approach which highlights the functional inadequacies of regional policy arenas, at least as long as these are not endorsed by strong and exogeneously provided national power resources. Schmitter and Streeck (1981: 156), for example, delineate the emergence of regional systems of governance in the context of 1992 as advancing, not the organization of encompassing interest associations, but rather its disorganization. This is because in the process of a Europeanization of regions or, for that matter, the regionalization of Europe, nationally legislated labour market and industrial policy regimes would likely lose much of their force. An argument of this kind would hold for those cases where the process of regionalization would go hand in hand with a loss of previously existing regulatory standards at the domestic level. In cases such as the Italian one, however, where capacities of this kind have never actually been built up, the argument loses its persuasiveness. Regional interest systems and a functioning regional administration being endowed with a number of regulatory resources which are presently not available would solve many of the shortcomings described earlier, rather than accentuating and adding to existing problems. In particular, they would enable firms and their representatives to provide for those collective goods whose production, under present circumstances, is held in short supply, not least as a result of vested interests by the central state to maintain its direct and unmediated relationships with individual firms and single local authorities.[43]

The weakness of an intermediate level of government and the absence of strong and cohesive regional interest associations are, however, not only and, perhaps, not even predominantly due to attempts by the centre to maintain existing relationships of basically unilateral dependence. Italy is generally characterized by strong localisms, weak regional identity and powerless regional administrative structures (Trigilia, 1989b: 174). Given this situation, even actors in the once glorified industrial districts find it increasingly difficult to generate capacities which could manage problems of both external economies and diseconomies of their respective territories. Yet, at the same time, there continue to be many disincentives to overcoming localist and parochial attitudes and to substitute politically mediated forms of grant allocation and assistance, that is, pluralistic mediation and a fragmented demand structure, with more proficient and profitable mechanisms. One of these is the constitutional, institutional and financial weakness of regional government itself.[44] Collective action at that level continues to be underdeveloped also, because entrepreneurs themselves have little interest in investing in public goods which would benefit the entire system of production and not just the single contributor alone – a disadvantage which, owing to the lack in capacities of regional government, can hardly be neutralized by forms of public coercion or other obligations to cooperate. Most entrepreneurs possess strong preferences for kinds of financial incentive which do not pose limits on their autonomy and can be organized and managed in the context of their specific local environment, where the benefits deriving from those incentives are also more visible and directly expropriatable (Trigilia, 1989b: 187). Attitudes of this kind, together with the lack of structures which could potentially contribute to a more cooperative spirit, that is, essentially regional government and organized interests, lead to a perpetuation of distributive policies – '*interventi a pioggia*' or raindrop interventions – and to non-decision-making in all cases where funds are not immediately divisible.[45] Since this concerns particularly those initiatives which try to control external economies and diseconomies, regional actors end up with a substantial under-utilization of resources which would otherwise be available.

Differences in the governance of the small enterprise domain in Italy and Germany, therefore, basically are of two kinds. They, first, result from rather distinct modes of production and, secondly, from an uneven endowment of regional institutions with regulatory capacities. As to the first aspect, flexible specialization and diversified quality production have already been distinguished on purely technological grounds and in terms of manufacturing strategies. Without going into much detail, further evidence can now be added to the distinctiveness of the two models.[46] The 'hard German model', as opposed to the 'soft' Italian one, is much less concerned with the communitarian voluntarism informing most of the work on industrial districts. It also does not claim to represent a historical fracture, ultimately leading to a dissolution of large enterprises. It is, rather, based on a peculiar balance between large but often decentralized firms being active in customized, quality-competitive production on the one hand, and a vast number of legally protected small artisan firms with very stable and mutually beneficial supplier relationships to bigger ones on the other.[47] Also, the German example is not characterized by the absence of conflict or the existence of a system of trust and solidarity, however ill-defined but, rather, sees conflict as an important input into processes of productive diversification, at least as long as it can be contained by encompassing mechanisms for its institutionalization as, for instance, the co-determination law. Diversified quality production is embedded in an overall industrial order materializing at the level of the *Länder* but, at the same time, being endorsed by strong national institutions which could only precariously exist on a voluntaristic-contractual basis. It generally rests on 'an affirmative polity in which major conditions of competitive performance are, and have to be, collectively created and maintained' (Streeck, 1991: 46). Such a polity which puts constraints on the hyper-rational interests of individual entrepreneurs in short-term benefits and immediate pay-offs, and which, thus, contributes to the general stability of a highly diversified and competitive mode of capitalist production, also helps to provide for the three basic ingredients necessary to combat market and hierarchy failure. These are, first, a 'congenial organizational ecology' putting a premium on strategic alliances and joint ventures between firms as well as promoting stable and enduring forms of cooperation between assemblers and suppliers; secondly, the creation and maintenance of 'redundant capacities' such as broad and high skills, a polyvalent organizational structure, decentralized competences and social peace; and, third, 'collective production inputs' relating to the generation of skills, of competence and of knowledge. As to the role interest associations play in a system such as the one just described, it is possible to hypothesize without much exaggeration, that diversified quality production essentially rests on a form of public–private collaboration which has best been described as 'private interest government' (Streeck and Schmitter, 1985) and, moreover, that there is hardly anything coming closer to this form of sectoral governance and self regulation than the system of *Handwerk* in the Federal Republic of Germany (Streeck, 1989b: 89).

As to the second aspect in which the two countries differ substantially, that is, that of political institutions at the regional level, it could be said that among the regions of the European Community, 'only the German *Länder* possess the quality of democratically enshrined statehood' (Scharpf, 1988: 1). In terms of full time public servants employed, they have become the best-staffed layer of the federal system during the course of the past 30 years. Mayntz reports a total of 1,559,500 *Länder* civil servants for 1986. That outperforms both the federal government (1,037,000) and the total of local administration (1,007,800). With respect to public expenditure at government level, the *Länder* governments (DM 262,615m) ranked only slightly below the federal government (DM 270,864m) (1987) (Mayntz, 1989, 1990). Although most of the constitutional power of the *Länder* lies with policy implementation, they are put in a position not only to co-determine but, actually, to determine industrial policy-making, and to establish legally binding public–private structures for the joint supply of small and medium-sized firms with the resources described above. The comparative advantage of federal organization, moreover, also implies a substantial capacity of the *Länder* and, for that matter, their *Land*-wide organized interest associations, to shape decisions at the transnational level. Germany is the only member state of the Community all of whose regional sub-units possess own *Länder*-offices at Brussels, each being equipped with a full time staff and considerable expertise concerning the industrial interests of their respective territories. Despite attempts by the federal government to block further moves in this direction, the *Länder* actually conduct a kind of 'complementary foreign policy' (*Nebenaussenpolitik*) having many implications for the emergence of a Community policy on small enterprises. None of the above could be said about the *regioni* in Italy.

The Role of Craft Associations in the Provision of Public Goods at Regional Level.

The inability of both private and public actors to arrange for more profitable institutional devices for the provision of collective goods at the regional level in Italy even occurs in those policy domains where the regions possess some regulatory authority as, for example, in the craft sector. A traditional and localist type of organization at the provincial level[48] and resulting underdeveloped demands for more comprehensive regional policy initiatives correspond to an insufficient supply of services for the entire territory which, in theory, could be jointly produced by public authorities and regional interest associations. Apart from eliciting the hegemonic role of the central state and from emphasizing parochialism and neo-localism, the 'generalized weakness of regional systems of interest representation' (Trigilia, 1989b: 185) in Italy can, of course, also be explained in historical terms. Lanzalaco (1989, 1990, and chapter 6 in this volume) provides for an encompassing explanation of the territorial structures of business interest associations in Italy, taking account of such determining factors as, for example, the country's late industrialization and the organization of the nation state. There is an additional factor, however, which appears to be rather under-researched. It relates to the strong ideological and political divisions between the main associations for the representation of craft interests. Apart from some insignificant and minuscule groupings, the Italian artisanat is represented by three major associations. These are the Confederazione Generale Italiana dell'Artigianato (CGIA), the Confederazione Nazionale dell'Artigianato (CNA) and the Confederazione Artigiani Sindacati Autonomi (CASA). A fourth association, the Confederazione Libere Associazioni Artigiane Italiane (CLAAI) holds such a minor share in organizing the category (about 0.5%) that it is not considered in this context.

In political terms, CGIA is predominantly Christian Democratic-orientated and can probably be termed the most traditional of the Italian associations, also with regard to its members, many of whom are artisans in the second or third generation. Especially in the areas of labour market policies and industrial relations, CGIA holds many contacts with Confindustria, the Italian peak association of business. Typical localist attitudes and a relatively weakly developed sense for cooperation probably dominate in this association. CGIA, which is the national peak association of the provincial Confartigianati, is a second-degree organization. Its members register with one of the provincial associations which, often, carry different names across the Italian territory and possess a high degree of autonomy from the centre. In 1987, the organization was composed of 33 national branch associations, 100 provincial associations and 13 so called '*associazioni mandamentali*', that is, associations being organized at a level between the province and the commune and falling under the direct jurisdiction of the central state (Baglioni et al., 1987: 326).

Despite its name, CNA has more of a federal-type nature. Its members directly adhere to the national peak association which, in turn, centrally structures the different provincial and regional federations. Capacities for policy-coordination and collective action, especially at the level of the *regioni*, appear to be better developed than in the case of CGIA. Unlike the latter association, which suffered slight membership losses throughout the 1980s, CNA constantly increased its numbers during the same period. The association is the successor of a sectoral federation of CGIL, the Italian Communist trade union, which had created a special branch for craft interests in the immediate post-war period. It became autonomous in the early 1950s (Brusco and Pezzini, 1990: 155). Most of the neo-artisans of the 'Third Italy', with the notable exception of the politically 'white' regions (especially the Veneto) are organized in this association. Organizational discipline and coherence is highest in CNA, particularly as a result of the fact that a large fraction of its members are ex-employees of large enterprises and, hence, more familiar with cooperation and collective action.[49]

CASA, although of catholic an origin as CGIA, essentially organizes those ex-members of the other two associations who prefer a greater degree of political autonomy. Interviews conducted with some of its officials revealed a political inclination towards the Republican Party. In 1987, CASA membership was composed of 65 provincial associations, 16 regional associations and 17 national branch associations (Baglioni et al., 1987: 331).

The least politically biased of the associations for the representation of small firm interests is probably the Confederazione delle Piccole Imprese. CONFAPI, however, does not predominantly organize craft interests but has its membership among small to medium-sized industrial firms. There is nothing corresponding to this association in Germany, where all non-artisanal firms, small, medium or large, are organized by the Bundesverband der Deutschen Industrie (BDI). Accordingly, CONFAPI's main competitor is not the craft associations, but Confindustria, the Italian peak association of industry. One of the main reasons for CONFAPI's existence is the exclusionary voting rules determining the leadership of Confindustria. They imply a weighting of the vote of each member in terms of annual turnover and number of employees and, thereby, lead to only marginal capacities of the very high number of small enterprises organized with Confindustria to influence the association's policies. Confindustria, as a result, is governed by not more than a handful of capitalists at the top of the few really large firms in Italy.

In general, the Italian system for the representation of craft interests appears to be a prime example for a typical pluralist form of interest intermediation: the associations possess competing membership, are voluntary organizations and are strongly divided in political terms. They also compete for recognition by the state and, accordingly, for services and grants being paid out to either of them. It has been difficult, if not impossible, to achieve some policy coordination between the associations, for example, for the pooling of resources and the combined supply of services to craft enterprises irrespective of their organizational adherence.[50] Interassociational cooperation is less developed than that occurrring between the three Italian trade union organizations which, originally, were split along the same ideological lines and, currently, discuss possibilities for creating a unitarian structure. In some provinces, the associational presence of craft is impressive. The Modena office of CNA in Emilia-Romagna, for example, employs as many as 540 employees (Brusco and Pezzini, 1990: 156). As Trigilia (1989b: 185) has shown with respect to the regions of Tuscany and the Veneto, it remains a fact, however, that the associational epicentre continues to be at the provincial level and that regional activities scarcely reach the needed degree of coordination and remain entrapped in narrow, neo-localist attitudes.

Both of the leading associations (CGIA and CNA) claim for themselves to represent the highest number of craft firms in Italy. It has been difficult to assess these claims since comprehensive data have never been published so far. Table 5.4 represents the first attempt to provide that data. It lists the relative shares of craft enterprises as a percentage of the total number of non-agricultural firms in Italy, as well as overall membership rates and the figures for each single association per region. Associationalism is highest

Table 5.4   *Density of craft associations per region and share of each single association in the total of craft enterprises (1990)*

Regione	Craft as % of total firms	Organized craft total (%)	CGIA	Associational membership as % of total craft CNA	CASA
Valle d'Aosta	37.7	13.1	7.6	5.5	0
Piemonte	41.2	31.1	8.0	17.3	5.8
Liguria	36.7	49.9	17.2	31.3	1.4
Lombardia	38.4	42.5	30.8	10.7	0.9
NORTH	38.5	34.6	15.9	16.2	2.7
Trentino-AA	36.7	74.6	65.5	9.1	0
Friuli-VG	40.1	62.0	50.7	11.3	0
Veneto	42.2	73.9	49.8	21.2	3.0
Emilia-Romagna	43.4	91.3	23.5	67.1	0.7
Toscana	40.2	77.5	27.4	48.8	1.4
Marche	45.4	84.7	37.4	40.3	7.0
Umbria	44.6	55.1	26.3	27.6	1.3
NEC	41.8	74.6	40.1	32.2	2.7
Lazio	31.9	47.2	12.4	25.5	9.2
Campania	26.0	50.2	18.2	26.9	5.2
Abruzzo	39.9	61.2	26.5	23.9	10.8
Molise	41.2	35.7	3.8	22.9	9.1
Puglia	36.8	53.5	27.4	21.3	4.9
Basilicata	46.2	94.3	45.1	37.7	11.4
Calabria	31.8	91.7	45.7	29.5	16.5
Sicilia	29.9	76.6	11.3	40.3	25.1
Sardegna	39.7	49.4	15.6	30.0	3.8
SOUTH	35.9	62.2	22.9	28.7	10.7
Mean	38.7	57.1	26.3	25.7	5.4

Note: data for Sicily does not include the provices of Messina and Caltanisetta. % values in the first two columns may thus be distorted.

Source: Author's calculations based on *CGIA, 1990* (for data on CGIA and CASA), CNA, 1991 and CERVED, 1991 (for craft enterprise data). For absolute figures, also including those of the Italian association for small and medium-sized enterprises (Confederazione Italiana delle Piccole Imprese – CONFAPI), see the appendix

developed in the North–East–Centre regions (74.6%) but, at the same time, membership density rates per single region do not allow for the building of direct relationships to economic performance and cooperative attitudes between craft firms. In Basilicata, Calabria and Sicily, hence in the most underdeveloped Italian regions, substantially more than 70% of craft enterprises are organized in one of the three associations. That strongly competes with figures for Emilia-Romagna, a region commonly identified as having an exceptionally high associational culture. Of course, the (roughly 97,000) organized firms in these three regions together do not measure up to the level of 122,000 organized enterprises in Emilia-Romagna and, given that almost 70% of the latter's artisans are organized by CNA, capacities for associational action are likely to be substantially more developed in this case.[51]

Quite obviously, in such a context, each association tends to promote its own 'organizational self interest' rather than the interests of the category as a whole (Ridolfi, 1985). The fact, for example, that all of the three organizations principally agreed to the implications of Law 443, that is to a non-definition of the artisanat as a specific category in terms of qualifications required and of specific production processes, might reflect a self interested bias of this sector's associations. The figures presented above would suggest, hence, that the role of associationalism among small firms and craft enterprises is precisely as insignificant for the economic performance of regions in general as for the arrangements of governance of regional economies. Compared to the German pattern of regulating the small firm domain, Italy's disadvantages would amount to, essentially, five, most of which being of a structural nature and therefore hard to surmount by deliberate political action and design. First, the absence of a specific policy for small and medium-sized enterprises and the continued practice of granting individual firms a form of special treatment which does not manage to impact on the productive tissue in which these firms are embedded. Second, the comparative disadvantage of a unitarian organization of the state which has failed to empower its decentralized units with the capacities absolutely critical for the management of subnational complexities. Third, a form of protectionism which puts a premium on smallness as such and, hence, inhibits a diversification in the range of products and production methods of craft enterprises. Fourth, partly resulting from and partly contributing to the above, the existence of extraordinarily strong neo-localist attitudes among both producers and politicians which promote 'free-riding' and do not allow for more profitable forms of organized collective action at the regional level. Fifth, sustained ideological divisions between the main representative organizations of the sector, resulting in the provision of selective goods, for the members of each single association separately, which scarcely go beyond the supply of such basic services as tax and pay-roll consultancy and do not manage to reach the critical mass of resources necessary for more innovative and technologically more sophisticated services.[52]

One of the most significant differences between Italian and

German craft associations lies in the fact that the role of the Italian Camera di Commercio, Industria, l'Artigianto e l'Agricoltura[53] merely goes beyond simple book-keeping, that is the maintenance of a register for licensed artisans, while the German Handwerks-kammern (HWKs), although possessing compulsory membership and a public status, are better understood as 'operating as the functional equivalent of the small business associations in other countries' (Coleman and Grant, 1988: 476). Streeck has given them the attribute of a 'mixture between a para-state agency and a voluntary interest association' (Streeck, 1989a: 69). As regards the wider context of small and medium-sized enterprises, the 45 territorial HWKs which form 11 associations (Klinge, 1990: 225) at the *Land* level (Landesvertretungen), together with the 81 Indus-trie- und Handelskammern (Chambers of Industry and Commerce, or IHKs) which form 9 regional associations, that is, Landeshand-werkskammertage or Arbeitsgemeinschaften (DIHT, 1987: 99) at the *Land* level, jointly provide for those non-economic production inputs which represent the specificity of German diversified quality production. It may be true that the regional level is the least important element of the artisanal associational system in Germany (Streeck, 1989a: 87), yet, cooperation at that level is extraordinarily high, as demonstrated, for example, by the *Land*-wide division of labour (*Federfuhrungsprinzip*) adopted by most of the provincial centres of IHKs and HWKs. This principle consists in each of the 45 and 81 chambers respectively, to assume responsibility at the regional level for a specific issue area, like technology transfer policy or the administration of vocational training programmes. Initial inquiries from member firms are directed to the appropriate chamber, regardless of whether the firm is a member of that particular chamber or not (Anderson, 1991: 83). Also, in most of the German *Länder*, the chambers participate formally in the *Land*'s regional policy-making process. For Nordrhein Westphalen, Anderson (1991) has observed that applications for federal and state assistance are gathered at the Ministry of Economics in Dusseldorf, and then sent on to the IHK representing the locality in which the proposed project would locate. The IHK assesses each application according to established criteria, including economic compatibility with the existing mix of industry in the area, and then submits its recommendations to the Economics Ministry which makes the final decision. In a general assessment of the chamber system, Mayntz (1989: 24, 1990) stresses 'that both neo-corporatist structures of decision-making and "private interest governments" exist at the regional level in the FRG [and that] Germany . . . is a thoroughly federalized country, not only in a political-administrative sense, but also in many fields of institutionalized self regulation.'

The associational system for the representation of craft interests in Germany, however, is not limited to compulsory membership organizations with public status as the chambers. There is an additional tier, or second column to the chamber system, consisting of 6,220 guilds (Innungen) being organized in 288 *Länder* guild associations (Streeck, 1989a: 72). Because guilds, unlike the chambers, also perform the function of employer associations, they are formally voluntary organizations although, in reality, non-membership is low, ranking at around 10–15%. In other words, only about 60,000–90,000 of the total of 611,000 craft enterprises do not belong to one of the guild associations. Since this figure strongly corresponds to the number of firms falling into the category of 'minor trade' (*handwerksahnliche Gewerbe*), it is very likely that many of the latter account for the non-organized fraction of total firms. That would raise membership rates of proper artisan firms operating in one of the legally specified 125 trades to almost 100% in the entire territory of the 'old' Federal Republic.[54] Most importantly, although having separate legal identities, the national peak associations of the two strands of compulsory and voluntary membership, that is the Federal Association of Chambers of Artisans (Deutscher Handwerkskammertag or DHKT) and the Federal Association of National Guild Associations (Bundes-vereiningung der Fachverbande des Deutschen Handwerks or BHG), jointly operate a third organization, the Central Association of German Artisans (Zentralverband des Deutschen Handwerks or ZDH) – a structure which is replicated in each *Land*. Hence, to summarize, German artisans are organized to nearly 100% in both voluntary and compulsory membership associations and these two types of association exhibit such an elevated level of strategic cooperation and administrative interpenetration that 'in practice they function as if they were one' (Streeck, 1989a: 73).

A European Enterprise Policy for Small Firms

Much space has been devoted in the preceding sections to a comparative analysis of markets, states, communities and interest associations as those mechanisms supplying the small firm econo-mies in Italy and Germany with the resources responsible for their disparate performances. As far as craft is concerned, we have not found much evidence for Schmitter's claim that the practices of capitalism in specific sectors are becoming more similar across national economies (Schmitter, 1990: 12). What, then, about the transnational dimension as an input which could provide for a more coherent organization of the small firm domain? While most of the chapters in this book mainly consider the format of domestic interest associations as determining factors for the capacity to act collectively at the European level, it can now be said that purely associational elements do not suffice for explaining transnational collective action, at least not in the case of craft. More than any other category of enterprise in Europe, artisan firms are so deeply embedded in one or more of the governance mechanisms outlined above that incentives to build up EC-level associations are strongly influenced by the way in which markets, states, communities and, of course, business associations themselves are structured at home and, moreover, that organizational formats may be determining in some cases but not necessarily in others. This leads to two implications for a European small enterprise policy. First, EC institutions presently responsible for this policy domain would have to consider mechanisms of sectoral governance other than those which have been attributed to the economic dimension in this chapter, namely markets, alliances and hierarchies. Secondly, interest associations representing small firms at the European level would have to include in their strategic deliberations some of those factors which go beyond the restricted competences and limited objectives some of their members possess and pursue at home. These are questions concerning the organization of markets and the appropriate means for achieving this organization, that is, the question of governance of regionally based small firm economies by public authorities and privately organized groups themselves.

As to the second implication, already the formal requirements for a comprehensive organization of small firms at the European level are far from being met. As demonstrated by Table 5.5, there are 11 EC-level associations representing SMEs which are officially recognized by DG XXIII, the directorate dealing with small enterprise policy. Although being the peak association of European capital at large, UNICE forms part of the list because many of its affiliated organizations also represent the interests of medium-sized industrial enterprises. Within the total of 50 specialized bodies and working parties, UNICE also operates a SME working party which is coordinated by its committee for industrial affairs. Both the minor importance of small firms in UNICE's national member associations, which has been shown with regard to the example of Confindustria in Italy, and the fact that only one out of 50 of its special bodies deals with the concerns of small firms, demonstrate that UNICE cannot actually be ascribed the virtue of representing the small firm domain in Europe. Yet, its organizational resources

Table 5.5   *European-level associations of SMEs*

1	Comité Européen de la Petite et Moyenne Entreprise Independante	EUROPMI *
2	Union Européenne des Classes Moyennes	EMSU *
3	Association Européenne des Classes Moyennes	AECM *
4	Comité de Coordination des Associations de Cooperatives de la CEE	CCACC
5	Union des Confederations de l'Industrie et des Employeurs d'Europe	UNICE **
6	Union Européenne del' Artisanat et des PME	UEAPME **
7	Federation des Associations Européenne du Commerce de Gros	FEWITA **
8	Confederation Européenne du Commerce au Detail	CECD **
9	Union Européenne de Chambres de Commerce	EUROCHAMBERS
10	Comité Européen des Cooperatives Ouvrières de Production	CECOP
11	Confederation Européenne des Independants	CEDI

* Contact group 1 (Eurogroup); ** Contact group 2.

Source: 'Lobbying list' of DG XXIII (summer 1991)

are substantial and many of the other groups may use them to increase their own impact on EC decisions.

Since some of the 11 associations which cover the entire range of sectors from trade and commerce to industry and craft simply lack the resources required for effectively running their own offices and, secondly, as it had become necessary to combat fragmentation, two coordinating groups have been created recently. Contact group 1, also called 'Eurogroup', combines some smaller associations representing middle-class and craft interests. Some of these possess a strong political orientation as, for example, EMSU and AECM, the latter combining the different '*Mittelstandsvereinigungen*' and '*comitati dei ceti medi*' of European Christian Democratic parties. Strange then that the Italian CNA, despite its Communist origin, has chosen a Christian Democratic-orientated association (EMSU) as its voice in Europe. The internal fragmentation of the Italian system of interest representation in the craft sector, no surprise, is reproduced at the European level with the three main organizations adhering to different EC peak associations. Apart from exotic exceptions of this kind, political cohesion is relatively strong in this contact group and members of 'Eurogroup' tend to cooperate more with each other than do members of contact group 2 (see Table 5.5). On the other hand, the organizational strength of the latter is considerably higher, and members of group 2 are more powerful even as single associations, a fact which might also explain the loose coupling occurring between them. While the creation of these two groupings has primarily been on the initiative of the associations themselves, more recent attempts to set up a joint structure for all of the 11 organizations are clearly resulting from problems of EC institutions in identifying and selecting appropriate partners for consultation and institutional incorporation, without triggering off discontent and opposition by competing groups. The 'Small and Medium-sized Enterprises Intergroup', having been created specifically for this purpose by some individual members of the European Parliament, has the 'objective to be a forum where interested MEPs, the Commission of the European Communities and organizations representing the SMEs can meet regularly and discuss the development of Community policies for their benefit'.[55]

Among the four private associations (EUROPMI, EMSU, AECM, UEAPME) representing proper small firm and craft interests, UEAPME is the organization with the longest track record and is also better resourced than its competitors. It should not come as a surprise that its most important national member is the Zentralverband des deutschen Handwerks which, actually, has been running the association since 1959, when its forerunner UACEE (Union de l'Artisanat de la CEE) was founded. While the ZdH, which also operates an autonomous office in Brussels, is the strongest and best equipped craft organization at EC level, the profile of Italian interest associations in any of the 11 Euro-associations is generally low, with the one exception of UNICE's working group for SMEs, which has traditionally been chaired by a member of Confindustria. To return to UACEE, from the late 1950s onwards, its main areas of work were the harmonization of sales taxes, the development of company law and EC initiatives in the field of anti-trust policy (Neunreither, 1968: 398). Still more important were those EC policies dealing with professional qualification and education where the association feared a drive towards demand-led planning and attacked all attempts of the EC to intervene by 'dirigism' thus undermining the standards regulating the profession in Germany. The working languages of UACEE were exclusively French and German and its office rooms and logistic facilities were supplied by the 'Comité National Belge des Petites et Moyennes Entreprises', a body being attached to the Belgian Ministère de Classes Moyennes. In other words, UACEE's staff members belonged to the Belgian civil service – a nice example of a form of private–public blurring known under the label of 'private interest government' in the context of some national arrangements. All further operational costs of the association accrued to the German ZdH (Neunreither, 1968: 407), which had such an interest in the collective good of running an EC association that it was prepared to contribute alone to its provision.

The organizational structures of UACEE underwent major modifications in 1979 when, at a conference in Madrid, its name was changed into UEAPME (Baglioni et al., 1987: 327) and membership was expanded to include non-artisanal firms, that is, the entire interest domain of SMEs. The association, whose Italian members are Confartigianato (CGIA) and CONFAPI, kept its headquarters in Bonn until 1990 when it moved to Brussels. Although representing the strongest and most influential EC-level association for small and medium-sized firms, UEAPME organized its activities from the German capital throughout the 1980s. That reflects an attitude characteristic of *Handwerk* and of the Federal government, both of which were rather reluctant to join demands for the creation of a new policy domain – 'SMEs' – under the responsibility of the Commission. This attitude prevailed until the mid 1980s, when, under the lead of the Thatcher government, attempts were being made to deregulate the SME domain in Europe. As confirmed by a leading official of UEAPME, 'a purely market-driven approach to the regulation of the domain would have implied the death of *Handwerk*'. The reluctance of the Germans, however, to support a European small firm policy before the time of the Single European Act and, accordingly, the hesitation of the ZdH to move UEAPME's headquarters to Brussels, was due to a number of additional reasons. In the first place, given the underdeveloped structures of the craft sector in countries such as Italy, a European policy for this domain would have implied substantial resource transfers to Southern member states and, hence, would have increased the Federal Republic's role as a net payer to the Community budget. Secondly, as long as there was no adequate institution to deal with SME concerns, the costs of running a proper European association would have been wasted.[56] Finally, but not less important, policy in that area in Germany falls under the jurisdiction of *Länder* governments, a fact explaining the wait-and-see stance adopted by the Federal government.

As already mentioned, the lack of eagerness with which the Federal government and the ZdH confronted the emergence of a European enterprise policy belongs to the past and UEAPME, meanwhile, has become the most influential EC-level association for craft and small firms. The German association has understood that the internal market implies not only competition between goods and companies but, more importantly, between different regulatory frameworks. Yet, the main issue at stake, in the present phase of defending the interests of organized craft, is not very different from the one already occupying the activities of UACEE during the initial years of its existence. It relates to Article 54 and Article 59 of the Treaties, that is, to the freedom of establishment and the freedom to provide services within the Community. A number of guidelines and recommendations were issued by the Community during the early days of European integration, whose objective was to dismantle the entry restrictions imposed on foreign artisans who wished to exercise their profession in other member states.[57] In many instances, the dismantling of restrictions in some member states would go hand in hand with successive policy coordination and harmonization at the European level. Yet, the existing incompatibilities between the different national provisions for professional training in the craft sector did not allow for harmonization and the mutual recognition of common quality standards. The guidelines, therefore, which originally were thought to be of a provisional and transitory character, meanwhile have become law and carry the same legal weight as any other EC directive. Although the enlargement of the EC to a Community of 12 has given more importance to positions arguing in favour of a market solution and of liberalization, there is little evidence for these guidelines being abandoned in the near future. For the interests of German artisans, they have proved to be more than sufficient, since only few foreign-based craft firms have so far made use of the transitory rules. While 807,275 craft enterprises have been founded in Germany between 1966 and 1987, only 2,754 permissions to register with the HWK were issued to professionals from other countries (Klinge, 1990: 36). Should UEAPME manage to convince the majority of craft associations and the Commission to maintain the existing system, no dramatic inroads should be expected into the well-protected system of *Handwerk* in Germany. On the contrary, recent initiatives undertaken by public authorities and organized craft in a number of member states indicate that the German variety of maintaining high levels of professional qualification via the master certificate seems to be an attractive solution also to Germany's competitors. Luxemburg has always made the master certificate an obligatory entry requirement for access to the profession. The province of Bolzano in Trentino-Alto Adige passed a *Handwerksordnung* in 1981 which, although later having been cancelled by the Italian constitutional court, still operates in practice (Klinge, 1990). Belgium adopted a craft law in 1970 which, albeit less restrictive than the German HWO, strongly regulates entry into the profession. Denmark possesses a number of trades where licensing is subject to professional qualification. Spain, where the legal category of craft was unknown until 1972, has recently started to regulate entry for a number of trades as well. Finally, France also shows a strong inclination 'to follow the German example' (Klinge, 1990: 32). It has introduced the titles of 'artisan' and 'maître d'artisan', and registration in the craft register requires a 'stage d'initiation à la gestion'. These are clear indications for an upgrading of the regulatory frameworks for craft production across Europe. Italy, as the country with the numerically strongest craft sector, has so far not made any move into this direction. It is hard to decide whether this is due to a form of 'free-riding' which expects the Community to come up with those regulatory standards the country seems neither to be willing nor able to provide on its own, or whether non-decision-making in this area has to be interpreted a result of 'suffrance' (Schmitter, 1985). The latter strategy would indicate that political (and economic) investments having already been undertaken in the domain are so high (sunk costs), and that benefits accruing to *all* actors from presently suboptimal arrangements are so 'satisficing', that the result is 'sitting tight and waiting', rather than 'voicing' the mechanisms which regulate the small firm economy in Italy. On the basis of what has been argued in the preceding sections, it is likely that both 'free-riding' and 'suffrance' contribute to the country's passivity.

To conclude the review of initiatives being undertaken in the small enterprise domain at EC level, some remarks are in order with regard to the institutional counterpart to associative action, not least because of the mutually determining influence one sphere has on the other. While the above examples demonstrate that most of the countries possessing a strong craft component in the overall economy are presently engaged in regulating the sector along the lines of the German example, activities by the EC Commission have just started to show some initial effects, but cannot yet be judged more comprehensively. Opinions of the kind that DG XXIII would be one of those directorates with the most evident features for corporatist interest intermediation, as being put forward by Andrews, tend to overstress that 'about half of its professional staff is on loan from the enterprises with which it deals and their associations' (1991: 13). Even if this information were based on hard facts,[58] it is questionable whether this alone would qualify DG XXIII to be a corporatist institution. The high penetration of the directorate with business representatives would, rather, reflect that it is still in its infant phase, and that it strongly depends on the expertise given by its regulatory targets, namely business, without being able yet to nominate a sufficient number of staff through the ordinary appointment procedure for EC officials.

Evidence for corporatist policies is also lacking in the field of legislation. The most relevant documents concerning small firms are the 'SME Action Programme' and, based on this, the SME Task Force's programmatic paper entitled 'An enterprise policy for the European Community'.[59] The latter has recently been amdended by DG XXIII and is presently waiting for approval by the Council.[60] In short, all of these documents converge around three topics, at the same time representing the major policy guidelines for action to be taken in the future. They could be summarized under the following headings.[61] First, traditional redistributive measures (that is, a separate Community budget for SMEs and financial support to firms), secondly, logistic assistance (that is, concrete support programmes promoting cooperation and strategic partnerships between firms) and, finally, regulation and legislation (essentially, elimination of unwarranted administrative, financial and legal constraints). Objectives relating to the first two of these guidelines have, in part, been achieved. These are the creation of a network of European Information Centres (EICs), 187 of which (including 16 regional liaison offices) had been established by 1991.[62] As regards the promotion of strategic alliances between small firms, two measures are worth mentioning. The first consists of the creation of Business Cooperation Centres (BCCs) and their computerized linkage via BC-Net which by now counts about 600 associated agencies.[63] The second consists in bringing together, about twice a year, a large number of entrepreneurs of SMEs, with the aim of 'stimulating cooperation among SMEs in regions that are underdeveloped or in industrial decline, and enterprises in other regions of the Community'.[64] About six of these meetings with an average participation of some 2,000 entrepreneurs each had been organized by the end of 1991. The Euro-Partneriat programme has recently been joined by an additional one called 'Interprise' which is modelled on the former. As regards the third general policy guideline, that is, regulation and legislation, very little has been achieved so far. Yet, it is unlikely that initiatives related to the first and second guidelines will be able to upgrade the productive environment of small firms along the lines of the German or any other model. With reference to the scheme outlined in the introduction, it can now be reaffirmed that a European enterprise policy for small firms is not likely to be successful unless the Commission goes beyond a system of incentives operating exclusively in the economic dimension, and unless it also includes into its deliberations those non-economic production inputs which are normally provided by either the interest associations of SMEs or public authorities managing the domain in the national or regional context.

Also, there is hardly any other area at EC level where the need to merge the economic, the spatial and the so called 'social dimension of the internal market' to one single and coherent policy domain is as important as in the traditional and small firm sector.[65] Yet, issues relating to the social dimension continue to be discussed in isolation within the services of DG V. The same applies to problems relating to the distribution of economic activity across the territory of the Community, that is, the spatial dimension, which fall in the area of responsibility of DG XVI and DG XXII, while problems resulting from small size are handled by DG XXIII. The splitting up of one genuine policy domain which, in theory, should be united, into different institutional fiefdoms is further nurtured by the fact that small enterprise policy was given a separate Directorate General in 1989. The 'institutional self interest' of DG XXIII in assembling and centralizing further competences for the domain presently inhibits moves towards more efficient coordination.

Problems of this kind are, of course, not unknown to the Commission itself. In order to avoid the policy effects of different directorates cancelling each other out, the Task Force SME, the forerunner of DG XXIII, introduced in 1986 an impact assessment procedure (fiche d'impact'), according to which each proposal for legislation drafted by one of the Commission's directorates has to be checked in terms of costs and benefits accruing to small firms. Yet, this procedure, which was modified and streamlined in 1990,[66] does not meet the expectations of industry. UNICE, in this case voicing the discontent of all European-level associations of SMEs, observed that even the renewed version of the 'fiche d'impact' does not entirely satisfy business and that more transparency would be required.[67] The objectives of organized business with respect to this practice are, first, that all associations representing industry should be consulted during the initial phase of the legislative process, secondly, that all services of the Commission whose activities potentially affect SMEs should be included into the procedure and, finally, that both the impact assessment sheets and the list of associations being consulted should be made public. Given the experiences with regional impact assessment (RIA) of the directorate dealing with regional policy (DG XVI), it is unlikely that even an improved version of this procedure will be able to prevent small firms continuing to suffer most from the lack of control and internal cohesion of the Commission's services (Grote, 1989a, b, 1990). The only way out of the present impasse would be a regionalization of industrial policy and a, so to speak, industrialization of regional policy, that is, the creation of a kind of super directorate which would combine the services of DG XVI, DG XXII and DG XXIII into one single agency. Steps in this direction, which would have to be accompanied by a simultaneous integration of the most relevant EC-level groups representing the interests of small firms and craft into one single association, are unlikely to be taken in the near future. As has been the case for many other policy domains under the responsibility of the Community, such as, for example, agriculture, it might be expected that those countries which have built up the necessary structures for the management of a specific category at home, will benefit most from EC policies, while those lacking them would seriously fail if expecting a substantial contribution to their creation from Brussels. For German *Handwerk*, there is a lot at stake in the context of impending regulation of the sector at transnational level. Accordingly, the 'yes' to Europe given by the Handwerkskammer is a form of conditional support and rests on the following conditions. First, maintenance of the HWO, secondly, introduction of a dual professional training system as a model for Europe, thirdly, no tax increases, fourthly, maintenance of existing assistance schemes and of regional development incentives for SMEs and, finally, no additional bureaucracy and paperwork.[68] Italian craft associations do not appear to have produced demands of this kind and hope that Community initiatives, such as the creation of Business Information Centres and Centres for Technology Transfer, help in upgrading the framework conditions under which artisans are operating. Whether this is a reasonable expectation or not will not be answered here. What seems to be clear, however, is that national policies and, where they exist, regionally diversified structures for their implementation, will continue to remain the most important devices for regulating the SME domain.

**Appendix: Absolute Membership Figures for the Three
Major Interest Associations Representing the Craft Sector
in Italy (1991)**

Regione	CGIA	CNA	CASA	Total	API
Valle d'Aosta	276	200	0	476	NA
Piemonte	9,974	21,500	7,176	38,650	4,000
Liguria	7,419	13,500	596	21,515	2,000
Lombardia	77,431	27,000	2,369	106,800	5,500
Trentino-AA	14,386	2,000	NA	16,386	NA
Friuli-VG	16,199	3,600	NA	19,795	3,000
Veneto	66,320	28,200	3,998	98,516	4,500
Emilia-Romagna	31,477	90,000	900	122,436	5,000
Toscana	30,937	55,000	1,524	87,461	2,000
Marche	19,007	20,500	3,539	43,046	700
Umbria	6,193	6,500	307	13,000	800
Lazio	10,466	21,500	7,792	39,758	3,000
Campania	14,200	21,000	4,036	39,236	2,000
Abruzzo	8,881	8,000	3,609	20,490	NA
Molise	280	1,700	673	2,653	NA
Puglia	21,193	16,500	3,774	41,467	1,500
Basilicata	6,574	5,500	1,663	13,737	1,000
Calabria	14,856	9,600	5,366	29,822	1,000
Sicilia	7,820	28,100	17,446	53,266	1,500
Sardegna	5,696	11,000	1,376	18,072	1,000
Total	371,677	390,800	66,205	828,682	40,000

Data provided by Confartigianato (for CGIA and CASA), CNA and CONFAPI.

Notes:

1. While 70–80% of all ESPRIT contracts of the first phase have been awarded to the big 12 European MNCs (Mytelka and Delapierre, 1987: 245), in subsequent Framework Programmes the SMEs' share has slightly been altered in the latter's favour. The only major scheme of the Framework Programme where SMEs exhibit a higher participation rate than the big 12, is BRITE whose problem definition and general framework have not been formulated by a handful of European multinationals and where also some, albeit indirect European trade union participation has been achieved (van Tulder and Junne, 1988).

2. This applies at least to the organizational elements being required to diversify the range of products and modes of production and eventually less to the technology itself. This paper elaborates on the social and, i.e. organizational, prerequisites for flexible specialization and diversified quality production, also because successful entrepreneurs first mastered the organization required to achieve flexible product strategies before starting to adopt flexible automation technologies (Kaplinski, 1990: 7). As regards the wider political and social organization which is of equal relevance, there is a strategic choice of how to organize production, employment and work.

'Which option is chosen is ultimately decided by "politics", i.e. the dominant groups in society, the power relations among them, and the institutions they create' (Loveman and Sengenberger, 1990: 5).

3. For a detailed account of types of actors, means of enforcement and modes of governance of sectors in modern capitalism, see Schmitter, 1990: 3–40.

4. See also the unproper use being made of the concept of region in Sabel (1990: 17–70). Region, in Sabel's work, is essentially set equal to industrial district, and where he speaks of a 're-emergence of regional economies', in reality, subregional agglomerations of small firms are meant.

5. See the 'Ahlemer Programm'.

6. As mentioned by Berger (1980: 108), for the year 1968, Sylos-Labini estimated 9.3 million electors belonging in one way or the other to the category of Italian small firms.

7. Law No. 860 of 25 July 1956 and Law 443 of 8 August 1985.

8. Provvedimenti per l'Artigianato. Raccolta di disposizioni legislative ed amministrative. Rome, 1991. See for a valuable comparison of the different artisan laws in the European Community, G. Klinge, 1990.

9. Unlike to the South of the country, the areas of the Third Italy with their particularly high shares of relatively successful minor enterprises, have never been the target of specific support by the central government (Bagnasco, 1988: 57–60). But even in the South, government policies exhibit a clear bias in favour of large public and private enterprises (see the public support given to FIAT's decision of 1990 to set up a new assembly plant in Basilicata).

10. Law 317 of 5 October 1991: 'Interventi per l'innovazione e lo sviluppo delle piccole imprese', Supplemento ordinario n. 60 alla Gazzetta Ufficiale n. 237 del 9 ottobre 1991.

11. Commissione Industriale, DDL no. 1524 of 20 April 1956.

12. Bellini (1990), for example, maintains that it is difficult to speak of an 'Emilian model' since the region is strongly fragmented into various provinces which jealously guard their political and economic autonomy.

13. Resources which regional government cannot control, or only to a limited extent, are the supply of public expenditure and special grants and credits or, in certain areas, also ordinary credits (see Pizzorno, 1975: 329).

14. The German Christian Democrats still operate a rather influential group being attached to the party and carrying on its banner the demands of small capital and the traditional sector. The Mittelstandsvereiningung of the CDU/CSU is represented at European level by AECM, the European Independent Business Confederation which is not, as suggested by the name, a business interest association but a group collecting the small business fractions of various European conservative and Christian democratic parties. Its Italian member is Confintesa.

15. Berghahn (1984: 180) mentions that it was actually due to the propaganda of the Bundesverband der Deutschen Industrie (BDI) that the CDU and especially the minister in charge of economic affairs, Ludwig Ehrhard, had been given the reputation of an exaggerated closeness to small business. In reality, the rebuilding of German industry, in Ehrhard's view, could not possibly be achieved without large enterprises, 'at least not within the framework of a competitive and internationally oriented capitalism' (1984: 182).

16. When modern industry entered the traditional markets of small craft enterprise during the last third of the nineteenth century, 'free trade began to be perceived by these as a threat to their independence'. This interpretation was shared

'by the Bismarck government for which the possible "proletarianization" of a group which was one of its staunchest allies presented a formidable threat' (Streeck, 1989a: 66).

17. That they may have survived in some of those *Länder* with strong Social Democratic or Christian Democratic party hegemony, is shown by Grabher (1990, 1991) who speaks of a 'pre-perestroika consensus culture' in Nordrhein Westphalen in the 1970s and, of course, also by the strange death of 'Späth-capitalism' in Baden Wurttemberg.

18. NB the German definition of the category, which includes firms with fewer than 500 employees while the new draft law on small and medium-sized enterprises in Italy sets the limit at 200 employees.

19. For example, small firms with less than 20 employees are obliged to conclude fixed-term employment contracts only after two years and firms with part-time workers are no longer subject to the rules of unfair or summary dismissal. Moreover, in the case of dismissal, in firms with between 20 and 60 employees at least 20% of the workforce must lose their jobs before the firm is obliged to draw up a social plan to assist those made redundant and small firms with up to 30 employees are now able to benefit from the compensation scheme for the costs of continued wage payments in cases of sickness (see Weimer, 1990: 137).

20. Unlike the chambers of artisans, voluntary membership remained one of the characteristics of the guild associations since this, together with private law jurisdiction, represented the key conditions for exerting the task of employer associations and engaging in collective bargaining (*Tariffähigkeit*). Yet, as shown later, almost 85–90%, if not more, of the firms adhere to one of the local guilds (*Innungen*).

21. The organizational structure given to the Reichsstand des deutschen Handwerks reflected most of what craft enterprises had strived for for decades.

22. Kubler et al. (1982: 16) note that a law on the reorganization of *Handwerk* without the master certificate (the official term being adopted in the HWO of 1953 is *Grosser Befähigungsnachweis*) would have made no sense at all and would have been useless. The *Grosse Befähigungsnachweis* had been first introduced on 18 January 1935 (RGBl.I, S.15).

23. See Bundesgesetzblatt Teil I No. 63 Jahrgang 1953 of 23 September 1953.

24. Adenauer assured the allies that the law, once accepted, would be made subject of a legal investigation by the constitutional court. For copies of the letter exchange, see Kübler et al., 1982: 46–9.

25. *Handwerk* in Germany is accredited the title of 'the training institution of national importance' (Klinge, 1990: 33).

26. That Italy has not only no adequate policy for the craft sector but for the entire category of SMEs is documented in Agenzia Industriale Italiana, 1986: 177–8; Burns and Dewhurst, 1986: 200–1; Partito Socialista Italiano, 1991: 35.

27. Whereby the term 'enterprise' relates to a separate legal entity, while 'establishment' means a single place of work which may also be part of a larger multi-establishment enterprise.

28. See note 12.

29. The concepts of small enterprise or of SME are elusive. 'They do in fact hide a large heterogeneity in the types of firms' (Loveman and Sengenberger, 1990: 5). In Italy, the recent Law on SMEs defines as the upper margin for the category firms with not more than 200 employees. In fact, if the OECD definition of SMEs were applied to the Italian case, the entire economy would form part of this group. The

German Institut fur Mittelstandsforschung (Small Business Research Institute) characterizes a small firm as one with up to 49 employees and a medium firm as employing between 50 and 499 employees (Kayser and Ibielski, 1986: 179). The German peak association of industry, the BDI, which also runs a special committee for SMEs, defines small firms as those with less than 500, medium firms as ones with between 500 and 1,000, and large firms as firms with more than 1,000 employees. This is, of course, a definition reflecting the industrial interests of the association. We follow here the OECD definition which comes closest to that of the EC Commission and the European Investment Bank, i.e. an SME is any firm with a workforce not exceeding 500, with net fixed assets of less than 75 million ECU, and with not more than one-third of its capital held by a larger company.

30. Note, however, that Weimer (1990: 99) calculates for Germany (1970) 44.2% of employment in small enterprises and 55.9% in the category 100 plus. Note as well that percentage shares in Germany remained rather stable over the period of the 1970s, so that the figures can actually be compared in the present form.

31. The following data all refer to the years 1970 for Germany and 1981 for Italy.

32. The fact that regional data are presented here, is due to our intention to elaborate on the relevance of the regional level for different types of production and for different mechanisms to achieve governance within the craft sector. More on that in the following sections.

33. For more detailed figures on the provincial level see CERVED, 1989: 21.

34. Note that these figures represent establishment and not enterprise data (Loveman and Sengenberger, 1990: 18).

35. The concept of flexible specialization, quite obviously, is based on the pioneering work of Piore and Sabel and on a vast array of earlier and subsequent studies by Italian regional economists. For one of the most recent overviews also containing a chapter by one of the toughest opponents (Amin and Robins) to the concept, see Pyke et al. (1990). After a first appearance in Sorge and Streeck (1988), the term of diversified quality production has been elaborated by Streeck (1989a, 1991). In another study on the German model, this has also been accredited the label 'organized flexible specialization' (Allen, 1989: 158).

36. The latter would apply, for instance, to countries as the UK whose lack of a SME policy also reflects the minuscule importance the small firm and craft sectors possess for the economy. It has often been underlined that the UK's economy is the most concentrated among the group of highly industrialized capitalist countries.

37. The cells of the table are filled by 'specialized component production', 'mass production' or 'Fordism', 'craft production' and 'diversified quality production'.

38. There is no complete agreement as regards a precise definition of an MID. Definitions converge around the issues mentioned here but differ in some respects. One category, however, is frequently mentioned in all contributions: the role of 'culture', 'social structure' and, more precisely, of 'community' as the main mechanism for the provision of internal coherence of these territories.

39. Most *'distrettisti'* are following Marshall's lead in this respect. A content analysis of 49 standard texts published on districts reveals that only a minor fraction of these explicitly consider trade unions as relevant actors (Farry and Streeck, 1991). That this also applies to other categories of interests, is confirmed by our own analysis of craft associations.

40. Pizzorno has highlighted this interesting twinning. *Omerta'* is the untranslatable word for a homage-like attitude known particularly from the personalized bonds which characterize the *'malavita'* of the south.

41. 'Undocumented labour often exposes children, pensioners, and women to unregulated and often unsafe working conditions, and depresses the general level of wages for all workers through the incorporation of vulnerable and more maleable secondary labourers into the labour market mix' (Blim, 1990: 254).

42. *Il Sole 24 Ore*, 12 October 1991: 7.

43. Political exchange circuits of the traditional type imply 'that there has actually been an interest in the ruling party to leave the central bureaucracy unreformed and local government short of resources' (di Palma, 1987: 155). For similar results with regard to institutional reforms and interest policies in the UK, see Anderson (1990a: 234–57).

44. This weakness is evident, if one considers that even in one of those areas where the region disposes of some, albeit insufficient, autonomy, as in the case of decisions concerning the location of craft firms (settlement areas) and of the creation of financial and industrial consortia, regional expenditure amounted to merely 0.35% of total national expenditure (Trigilia, 1989b). This, of course, discourages any form of collective action by private firms at that level.

45. That this also has impacts on the composition of the technological assets of small enterprises is demonstrated by Patrizio Bianchi (1990).

46. Most of the following arguments are taken from Streeck (1989b, 1990a, b, 1991).

47. Note, that Volkswagen, for example, does not allow for more than a third of the total output of its supplier companies to be submitted to the customer, i.e. VW itself, in order to avoid any form of threatening and unilateral dependence so typical of subcontracting networks.

48. Most of the organizational power, of financial resources and of organizational staff resides at provincial or other local levels. This is, at the same time, the level that is also most important for political decisions to be taken for small firm and craft concerns.

49. Some 80% of the owners of craft firms in Lombardia have been dependent workers in one of the large enterprises in the North (Weiss, 1988).

50. There are exceptions to that rule, but most attempts to create an interassociational structure have failed so far. See for that the regional agreement between CNA, CASA, CGIA, CLAAI, CGIL, CISL and UIL in Sicily which did not even survive its first year of existence (Protocollo Interconfederale, 21 December 1983). Only recently (7 November 1990), there has been an agreement at the national level between CONFAPI and the main craft associations, aimed at improving coordination and increasing the combined power of organized SMEs versus the central government (API Toscana, 1991).

51. The author's view is that membership figures for craft associations in Italy in Table 5.4 may have been somewhat exaggerated by the associations. They do, however, represent the best available information in the absence of a central data bank.

52. A survey by the Tuscan branch of the CONFAPI among 200 SMEs of the region reveals that for 90% of the firms franchising assistance is completely unknown, for 58% P&R assistance has never been used, 55% do not even make use of industrial design services and almost 50% do not care for marketing. The report concludes that relationships between individual firms and their interest associations appear to be 'trustful but non-participatory' (API Toscana, 1989: 6). Entrepreneurs would not be prepared to cooperate beyond issues which are not directly related to production.

53. Note that the Italian system foresees only one encompassing chamber for all economic categories (trade, industry, craft and agriculture). That makes the chambers much less competent for the representation of craft interests than in Germany where they represent the main interest organization of artisans. The organization of the craft fraction of the chambers into different trades, however, is similar to Germany. In Italy, chamber membership is divided among 13 professional groups (metal, wood, textile, etc.) which represent 102 different trades while the respective figures for Germany, established by the artisan law, are seven groups and 125 trades.

54. This is one of the reasons why no exact membership figures for guild associations are presented in this text. Approximate figures can easily be deduced from Table 5.2.

55. Euro-Info SME Craft Industry, no. 37, 1991: 6.

56. In the case of UACEE, whose operating costs were substantially lower than that of its successor UEAPME, Belgian and German bodies commonly shared the burden.

57. For a complete list of the seven most important guidelines, see Klinge, 1990.

58. Andrews maintains that 'such staff are part-time, continuing their work for their home organization and being paid fully by it' (1991:13), but the author fails to provide reliable data.

59. 'SME Action Programme', August 1986. COM(86)445 final; 'An Enterprise Policy for the Community', June 1988; COM(88)241 final. Work in this area started immediately after 1983, the European Year of SMEs and Craft Industry. Documents predating the Action Programme are SEC(85)1592 and subsequent reports on the implementation of the Programme are COM(87)238 and COM(88)64.

60. 'Enterprise Policy: a New Dimension for Small and Medium-Sized Enterprises', Winter 1990; COM(90)528 final.

61. See 'The Enterprise Policy: the priorities in 1991', in: Euro-Info SME Craft Industry, no. 37, 1991: 3.

62. Euro-Info-Centres Network – Activity Report for 1990.

63. Euro-Info SME Craft Industry, no. 38, 1991: 3. By 1991, about 30,000 cooperation profiles had been processed.

64. Europartnership: Results and Assessment, Communication from the Commission. COM(89)76 final: 4.

65. For a description of how effects generated under the umbrella of the social dimension of the internal market are cancelled out by the spatial and economic effects of other transnational policies, see Streeck 1990a.

66. The Commission intends to make use of such sophisticated tools as 'cost–benefit analysis' and 'necessity tests' (An Enterprise Policy for Europe, 1988: 26).

67. UNICE 1990: 3. See also the Annual Report of UEAPME 1990, raising many doubts with regard to an improvement of the procedure.

68. Niedersachsischer Handwerkstag; Wunsche und Forderungen des Niedersachsischen Handwerks an den 12. Landtag und die Landesregierung von Niedersachsen, 1990.

6
Coping with Heterogeneity: Peak Associations of Business within and across Western European Nations

Luca Lanzalaco

Introduction

Corporatist theory and empirical research about the organizational structuring of systems for business interest intermediation have usually focused on two dimensions of analysis, namely the sectoral and the national one (Schmitter and Streeck, 1981: 121, 141; Streeck, 1989b: 61). The forms of interest aggregation above and below the national scale and those across different sectors of the economy are substantially understudied. Omitting them is not justified for at least two reasons.

First, the choice of the national scale as the 'natural' level of analysis is not very far-reaching, as has been highlighted by the relevance simultaneously assumed by subnational (local and regional) and supranational forms of governance and interest intermediation during recent years.[1] This lacuna has at least been partially filled with regard to subnational levels (Cawson, 1985b; Coleman and Jacek, 1989a; Hernes and Selvik, 1981; King, 1985; Saunders, 1983), while the study of transnational interest organization continues to remain relatively underdeveloped. Secondly, the rejection of any form of societal-economicism – that is, of those approaches hypothesizing that modes of interest representation are primarily the product or reflection of prior and independent changes in economic and social structures (Schmitter, 1977, 1991), and of the assumption of the autonomy of political and organizational processes – implies that the structuring of a class or other social group and the establishment of its political organization must be conceptualized as components of a single and unique process, namely the transformation of the class in itself (*Klasse an sich*) into a class for itself (*Klasse für sich*). It is not the class that brings about the organization on the basis of its member 'real' and 'objective' preferences, but it is the organization that structures and shapes the class, moulding the subjective perceptions it has of its interests and the way in which they are transformed into collective strategies (Lange, 1983; Sartori, 1969; Schmitter, 1977, 1983).

It is curious that this way of conceptualizing collective action, which is taken for granted when the labour movement is at stake, is usually (even if not always) ignored when capitalists are the object of study. Nevertheless, if no theoretical difference may be established between labour and capital logics of action and organization (Streeck, 1988), then the analytical tools on which the study of the labour movement is based, and the substantive questions by which it is inspired, should be extended to the analysis of associative action by business interests as well. The first step in this direction is just to give relevance not only to interest intermediation within specific sectors, that is the typical topic of corporatist theory and research, but also to sector-unspecific (that is, intersectoral, general, 'horizontal', comprehensive, encompassing or inclusive, according to linguistic preferences) forms of interest organization, namely peak associations and the sector-unspecific associational systems[2] in which they operate (Coleman and Grant, 1988; Schmitter and Lanzalaco, 1989). In fact, it is mainly by means of the sector-unspecific aggregation and organization of interests that capitalists try to smooth the differences and clashes among their conflicting interests as competitive producers of goods and services, and to identify and emphasize their common interests as employers (Streeck, 1988). By analysing 'from above' the sector-unspecific organization of business interests it is possible to highlight and explain cross-country similarities and differences in the mode in which capitalists perceive and organize themselves as a class.

The relevance of the sector-unspecific organization of business interests is even greater from the perspective of European integration. Europe's Internal Market will involve an institutional restructuring of both product and labour markets that will affect in different ways the firms of different sectors, branches, size and regions and, hence, will bring about internal conflicts and centrifugal trends. The 'management of diversity' among business interests will become more and more difficult and the 'unity of the capitalist class' – already a precarious matter at the level of most countries – will be jeopardized both at the national and at the transnational level. The task of balancing these disaggregating forces will pertain mainly to sector-unspecific associations. Thus, it is because of the interplay between the process of structuring of a social group and that of establishment of its political organization that, regardless of the scenario we forecast, the future 'features' of the capitalist class (for example, alternatively, the emergence of a relatively united Euro-bourgeoisie or the resurgence of national capitalisms or the emergence of cross-national clashes among the capitalists of different sectors and regions) will be significantly affected by the more or less cohesive and proactive associative response capitalists will give to the so-called 'challenge of 1992' (Lanzalaco and Schmitter, 1992).

This chapter is an attempt to analyse the characteristics and the logics of the sector-unspecific organization of business interests at the transnational level in Western Europe. In this the chapter starts from four general questions:

1 What are the main characteristics of the sector-unspecific associational system of business interests at the European level? What factors account for these characteristics?

2 Are there significant differences between the sector-unspecific organization of capital and that of labour at the EC level – and if so, why?

3 Are there similarities between the national and the transnational sector-unspecific organization of capital – and if so, why?

4 Are there differences in the sector-unspecific organization of business interests across European countries? Do these differences affect in some way the modes of intersectoral associability at the transnational level – and if so, why?

The Transnational Organization of Interests and the Logics of Collective Action

According to Schmitter and Streeck (1981), the organization of business interest associations (BIAs) may be conceptualized as a compromise between the logic of membership, leading to associative structures that reflect the fragmented and specialized preferences of members, and the logic of influence, which tends to produce more unitary and encompassing structures in response to the demands of the principal interlocutors, namely state agencies and trade unions. Furthermore, in mediating between these two conflicting logics, BIAs are subject to the imperatives of the logic of goal formation, and the logic of implementation. These indicate that a BIA must structure itself functionally and spatially in such a manner to allow, with the most efficient and efficacious use of its resources, both the formation of goals for a particular category of members and before a particular set of authorities, and the implementation with certainty and continuity of a particular mix of goods and services over a particular territory (Figure 6.1).

Even if the logics of membership and of influence call for conflicting organizational properties (Schmitter and Streeck, 1981:

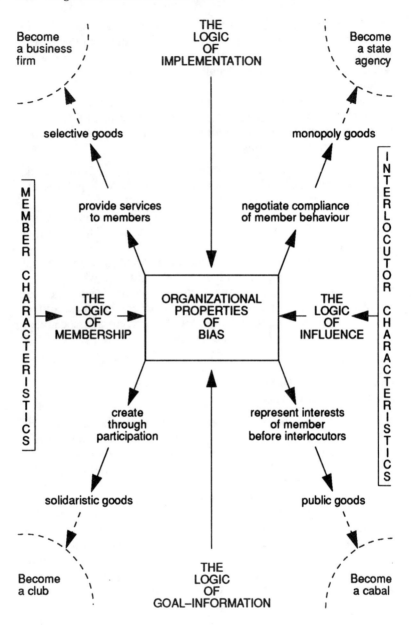

Figure 6.1 *The four logics of associability (Schmitter, 1981: 51a)*

132–40), the relationship between them cannot be interpreted as a zero-sum game, but as a variable-sum one, since their impacts on the organizational properties of BIAs do not cancel each other out but are, rather, of a cumulative nature. In fact, if both the logic of membership and the logic of influence are pressing, namely if BIAs are requested to develop their intermediation functions, the joint pressure of the two contending logics will be stronger. In turn, this will require a greater organizational development of the associations. In general terms,

> organizational structures are more 'developed': the more encompassing they are in scope and purpose (the more 'external effects' and interdependencies they 'internalize'); the more specialized and coordinated they are internally; the more safely their supply of strategic resources is institutionalized; and the greater their autonomous capacity to act and to pursue long-term strategies regardless of short-term environmental contraints and fluctuations. (Schmitter and Streeck, 1981: 124)

By analysing the organized complexity (associative domains and structural interrelatedness) and the autonomy (resource control and policy capacity) of an associational system, it is possible to assess its degree of organizational development and, hence, how much associative action is important for business interests in a particular country or sector (Schmitter and Streeck, 1981: 124). In this chapter, such an analytical framework is utilized beyond the borders of sectors and countries in order to evaluate the degree of organizational development of the sector-unspecific associational system of capitalists at the transnational level within Western Europe, and to identify the factors accounting for it.

The creation of a sector-unspecific associational system on a transnational scale implies a twofold and joint process of organizational integration (Schmitter and Streeck, 1981: 171–202) along the sectoral and the territorial dimension, namely across both different national territories and various sectors of the economy. In analysing the process of integration of a sector-unspecific associational system at the transnational level three types of variables must be considered: the type of integration; the degree of integration; and the dimension along which the process of integration is occurring. Different types of associative integration may be:

> horizontal, to the extent that there exist institutionalized relationships between its component associations that are not mediated through hierarchically superior, more general associations . . . or hierarchical, to the extent that the component associations are affiliated to, and controlled by, higher-order associations. (Schmitter and Streeck, 1981: 195,199)

Table 6.1   *Characteristics of the forms of associative integration*

The process of integration among associations involves:	Hierarchical integration	Horizontal integration				
		Ad Hoc alliance	Joint task force	Joint venture	Alliance	Staff sharing
Exchange of information and strategy coordination	Yes	Yes	Yes	Yes	Yes	Yes
A multi-issue (vs issue-bond) cooperative relationship	Yes	No	No	No	Yes	Yes
A permanent (vs temporary) cooperative relationship	Yes	No	No	Yes	Yes	Yes
Elected or paid staff sharing	Yes	No	Yes	Yes	No	Yes
Establishment of a joint organization unit	Yes	No	Yes	Yes	Yes/No	No
Hierarchical control of this joint organization upon constituent associations	Yes	No	No	No	No	No/Yes[1]

[1] The hierarchical control may be wielded not by a joint organization unit but by a constituent association upon another.

Horizontal integration may give rise to different cooperative relationships (*ad hoc* alliances, joint ventures etc.) with varying degrees of stability and institutionalization. In Table 6.1 the properties of these organizational arrangements are compared and contrasted with those of hierarchical integration. The degree of associative integration varies according to the type considered. The degree of horizontal integration of an associational system is measured both by the stability of cooperative relationships (alliances, staff sharing, joint ventures) among the associations and by the share of its component associations taking part in these stable relationships.

The more stable the relationships are and the more numerous the associations involved, the more horizontally integrated appears the associational system. The degree of hierarchical integration of a system is measured by the number of hierarchically unaffiliated higher-order associations.[3] If this number is low, the associational system is highly hierarchically integrated; meanwhile if this number is high the system is fragmented into many associations and 'each hierarchically unaffiliated higher-order association stands for an *interest subsystem* not linked into a more general level of interest representation' (Schmitter and Streeck, 1981: 200, emphasis added), and the associational system is scarcely integrated.

Finally, the process of integration of a sector-unspecific associational system must involve both the territorial and the sectoral dimension, and there may be asymmetry between what happens on the two dimensions. Hence, the associational system may present cross-nationally and cross-sectorally both a different degree and a different form of integration. The following section will be devoted to assessing the degree (high or low), the type (horizontal or hierarchical) and the dimension (cross-nation and/or cross-sector) of integration of the sector-unspecific system of business interest representation in Europe. Then, in the following two sections, those factors related to the logic of influence and the logic of membership that may account for these features will be discussed. Finally, the last section will deal with some general questions concerning the meaning of the transnational dimension and the organizational problems of BIAs at European level.

The European System of Business Interest Intermediation

The System of Business Interest Representation
While labour is represented by one encompassing peak association, however weak and precarious the European Trade Union Confed-

eration (ETUC) may ultimately be (see chapter 7), the system of business interest representation comprises at least 20 sector-unspecific peak associations. The main EC peak associations of capital (UNICE, COPA etc.) were founded much earlier than those of labour and, in general, EC business interest associations are the greatest part of all the interest organizations (trade unions, consumer associations, professional associations etc.) (De Vroom, 1987). Hence, the high degree of fragmentation of the business interest intermediation system cannot be ascribed to a backward development. According to the typology of national interest representation systems adopted below, the European system of business interest representation may be defined as a homogeneous associational system, since the cleavages among peak associations are brought about by one main axis of differentiation, the sectoral one. There are peak associations which specialize in the representation of industry, public enterprise, crafts, small and medium-sized firms, insurance and credit, agriculture and trade. And often the general interests of the capitalists of these sectors are promoted and defended by more than one peak association. Hence, the system is also characterized by a high degree of intra- and intersectoral differentiation.

Some sectors present a degree of fragmentation greater than others. The industry sector has the most fragmented system of representation, since there are six sector-unspecific peak associations. These are the Union of Industrial and Employers Confederations of Europe (UNICE); Eurochambres; the European Round Table; the European Centre of Public Enterprises (CEEP); the European Community Services Group; and the American Chamber EC Committee. In addition, employers are also represented by the Employers Group of the Economic and Social Committee, the members of which 'are appointed by personal capacity and do not necessarily reflect the view of UNICE' (Oeschlin, 1980: 204; Tyszkiewicz, 1990). At the other extreme, we find the agricultural sector, represented by the Committee of Agricultural Organizations in the European Community (COPA) and the General Committee of Agricultural Cooperation (COGECA), which together form a unique great peak association, considered the most powerful of the Community-level pressure groups (Grant, 1990: 13).

Between these two extremes we find trade, craft and small and medium-sized enterprise, as well as the credit and insurance sectors, each being characterized by an intermediate level of fragmentation. Banks and insurance companies are represented by three peak associations: the Banking Federation of the EC (BFEC), the European Insurance Committee (CEA) and the Association of

Cooperative Savings and Credit Institutions. The Confederation Européenne de Commerce du Detail (CECD) and the Federation of European Wholesale and International Trade Associations (FEWITA), both established after the demise of the Comité des Organisations Commerciales de la CEE (COCCEE) in 1978, represent, together with the International Federation of Small and Medium-Sized Commercial Enterprises (FIMPEC), the commerce sector. Finally, as demonstrated by Grote in chapter 5, the European Association of Crafts and Small and Medium-Sized Enterprises (UEAPME), the European Committee for Small and Medium-Sized Enterprises (EUROPMI), the European Union (EMSU) and the European Association of the Middle Classes (AECM) are the main Community-level peak associations of artisans and small firms. To cope with this high level of fragmentation there is only one weak organ of coordination, the Employers' Liaison Committee (ELC), which facilitates contacts among the capitalists of commerce, insurance, banking and crafts as regards Community-related social questions. The ELC is substantially an emanation of UNICE, which guarantess its secretarial staff (Confindustria, 1980; Oeschlin, 1980). It is a rather weak body since 'membership of the ELC does not require any European interest organization to surrender its autonomy, as any collaboration fostered under the auspices of the committee is purely voluntary' (Sargent, 1985: 233). Furthermore, excluded from the ELC are the confederations representing agriculture and the public sector, represented respectively by COPA and the CEEP, even though some of UNICE's member associations also represent fractions of the two former sectors. This further weakens the representativeness of ELC.

The members of European sector-unspecific peak associations are the corresponding sector-unspecific national peak associations. For example, UNICE's members are the national peak associations representing industry and employers, while COPA's members are the national confederations of farmers. Apart from this similarity, however, these Euro peak associations widely differ from one another, because they do not cover the same number of countries and they are not equally resourced.

At the national level, sector-unspecific peak associations usually combine the sectoral and the territorial associative units present on a given national territory, whereas at the transnational level they combine only territorial ones, that is national sector-unspecific peak associations. Sectoral national associations are affiliated to transnational product, branch, or sector-specific associations (see Figure 6.2). The latter may combine into federations, but they cannot join

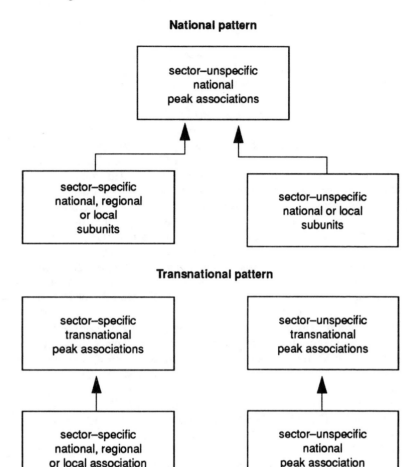

Figure 6.2   *Patterns of peak associations*

sector-unspecific Euro peak associations. In other words, at the national level peak associations act as channels of integration between the sectoral and the territorial dimension (Schmitter and Lanzalaco, 1989), while at the transnational level the processes of transnational aggregation along the two dimensions are kept separate.[4] And if we compare the number of sector-unspecific Euro peak associations (not more than 20), with that of sector-specific Euro associations and federations (more than 300) we may infer that the representative system is much more fragmented along the sectoral dimension than along the territorial one.

This peculiar arrangement has two consequences. First, it gives rise to a double associative channel of access to decision-making. National or local sector-specific associations, in order to put pressure on EC bodies, may utilize both transnational sector-specific associations and national (and then transnational) sector-unspecific associations. Secondly, it weakens the representativeness of Euro peak associations as a 'voice' of the European business community (Tyszkiewicz, 1990). This distinction between sectoral and territorial forms of aggregation could be effective only to the extent that the social dimension acquired a greater relevance, and a form of functional specialization emerged, with sector-specific Euro federations dealing with economic and trade matters, and sector-unspecific Euro peak associations with social ones. In this case, the territorial orientation of sector-unspecific BIAs would not only be functionally effective, but would also confirm the patterns of European countries where employers peak associations tend to be more differentiated by territory (and less by sector) than trade peak associations (Lanzalaco, 1990: ch. 3). But at the moment this form of functional specialization is absent and the distinction between the two realms of action, the social and the economic one, tends to blur.[5] So, the lack of integration among territorial (national) and sectoral associations at the transnational level is only an indicator of the weak hierarchical integration of the transnational associative system.

The Case of UNICE

In order to assess the characteristics of the sector-unspecific organization of business interests at the transnational level it is not sufficient to analyse the overall system of interest representation. In addition, the features and problems of the single peak associations operating within it also have to be taken into consideration. In fact, the transnational associative integration is both an inter- and a intra-associative process. Thus, it makes sense to examine the integrative capacity of the single associations as well.

In this context, the structure of UNICE will be analysed, comparing it with that of other European peak associations. UNICE, the most important of the peak associations representing the employers of the industry sector, was created in 1958 by the national employer federations of the six original EC member states (Belgium, the Federal Republic, France, Italy, Luxemburg, the Netherlands). UNICE is not, however, the first form of business interest representation at European level. The Council of European Industrial Federations (CIFE) was founded in the immediate post-war period (1949) and, after its demise in 1961, part of its functions were accomplished by the Business and Industrial Advisory Committee (BIAC). As Article 5 of its constitution underlines, UNICE was created as a coordination body among industrial confederations versus the institutions of the EC. Thus, even if it operates both in social and economic fields, its main interlocutors have always remained Community institutions and not, as might be expected, European trade unions. Even if its primary objective has been to canvass and influence EC institutions, membership of UNICE goes beyond the borders of the Community. As early as 1962, the Federation of Greek Industry was associated with its work. In 1972–73 the employers organizations of the three new member states – UK, Denmark and Ireland – joined UNICE, while employer associations from western European countries outside the Community also decided to become associated members (Oeschlin, 1980: 204). Nowadays the present membership consists of 32 central federations of industry and employers from 22 countries, that is, the 12 EC members, the six EFTA countries, Turkey, Cyprus, Malta and San Marino (Tyszkiewicz, 1990). Hence, 'UNICE is more than an organization of EEC employers but also an organization of European employers' (Oeschlin, 1980: 204).

It is precisely this 'over-representativeness' which raises doubts about the actual capacity of the association to manage the diversity among European countries. The logic of goal formation requires that in order to minimize the transaction costs involved in defining collective goals, the membership of an association mirrors the range of interests affected by a given decision-making body. If association-al membership is larger than the community of policy-takers, internal decision-making risks being overloaded because of the presence of redundant members. This equally applies to the fact that there exists no discrimination between the decisional powers of EC and non-EC members. The latter possess the same right to veto decisions as do associations of EC member states, even in Community-related matters.

The structure of UNICE, just as that of any other BIA, is based on the double tier of elected representatives and paid officials – on the one hand the President, the Vice-Presidents etc., and on the other hand the Secretariat, the Directors etc. (Windmuller and Gladstone, 1985). In general terms, the more relevant the former group are, the more the association depends on its membership, and the more relevant the latter group, the more the organization is autonomous and institutionalized. A further distinction may be added between the agencies endowed with direct legitimation (either directly elected if representatives or paid by UNICE bodies themselves if officials) and, on the other hand, those bodies possessing only an indirect legitimation, since they are formed by representatives and officials chosen separately and sent as spokespeople by each member association. Again, the more relevant directly legitimated bodies are, the higher the association's autonomy from its membership.

The complex organizational chart of UNICE (Figure 6.3) can be analysed in terms of the above two-dimensional typology in order to assess the association's degree of relative autonomy (Figure 6.4). As expected, the degree of autonomy of UNICE is relatively low, since

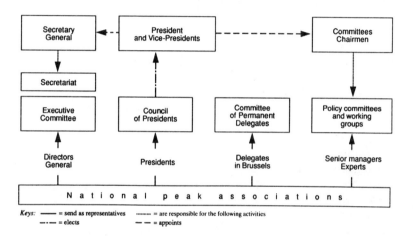

Figure 6.3   *UNICE's organization chart*

	Organs appointed by:	
	Member associations	**UNICE bodies**
Paid officials	(a) Executive Committee Committee of Permanent Delegates Policy Committees	(b) Secretary General Secretariat
Elected representatives	(c) Council of Presidents	(d) President Vice-Presidents

Figure 6.4   *A typology of UNICE bodies and organs*

many of its bodies are composed of delegates of member associations. Only the top levels of the hierarchy, that is President and Vice-Presidents, are directly elected by UNICE agencies themselves. Yet, comparing cells (a) and (c) of the typology, it appears that many of the committees possessing indirect legitimation are formed by officials and not by representatives.

The decision-making processes of UNICE are precisely the cornerstones of its activity (Tyszkiewicz, 1990). In order to evaluate this structure, we shall confront it with the structure of other European peak associations. In some respects, the structure of other EC-level peak associations is more simple than the UNICE case. Most of these are organized around an agency composed of the representatives of national associations. These are, for instance, the Comité des Délégués of the CEEP (CEEP statute, Articles 9–16), the General Assembly of the CECD (CECD statute, Article 6), the Réunion des Chefs de Délégation of the CEA (CEA statute, Articles 7–8). Usually these agencies elect the President, the Vice-President and the Treasurer. It is mainly the representatives of national associations which are of relevance here, and choices for their appointment or re-appointment are left to the member associations.

Contrasting this very simple organizational model are some other and more complex ones. First, there is both an agency exclusively composed of representatives, and another formed by the director or the general secretary of the associations. This creates a substantial difference between the board and the committee of permanent representatives of FEWITA (FEWITA statute, Articles 14–15, 16–20); the assembly and presidency of COPA (COPA statute, Articles 9–10); and, finally, the presidential council and the executive committee of UNICE. Secondly, in some cases associations possess separate agencies and working groups to deal with more specific problems, such as the special commissions and expert groups of UNICE, or the technical working groups of FEWITA. Summing up, UNICE has reached a degree of organizational development greater than that of other associations. This relates, first of all, to its structure which is relatively more complex than that of other groups. Secondly, agencies composed of officials and directly legitimated by the association itself possess an authority which cannot be found in other organizations.

These traits are confirmed and strengthened by recent organizational reforms under way since 1989. The cornerstones of this reform are essentially twofold (Tyszkiewicz, 1990: 20–1). The first is the strengthening of the Secretariat with a 40% increase in UNICE's budget. Secondly, direct relationships with single firms have been set up via the establishment of the advisory and support group which is composed of companies. Both these changes contribute to a greater autonomy of UNICE, since they strengthen its capacity for controlling organizational power resources such as direct membership contacts and a more efficient staff of officials.

Hierarchical or Horizontal Integration?

For a number of reasons, the degree of organizational development of the sector-unspecific system of business interest representation at the EC level is relatively low. Associational domains continue to be quite narrow, associational resources are basically controlled by their national constituent units and their internal structures are scarcely interrelated both because sector-specific associations are not affiliated to sector-unspecific ones, and because the latter are scarcely integrated among themselves. The dimension in which integration is most developed is the territorial one. This is because cross-national forms of integration are relatively strong within sectors, but are weak between them. In fact, while forms of cross-national integration have emerged (which often also include non-EC members), cross-sectoral integration mostly does not go beyond the weak experiments made with the ELC. Instead of a unique sector-unspecific peak association such as ETUC (in the case of labour), we find a loosely coupled network of transnational associational subsystems horizontally differentiated along sectoral lines. Furthermore, even if the peak associations should acquire more resources and capacities for intermediation, as UNICE is trying to achieve, the degree of hierarchical integration is likely to remain very low. The number of un-affiliated higher-order associations (UNICE, COPA etc.) is doomed to remain very high (Tyszkiewicz, 1990). The form of integration (see Table 6.1) prevailing at the EC level is quite an ambiguous one. National peak associations are affiliated to higher-order associations, thus fulfilling one of the prerequisites of hierarchical integration. The second condition, however, is absent, since it can hardly be said that national peak associations are controlled by higher-order associations. If there is any form of control, it exists in the opposite direction. In addition, in the more complex and relatively autonomous Euro peak associations such as UNICE, the decision-making bodies are predominantly formed by elected or paid representatives appointed by each constituent association. The same thing may also be said with regard to ELC, whose staff are provided by UNICE.

Therefore, in spite of the existence of formally autonomous transnational peak associations, what appears to be the case in reality is a form of horizontal integration, which Schmitter and

Streeck (1981) have defined as 'alliance' (see Table 6.1).[6] National BIAs look at transnational peak associations more 'as channels of representation to their respective sister federations than as channels of representation to EC or national bodies to which the groups could and did establish individual channels of representation' (Sargent, 1987: 232). As regards industry, when national peak associations need to establish contacts with one another, resort is not always made to associative channels but, rather, to bilateral relations between sister associations (Grant, 1990: 9). Subsequently, instead of empowering their transnational peak association UNICE, they actually preferred to locate and enlarge their individual headquarters in Brussells (Tyszkiewicz, 1990). The result is that many of the relationships among national peak associations are not necessarily mediated by hierarchically superior and more general transnational associations. Usually, 'an alliance, even if embodied in a joint organization, differs from a higher order association in that . . . it has no staff or elected leadership of its own, but operates exclusively by personnel belonging to its member associations' (Schmitter and Streeck, 1981: 196). This does not contradict what has been argued before, namely that transnational associations do actually have paid staff with part (sometimes only the President) of the leadership being directly elected by the members of the associations. In fact 'the boundaries between an alliance and a higher-order association are probably shifting, and it is possible that alliances turn into higher-order associations as they develop their organizational properties' (Schmitter and Streeck, 1981: 196). Thus, the question is whether transnational associations will eventually assume patterns of hierarchical integration or, rather, remain horizontally integrated.

Taking as an indicator the date of foundation, the degree of horizontal integration at the transnational level – at least with regard to the stability of the cooperative relationships – is relatively high, but remains very low with respect to the number of associations being involved in these relationships. First, at the transnational level, unlike the national one, sector-unspecific peak associations only connect territorial units (national sector-unspecific peak associations) and not sectoral ones (transnational sector-specific associations). Secondly, ELC, as the only real attempt at intersectoral integration, does not comprise many transnational peak associations.

This contradictory pattern of horizontal integration may be explained if we compare the timing of foundation of sector-unspecific associations with that of sector-specific ones at the transnational level. At the national level, peak associations had been founded after a more or less extended (Lanzalaco, 1990) period of diversification and diffusion and only then, in a second step, have they started integrating with territorially and sectorally diversified associations. At the transnational level, the process appears to be inverted – initially, peak associations are set up, while sector-specific ones are added only in a subsequent step (De Vroom, 1987). This anomaly may be due to the fact that sector-unspecific associations mainly performed such symbolic functions as, for instance, the 'mirroring' of new Community institutions, while the tasks of pressure and lobbying were, subsequently, left to sector-specific associations, in each case matching the pace with which EC institutions had been endowed with regulatory capacities. This hypothesis is confirmed in so far as sector-specific associations are generally better resourced than are sector-unspecific ones. Given the relatively low degree of organizational development of the latter at transnational level, it would be misleading to speak of a process of transnational aggregation of business interests. What emerges in reality, is, rather, the existence of a dualist and scarcely integrated network of international connections between different national and sectoral peak associations.

Institutional Constraints and Opportunities for Sector-unspecific Collective Action

A first set of factors accounting for the fragmentation and loose coupling of the sector-unspecific system of business interest representation in Western Europe is related to the 'logic of influence' as described by Schmitter and Streeck (1981). This concerns the characteristics of private and public interlocutors with which BIAs usually interact, that is trade unions and public authorities. At the national level, the factors that have fostered the emergence of centralized business interest peak associations are of a twofold nature. First, the encouragement and support given to them by agencies of the state (for example, France or Spain) or, secondly, the threat employers encountered in the political arena through either electoral mobilization and access of pro-labour parties to government, or the existence of a strong union organization (for example, Sweden). The absence of both of these factors at the European level is conspicuous (Schmitter and Streeck, 1990). As shown by Visser and Ebbinghaus in chapter 7, the labour movement is rather weak at that level, and it can hardly be said to represent a serious threat for capitalists (Grant, 1990; Sargent 1985). Given that 'labour at the EC-level has always been (and remains) highly disorganized as a class' (Schmitter and Streeck, 1981: 8), it is not clear at all why capitalists should seek to reinforce their class (namely sector-unspecific) organization on a transnational scale. The minor weight accruing to the defence of class interests of capital at that level is further diminished by the relatively marginal role of the European Parliament, despite the socialists forming its largest voting bloc. The only period during which there might have been some more substantial incentives for a more coherent form of sector-unspecific organization was between 1970 and 1978, when attempts had been made to establish a kind of Euro-corporatism. Experiments of this kind, however, elapsed rather soon and were hardly perceived as initiatives which would make an acceleration in the process of building inclusive and encompassing peak associations compelling for capitalists. Furthermore, both the scarce relevance of social issues and the absence of collective bargaining at the EC level implied for BIAs the need to emphasize producer interests at the cost of defending their interests as employers. It appears, in fact, that EC-level business associations are mainly, if not exclusively[7], trade associations (Grant, 1990; Kirchner, 1986a) representing the producer interests of capitalists. Since the latter are more divisive than the class interests usually represented by employers associations (Lanzalaco and Schmitter, 1992; Streeck, 1988), fragmentation rather than the emergence of centralization results. Not surprisingly, therefore, the main attempts having been made to coordinate and integrate the various peak associations, represented particularly by the Employers' Liaison Committee, are mostly related to social matters rather than to ones of an economic nature.

The trade orientation of EC-level associations may also explain why sector-specific associational systems possess a strikingly higher sectoral differentiation at the transnational level than they do domestically (De Vroom, 1987). In fact, the development of a sector-specific associational system at the national level has often been affected by the – sometimes strong and pervasive – existence of sector-specific employers associations (Windmuller and Gladstone, 1985), whereby the latter were usually more orientated towards unity and cohesion than trade associations. There had been permeability between the two logics of associability, also because sector-specific associations, at least in some countries, are both trade and employers associations at the same time. In other words, while centrifugal and divisive tendencies brought about by the producer interests of capitalists and represented by sector-specific trade associations had been limited and equilibrated at the national level, they fully emerged at the level of the Community where employer associations do not exist.

If the labour movement has provided only little incentive to a more straightforward type of associative centralization, the role played by public policy intervention in this respect has been even weaker. If there was anything that has been fostered by the existence of public actors, it was not the intersectoral integration of business interests but, rather, their intrasectoral differentiation. As demonstrated by Grote (1989b, 1990), the Commission has substantially increased the number of committees and working parties dealing with various and specialized issues. This process, partly because of its spontaneous and uncontrolled nature (1989b, 1990), has resulted in a proliferation in the number of organized special interests (De Vroom, 1987; Schmitter and Streeck, 1990). Neither the Commission, however, nor any other Community institution appears to have contributed to a simplification of the way capital organizes at the European level. For example, 'there has been no encouragement of mergers across organizations which represent similar interests, nor support for a greater hierarchical ordering of European representatives of capital' (Sargent, 1985: 233). This is further corroborated by the failure, partially questioned in some chapters of this book, of attempts to establish processes of corporatist policy-making at EC level (Grote 1989b, 1990; Schmitter and Streeck, 1990). Another factor contributing to a reduction of the need for sector-unspecific organization is the character of EC-level decision-making itself. First, its complex, multilayered, overlapping and somewhat disordered structure itself elicits diversification of the forms of collective action: 'pluralism . . . is literally written into the structure of authority' (Schmitter and Streeck, 1990: 28). Secondly, the dissociated forms of governance at the transnational level provide interest groups with multiple channels of access to decision-making and triggers off a high variety of influence strategies. In very schematic terms, two channels of access to EC decision-making are available to national interest groups: either they act through national governments which may use their veto power in the Council of Ministers, or they resort to their transnational counterparts in order to interact directly with Community institutions, in particular with the Commission and its committees. The mere presence of EC institutions does not in itself entail that transnational channels are privileged a priori. On the contrary, national channels of pressure have actually maintained their 'attractiveness' (Grant, 1990; Kirchner, 1986a) as effective means for influencing Community decisions.

The assumption which could be advanced is that interest associations are likely to choose the strategy of getting access that is most rewarding in each specific case. Given the multiplicity of points of access, strategies are equally numerous. Associational activities falling under the 'logic of influence' are not shaped by the simple presence of EC institutions *per se* but, rather, by more rewarding opportunities offered by supranational institutions relative to those offered by national ones. Two characteristics of the EC system make the use of national channels advantageous for business interest groups. The first is the relative centrality of the Council of Ministers in EC decision-making. Acting via their national government, business interests may avoid interaction with the European Parliament where pro-labour parties are well represented and trade unions find favourable interlocutors. Secondly, within the Council of Ministers, decisions affecting business have mainly been taken by unanimity, which has led national BIAs to convince their respective governments to exploit their veto power. This procedure has turned out to be more rewarding and less costly than trying to reach agreements with associations of other member states. Accordingly, a form of proper transnational interest aggregation was neither required within sectors nor across them. With the coming into force of the Single European Act in 1986, the 'attractiveness' of national access routes is declining. In fact, the increasing relevance of the European Parliament as a decision-making body, together with the extension of qualified majority voting to virtually all issues concerning business and industry, produce major changes in the influence strategies of capital (Grant, 1990; Mazey and Richardson, 1991; Tyszkiewicz, 1990). Since veto powers are reduced, acting through national governments is now becoming more uncertain and reaching agreements with the affiliates of other member states is increasingly becoming advantageous. In other words,

> by reducing the extent to which national governments within the Council are either willing or able to obstruct proposals, the greater use of majority voting has increased the incentive for groups to seek allies in other member states in order to achieve either a blocking minority or qualified majority. (Mazey and Richardson, 1991: 7)

This is likely to increase the relevance attached to the transnational definition, aggregation and coordination of business interests. Equally important is the growing centrality of Parliament, where trade union influence is particularly well developed in social policy areas. Both of the above, hence, represent developments that make the upgrading of the pressure capability of business interests mandatory. More frequent recourse to transnational channels of influence not only calls for improvements to be made in the action capacity of sector-specific associations and federations but, equally, for a strengthening in the guidance and coordination of sector-unspecific associations. Recent organizational reforms adopted by UNICE have to be interpreted as reactions to this new institutional arrangement (Tyszkiewicz, 1990). Thus, on the one hand, factors related to the logic of influence may account for the fragmented character of the sector-unspecific organization of business interests at EC level, while on the other they will also represent a serious challenge in the future for this organizational asset.

The Heterogeneity of Business Interest Organization in Western Europe

A Typology of Systems of Interest Representation
In general, while the 'logic of influence' only offers few incentives to sector-unspecific transnational collective action by capitalists, the 'logic of membership' creates still greater problems. There are, indeed, serious differences among the sector-unspecific association-al systems which represent capitalists in European countries and, moreover, these differences are considerably deeper than those which exist among national labour movements. While labour has greater incentives to seek unity and cohesion, since it views organized action as an important political resource, for capital it is much more costly and less rewarding to establish large and inclusive associations (Streeck, 1988). In fact, as confirmed by empirical evidence, national systems for the representation of business interests are more fragmented than those of labour at both the sectoral (Streeck, 1988) and the intersectoral level (Lanzalaco, 1990: 58–9). That implies that the potential members of transnation-al associations, that is, the different national peak associations, are much more fragmented among themselves in the case of capital than in that of labour. As a consequence, for capital it is a much more complex and complicated task to build up unitarian systems of representation at transnational level because the interest variety to be internalized and managed is greater than that of labour.

In a comparative perspective, it is possible to distinguish between three systemic types of business interest representation.[8] Depend-ing on the number and configuration of cleavages present in these systems, these are segmented, homogeneous and hegemonic forms of representation (Lanzalaco, 1990). Segmented (or sectional) systems prevail in countries such as Belgium, Italy and the Netherlands. They are characterized by the presence of two or more cleavages which crosscut one another and bring about a number of different peak associations. Possible axes of cleavage may be by category (that is, either sector, size or type of ownership of firms, or religious, ethnic and political allegiance of entrepreneurs) or, more rarely, of a functional nature (employers versus trade associations). On the other hand, homogeneous representational settings are characterized by only one primary cleavage which crosscuts the entire system. Additional cleavage lines produce divisions exclusively within those segments that have already been generated by the dominant split, that is within the group of peak associations of a specific type. For instance, the main type of cleavage in the 'German' model of business interest associationalism, a model being replicated in countries such as Denmark, Norway, Switzerland and Sweden, is the functional one. It cuts across the entire organizational population. In other words, associations are either trade or employers' associations. There is only one large and inclusive peak association among the latter type which represents all sectors of the economy: the Bundesvereinigung der Deutschen Arbeitgeberverbände (BDA) in Germany and the Svenska Arbetsgvareforeningen (SAF)in Sweden. In the case of trade associations, one is confronted with a high number of different peak associations, each being specialized in the representation of a single sector of the economy – for German industry the Bundesverband der Deutschen Industrie (BDI), and for the Swedish industry the Sveriges Industriforbund (SI). While there are also sectoral cleavage lines in these cases, they generate specific peak associations only within the category of peak associations of trade. The French system is rather homogeneous as well but essentially converges around sectoral cleavage lines. The interest domain of the Conseil National du Patronat Français (CNPF), which is both a trade and an employer association, does not include agriculture and the craft sector, which both have their specific peak associations. In addition to the CNPF, there are two peak associations specialized in the representation of small firms, the Confédération Général des Petites et Moyennes Entreprises (CGPME) and the Syndicat National de la Petite et Moyenne Industrie (SNMPI), whose interest domains overlap with that of the CNPF but not with that of the peak associations of agriculture and crafts. Hence, size as a potentially dividing element is relevant only within the partition already being produced by the sectoral specification. Hegemonic systems, finally, are characterized by the presence of one comprehensive peak association, for example, the Confederacion Española de Organizaciones Empresariales (CEOE) in Spain, or the Confederation of British Industry (CBI), whose potential interest domain includes almost the entire range of capitalists from all economic sectors, and whose functions cover both trade and employers' interests. In these cases, there may be some other and competing peak associations, but they are normally of relatively small size and do not control specific domains from which the dominant one would be excluded.

Of course, these differences in the configuration of representative systems are paralelled by significant differences among the organizational properties of the peak associations that operate within them. Hence, characteristics of the peak associations affiliated to the same transnational sector-unspecific peak association are anything other than homogeneous and are hardly compatible with each other. Let us briefly take into consideration, for example, the organizational properties of the peak associations affiliated to UNICE. In Table 6.2 the main organizational properties of some peak associations affiliated to UNICE are synthesized. The differences are impressive. Apart from their different type of membership, in some cases only associations are admitted as members, whereas in others the direct affiliation of firms is allowed. The main difference concerns their domain. Some peak associations (for example, the British CBI, the German BDA, the Spanish CEOE) include almost all sectors of the economy, while in other cases (for example, the German BDI, the Italian Confindustria) their domain is confined only to industry.

Of course, domain-specific differences are mirrored by membership size as well. This emerges from a comparison of the number of firms represented by the Italian Confindustria, the French CNPF and the German BDA. Since it is quite a different thing to represent 120,000 industrial firms or to combine 1,000,000 employers of all economic sectors, the internal structure of these associations varies considerably. In fact, these peak associations differ in terms of the influence exerted by the central confederation versus its affiliates and, secondly, in terms of the relative weight that territorial and sectoral structures possess (Schmitter and Lanzalaco, 1989). As mentioned, additional differences occur with regard to the functions being accomplished by these peak associations. Some of the latter are specialized either as trade or as employers' associations, while others accomplish both of these functions, whereby functional specialization is independent from domain specificity. For example, while the Italian Confindustria and the German BDI exclusively represent industry, the latter is a trade association, whereas the former combines the functions of both a trade and an employers' association.

As is easily understandable, the cross-national variation and heterogeneity in the structure of different associational systems and of peak associations create serious problems to transnational collective action. Domain-specific incongruencies and functional diversification among different national peak associations weaken

Table 6.2 *The heterogeneity of UNICE's members: main characteristics of some affiliated peak associations*

Country	Association	Function	Membership characteristics				
			Sectors	Ownership	Affiliation	No. of firms	No. of employees (millions)
Italy	Confindustria	1.1, 1.2	2.2, 2.3, 2.4, 2.5, 2.7, 2.8, 2.10	3.1, 3.2	4.2	110,000	3
Belgium	FEB	1.1, 1.2	2.2, 2.3, 2.4, 2.5, 2.6, 2.8, 2.9	3.1, 3.2, 3.5	4.2	30,000	1
France	CNPF	1.1, 1.2	All but 2.1	3.1, 3.2, 3.5	4.2	Over 1m	13.6
FRG	BDA	1.1	All	3.1, 3.2, 3.5	4.2	1.2m	18
	BDI	1.2	2.2, 2.3, 2.4, 2.5	3.1, 3.2	4.2	80,000	5.6
UK	CBI	1.1, 1.2	All	3.1, 3.2, 3.4, 3.5	4.1, 4.2	260,000	10
Spain	CEOE	1.1, 1.2	All	All	4.2	1.2m	Over 5
Sweden	SAF	1.1	All	3.1, 3.2, 3.3, 3.4	4.2	49,625	1.2
	SI	1.2	2.2, 2.3, 2.4, 2.5	All	4.2	4,400	0.7

Key:

1 Functions
1.1 Employers' association
1.2 Trade association

2 Sectors
2.1 Agriculture
2.2 Mining
2.3 Manufacturing
2.4 Utilities
2.5 Construction
2.6 Commerce
2.7 Food and tourism
2.8 Transportation
2.9 Banks and insurance
2.10 Services

3 Type of Ownership
3.1 National and private capital
3.2 Foreign and private capital
3.3 Cooperative
3.4 Public
3.5 Public–private

4 Affiliation
4.1 Direct (also firms)
4.2 Indirect (only associations)

Source: Organisation Internationale des Employers (1984); for Sweden, Pestoff (1988).

associative action and jeopardize its effectiveness, since the overlapping area of common interests (the 'interest core') among associations with widely different domains is too tight to bring about mobilization around collective goals. As demonstrated by the fragmentation of transnational sector-unspecific systems, sectoral overlaps among their domains neutralize the aggregative capacity of national peak associations. Put differently, transnational collective action not only involves transaction costs deriving from divergences within single national systems, but also ones that are produced by cross-national differences in the precise definition of the same interest domain. For example, sector-unspecific transnational associations not only have to mediate between the divergent interests of German and Italian capitalists, but also between the different ways in which these perceive and organize themselves as a class. It is precisely these elements which make the costs of cross-sector integration prohibitive.

At the same time, there have, of course, also been trends towards convergence among the organizational properties of national peak associations. Two examples may be mentioned in this respect. On the one hand, there are certain similarities in the ways in which the CBI, the CNPF and Confindustria managed their organizational reforms during the 1970s in order to increase their political influence. On the other hand, many peak associations have continued to strengthen their regional sub-units in recent years. Yet, owing to two structural factors, differences among national peak associations are likely to stay for a long time to come. First, the differences among sector-unspecific peak associations mirror the disparate configuration of systems for business interest intermediation. What is at stake, hence, is not just an organizational reform of peak associations but, rather, an overall restructuring of quite consolidated systems of representation. This is very hard to achieve. Secondly, the different configurations are deeply rooted in the historical trajectories of each country.

The Historical Roots of Hetereogeneity
Paraphrasing what Lipset and Rokkan (1967: 50) assert with regard to European party systems, it might be said that systems for business interest representation at the beginning of the 1990s reflect the cleavage structures of the late 1950s and before. Most of the peak associations currently operating in European countries had been founded either during the first decades of this century or, sometimes, long before. Although the structural configuration of systems for business interest representation and peak associations certainly underwent considerable change – being induced either by

war and the emergence of authoritarian regimes (Schmitter, 1977) or by sustained challenges on the part of the labour movement – genetic differences continue to prevail and cross-national differences are not substantially reduced as a result. For example, Germany, Italy and Spain, all having suffered under authoritarian rule, continue to exhibit many differences in the organization of their associational systems as regards the domain, the function and the strength of peak associations.

There is a striking disequilibrium between the significant efforts made to explain, in a historical and comparative fashion, the centralization of national labour movements (for example, Kendall, 1975; Shalev, 1980; Visser, 1990), and the negligence with which the same topic has been treated as far as collective action by capitalists is concerned.[9] From many of the contributions to the study of organized labour the state of capitalist development emerges (Shalev, 1980) as a key variable for the explanation of different traits of the trade union movements. As noted by Commons as early as 1932, 'the labor movement is always a reaction and a protest against capitalism. But capitalism is not a single or static concept . . . Labor movements reflect these capitalistic movements' (Commons, 1932: 682). If the mode of capitalist development has affected the way in which workers organized, it is likely to have a similarly determining influence on the way capitalists organized their class interests. That would imply that the reasons underlying the impressive heterogeneity in systems of sector-unspecific business associations have to be looked for in the different formats capitalist development has assumed across the member states of the Community. The high variation in cross-sectoral business interest organization in Western Europe may simply be due to the fact that capitalism has developed in making recourse to radically different models. This development proceeded at highly different speeds, including 'first-comer' countries, such as the United Kingdom, as well as 'late starters', such as Italy or Spain.

The variety in the capitalist mode of development may also explain the heterogeneity with which capitalists organize themselves as a class. Sector-unspecific collective action is contingent on these types of factors in at least two respects. In the first place, as demonstrated also by Grote in chapter 5, the specific type of capitalist development had an impact on the relative weight assumed by the traditional middle classes such as artisans, shop-keepers and farmers (Berger, 1975, 1980; Pizzorno, 1975), in comparison with the industrial bourgeoisie. Middle classses mainly flourished and persisted in countries with late industrial development in which capitalist relationships of production did not penetrate agriculture, craft and commerce. The presence of large strata of small entrepreneurs creates a vast potential membership for highly specialized confederations and, hence, fosters associative fragmentation and inhibits cross-sectoral aggregation. Given their unclear collocation around class cleavages, these social groups represent a factor of political instability and, not surprisingly, the state tends to regulate their behaviour directly. This is the case for German *Handwerk* (Streeck, 1989a) and Swiss *Gewerbe* (Kriesi and Farago, 1989), but equally applies to Chambers of Commerce which are public bodies in non-Anglo-Saxon countries and, not least, to the intensive interplays between state, political parties and the associations representing these sectors in countries such as France, Italy and Germany (Berger, 1981; Trigilia, 1986). State intervention, as demonstrated by the French, German and the Italian cases, tends to reinforce and shape the overall configuration of the sector-unspecific associational system. Secondly, the timing of capitalist development also determined the genesis of associational systems, in that it affected the complex intermingling between class conflict (workers versus employers) on the one hand, and sectoral conflict (capitalists versus capitalists) occurring across different branches on the other (Schmitter and Brand, 1979; Sisson, 1987).

In general, where development of capitalism has been early and gradual, the first forms of associationalism were not aimed at coping with the 'challenge' of the labour movement, but were 'attempts to avoid cut-throat price competition on the market, efforts to limit or prevent altogether the access of foreign competitors to the domestic market, endeavours to form a common front vis-à-vis the sellers of basic raw materials and other supplies, and the like' (Schmitter and Streeck, 1981: 16). The main problem was not to organize against an external enemy, represented by the labour movement, but against an enemy that was internal to the capitalist class itself, that is, producers of other sectors and other countries. In cases of this kind, trade associations and sectoral forms of aggregation prevailed. Where capitalist development has been late and rapid, capitalists got organized predominantly as a response to the labour movement. First forms of associationalism and early processes of organizational centralization were class-conflict-led. In cases of this kind, where unity and cohesion against a common external enemy was required, employer associations and territorial modes of organization prevailed. The above are two examples of a more numerous menu which demonstrates how the mode of development of capitalism has impacted on the way in which capitalists have organized themselves as a class. The crucial point to be underlined is that the characteristics of sector-unspecific associational systems and peak associations are deeply influenced and determined by the socio-economic and political history of each single country. Most importantly, this implies that the potential membership of trans-national sector-unspecific associations can be hardly 'homogenized'.

The Transnational Dimension and the National Legacy

Given the modes of operation of 'the logic of membership' and the 'logic of influence', one arrives at a paradox conclusion. What has to be explained is not the absence of a European sector-unspecific confederation of capitalists but, on the contrary, the presence of forms of transnational integration represented by associations such as UNICE, FEWITA and COPA. Lack of incentives to get together in sector-unspecific organizations and a multitude of inducements favouring fragmentation and differentiation have made the process of aggregating business interests at a European level a precarious exercise, and many problems still persist today. In general terms, the main problem for transnational associations is to internalize the conflicts among different nationally based interests and to reduce the relevance possessed by national allegiances for further cleavages and divisions. This is much easier to achieve in those cases where another strong parameter for the definition of interests is present, namely a sectoral one along which associational domains are more easily demarcated and interest aggregated. Where such a strong 'counterbalancing' parameter is absent, especially in cases where sector-unspecific organizations have to be established, the process of 'transnationalization' is likely to be very difficult. In these cases, the only factors able to stimulate more cohesive forms of interest aggregation would appear to be external enforcement mechanisms, such as either the challenge of organized labour or the presence of powerful political institutions endowed with authority over a wide range of issues. There is hardly any other motive which could be thought of as contributing to an increase of intersectoral inter-dependencies and which could, subsequently, lead to the need to govern them by means of sector-unspecific associations. In the absence of these factors, transaction costs for transnational collec-tive action are simply too high. As regards Community-level associations, both of these external factors have been absent and, not surprisingly, the process of 'transnationalization' of business interests has been much more successful within sectors than across sectors.

However, attempts which would resort only to the 'logic of influence' to explain the sparse inclusiveness of EC-level BIAs would be reductionist and misleading. Our argument has been that factors related to the 'logic of membership' have resulted in the past, and are likely to remain important for the absence of an ETUC-like confederation of capitalists. In fact, the 'transnationalization' of BIAs has to be understood as one of many phases of a long historical process during which capitalists have been 'experimenting with scale' (Schmitter, 1985) of associative action, in order to adapt their organizations to environmental challenges and changes while, at the same time, trying to manage internal diversity and interdependencies. This process has its origin in the nineteenth century and its main stages have been – in chronological order – the progressive transformation of craft associations into industrial associations (Sisson, 1979); the rapid and spontaneous germination of territorially specific or product-specific associations; the progressive integration of these specialized and diversified associations into more inclusive sectoral and regional federations; and, finally (albeit not in each single instance), the establishment of inclusive peak associations.[10] It is since the First World War that the 'genetic' phase has come to an end. In virtually all countries, the subsequent process of integration, centralization and the establishment of central peak associations was triggered off either by the existence of powerful trade union organizations (Sweden, Germany, Switzerland) or by threats to organizational stability in climates of increasing state intervention (France). The other side of the coin of organizational consolidation was the 'freezing' of interest spaces in each country, that is the progressive stabilization in the configuration of systems for business interest representation and a firmly institutionalized demarcation of associational domains as a result of wartime mobilization (Schmitter, 1977: 72). The second phase is essentially limited to the inter-war period, during which European systems of interest intermediation either assumed authoritarian or liberal-democratic patterns (Maier, 1981). Despite these different paths of development, one trait has been common to all European countries, namely the persistence of the national level as the highest level of business interest associability. Only in the course of this phase does the centralizing process in the organization of business interests stabilize throughout Western Europe. At the same time, the domestic level appears to be the 'natural' one beyond which business interests were not likely to be 'associable'. This predominance of national associations was then questioned during a third phase which started at around 1945 and has not yet come to an end. Capitalists, again, began experimenting with scale, this time both below and above the level of the nation state, and started to establish subnational and transnational interest associations.[11]

Social experiments, unlike laboratory experiments, cannot be arranged in terms of strict timing and, once commenced, are irreversible. Results of past experiments affect the outcome of the successive ones. The way in which capitalists are currently 'experimenting with scale' of associability at transnational level is strongly determined by what happened in the previous phases. The 'raw material' of transnational associations is interests that have been defined and shaped by very peculiar and often incompatible institutions and national associational systems. Processes of 'transnationalization' are, therefore, constrained by the legacy of 'deep frozen' patterns of associationalism at the national level. As has previously been the case at the national level, when trying to build up capitalist class unity at a European scale, transnational sector-unspecific associations have not only to cope with internal divisions and clashes occurring among firms differentiated by size, sector, product, branch, ownership and region but, in addition, with the wide heterogeneity in which capitalists have perceived and organized themselves as a class in different nations. This has not created substantial problems as long as national channels of influence could provide business interests with effective and efficient access to EC decision-makers, but is likely to undergo many changes as a result of the Single European Act, which has posed limits to the capacity of single governments to steer the boat in favour of particularistic interests. Hence, the need for improving the capacity of intermediation of sector-unspecific peak associations, at a time when the 'deep frozen' formats of individual domestic associational systems are unlikely to assume a more equal and compatible shape. In this context, Schmitter (1988: 50) has emphasized that

> capitalism may not have designed the nation-state and has had repeated difficulty in adapting to it, but it has been very deeply impregnated with this way of organizing political authority. It will take more than the removal of barriers to trade, the liberalization of finance, the globalization of production and the standardization of consumer tastes to extirpate capitalism's national orientation. Firms (not to mention, individual capitalists) will still identify themselves with a particular society and seek the special protection of a particular state for the foreseeable future.

The link between capitalism and the nation state is likely to persist also with respect to the organizational format associative action is going to assume in the future. This probability is higher where representation of the entire class is at stake. In fact, the transnational dimension can neither be imagined in terms of shifting along the territorial axis nor as an international relationship. This is because the territorial level represented by the nation state is too special a case as to consider the transnational organization only in terms of a matter of small changes in the scale of organization. Imagining associative action as a variety of international relations is made impossible by the fact that it involves not merely simple coordination among capitalists of different states but, rather, the identification of common interests ranging beyond the institutional shell within which capitalism has developed and flourished and, also, beyond the national community within which capitalists' identity continues to be formed. Forecasting scenarios is a difficult task to accomplish, not only because of the uncertain impact the Internal Market might have on the two logics of business interest associability, but also because the organizational response of capitalists does not just involve simple adaptive reactions of a kind of 'organizational engineering', but more complex and wide-ranging strategic choices. In restructuring their associative action to meet the exigencies of the Europe of post-1992, capitalists will, first and foremost, have to decide whether to pursue the representation of their class interests or that of their production-related interests. As a result of their very strategic nature, choices of this kind do not only involve dramatically different organizational outcomes but, also, provide actors with wide margins of manoeuvre and discretion (Lanzalaco and Schmitter, 1992).

Two general considerations may be drawn from the above with regard to the future of sector-unspecific associability of business interests. First of all, the national legacy is not only the outcome of organizational inertia and of the constraints posed by historical trajectories, but may also represent a rational response to future events. The Internal Market will produce interest fragmentation among firms of different size, sectors and regions. In order to counterbalance this trend, and preserve the unity of their class, capitalists could react 'proactively' by strengthening their national peak associations such as the CBI, BDI and BDA, and CNPF.

This strategy would result not so much from easily perceptible impacts of the 1992-package but, on the contrary, from the uncertainties by which the event is surrounded. When actors perceive uncertainty, they usually cling to old and well-consolidated institutions (Crouch, 1986). Existing and well-established national peak associations readily offer a familiar and reassuring framework for collective action. The adoption of such a strategy is likely to emerge to the extent that transnational regulation of the Europe of post-1992 will follow the pattern of 'mutual recognition' rather than that of harmonization of nationally incompatible rules (Schmitter and Streeck, 1990; Streeck, 1989a, b). Mutual recognition would involve harsher competition among 'national regimes' and competitiveness of firms would, more than ever, depend on the economic and social policies of their home countries. Should national associations succeed in protecting the basis of national productivity from 'social dumping' and 'regime competition' by means of the influence they exert on their home governments, their relevance would increase rather than diminish.

Secondly, changes forthcoming in view of the factors which determine the 'logic of influence', that is, the enhanced role of Parliament and majority voting in the Council, are likely to produce more inter- and intraorganizational strains than opportunities for transnational action for sector-unspecific associations. In order to overcome these inconveniences and to bring influence and membership into balance, one possible solution could be to act on the 'logic of membership' side, that is to reduce the organizational heterogeneity across national peak associations. This solution, however, being rather optimistically recommended by UNICE's General Secretary (Tyszkiewicz, 1990), does not seem to be feasible because of the, largely, incompatible national legacies. Associative systems are deeply rooted in national history and specificity. 'Homogenizing' these systems, hence, appears to represent a rather remote option. Once heterogeneity among national peak associations is given and once this heterogeneity is a stable and persistent feature being deeply rooted in national specificities and historical trajectories, then Euro peak associations will be badly advised in shifting the burden that results from processes of adaptation to new institutional arrangements to their national constituencies. It is not primarily domestic associations which will have to reorganize their internal structures but, rather, the Euro associations themselves.

Notes

I am indebted to Justin Greenwood and Jürgen Grote for a careful revision of my English text.

1. It is not surprising that the sub- and transnational level of policy-making and interest intermediation assumed simultaneous relevance, since both of them are responses to the 'decomposition of the nation state'. On the point see Wassenberg (1982) and Greenwood, Grote and Ronit (1990).

2. An associational system is 'the universe of all business interest associations (BIAs) representing interests from a given sector or category' (Schmitter and Streeck, 1981: 125, 141). A sector-unspecific associational system is the universe of all the BIAs representing the common, general, cross sector interests of capitalists on a given (national, subnational or transnational) system. In this chapter these systems will be analysed 'from above', i.e. focusing attention only on peak associations.

3. Schmitter and Streeck (1981: 200) use another indicator of hierarchical integration, namely the percentage of first-order associations in the system that are affiliated to a higher-order association.

4. Of course, in national associative systems there are also sectoral associations which do not converge into peak associations, but they are not the rule, they are the exception. In a transnational system, on the contrary, it is the rule.

5. From this point of view 'the model of organization at European level is different from a dualist system at international level . . . As in many national situations there are two organizations representing the interests of employers at international level, one in charge of so-called social questions, the International Organization of Employers (OIE) and one specialized in economic questions, the International Chamber of Commerce (ICC)' (Oeschlin, 1980: 202, 204).

6. The organizational form prevailing at the European level could be considered also a joint venture (see Table 6.1), for the presence of staff sharing. But, contrary to alliances, joint ventures are issue-bond cooperative relationships, meanwhile Euro peak associations cover a relatively broad range of issues.

7. There are some exceptions, such as the Western European Metal Trades Employers Organisation (WEM) that is specialized on social matters.

8. Only the main peak associations and cleavages will be taken into consideration here. What we are interested in is not a careful description of each associational system, but a comparison of their overall configurations.

9. Apart from some exceptions, as Jackson and Sisson, 1976; Lanzalaco, 1990; Schmitter and Brand, 1979; Sisson, 1979, 1987).

10. Of course, both the process of spontaneous germination of associations and that of associative integration assumed very different features in various European countries.

11. A first attempt at transnational action by capitalists dates back to 1911, when the Industrial League of Turin (Italy), responding to the creation of the International Association of Workers, sponsored an International Conference in order to establish an International Association of Employers.

7
Making the Most of Diversity? European Integration and Transnational Organization of Labour

Jelle Visser and Bernhard Ebbinghaus

Introduction: the Double Challenge of Political and Economic Integration

The trade union movements of Europe are in a particularly dramatic episode of their century-old history. The challenges which confront trade unions in this last decade of the twentieth century are comparable with those of the early years when, before the development of national collective bargaining and universal suffrage, the capacity of unions to forge alliances beyond their own group, occupation or town was heavily taxed. The 1980s have been difficult times for unions, in Europe as elsewhere (Freeman, 1990; Goetschy and Linhard, 1990; Müller-Jentsch, 1987; Visser, 1988). Intensified global competition, high unemployment levels, changing technologies, neo-liberal government policies, and ongoing social and cultural shifts in labour supply and workforce composition are among the factors that tend to weaken union representation and to erode the traditional sectoral and interoccupational structures of interest aggregation and solidarity. Union density levels in Western Europe, although significantly higher than in the United States and Japan, have fallen (Visser, 1991; see Table 7.1). The erosion of union support was particularly severe in the private sector and has reduced the ability of trade union movements to influence the political and industrial agendas of employers and governments, both 'friendly' as in France or Spain, or 'hostile' as in Britain (Baglioni and Crouch, 1990).

From a weakened position at home, trade unions face the double challenge of Europe: the further political and economic integration of the 12 member states of the European Community, and the demand for aid, development and support from Central and Eastern European countries. With the advance of economic integration and a European Monetary Union, national sovereignty in matters of economic and social policies risks being limited, and customary union avenues for protecting and enhancing employee welfare and security in the national agenda will become more and more restrained. The internationalization of organizations and markets has eroded, and will further reduce, the remaining zones of national autonomy in social and economic policy-making. Given the advance of multinational firms and within-firm centralization of decision-making on strategic issues, and the arrival of supranational decision-making in the European Community on the main economic and monetary issues, trade unions have no choice but to develop some transnational capacity for organization and action. Organized Labour in Europe will have to become transnational, or it will not be part of the future.

Table 7.1   *Union density rates in Western Europe, the United States and Japan, 1970–1989*

	1970	1975	1980	1985	1989
EC-6	32	37	36	34	30
EC-9	36	41	41	38	34
EC-12	–	40	40	36	33
EFTA	54	58	60	60	59
Western Europe	38	43	44	40	38
USA	30	25	23	18	16
Japan	35	34	31	29	26

Weighted averages on the basis of size of dependent workforce; EC-6: BE, GE, FR, IT, LU, NE; EC-9: EC-6 plus DE, IR, UK; EC-12: EC-9 plus GR, PO, SP; EFTA: AU, FI, IC, NO, SW, SZ; Western Europe: EC-12 plus EFTA.

Sources: Visser, 1991

Current developments in Eastern and Central Europe reinforce this conclusion. Without a high degree of international cooperation in Western Europe and a common vision on how to share the burden of aid and support, trade unions in Western Europe will have to prepare themselves for a large supply of cheap labour, further pressures of deregulation and downward bidding of legal and customary restrictions on the free and unlimited use of labour, as well as for a conservative reaction among the 'marginalized' and 'underprivileged' in their own ranks. The challenges of the 1990s are also comparable with those of the 1910s and 1930s. On both occasions organized labour in Europe failed the test and abandoned international policies and transnational structures of solidarity. Are today's trade unions better prepared?

In this chapter we analyse the developments and prospects of transnational organization and action of trade unions in Western Europe. Differing from many conventional analyses of transnational organization that look only at the structure of interest groups at the Community or international level, we start our analysis by looking at the differences in union organization at the national level and the possible (organizational) obstacles for integrating these diverse interests at a supranational level. Seen from this perspective, our attention is then especially directed towards the achievements and difficulties of the European Trade Union Confederation (ETUC), Europe's main transnational peak association of national trade union movements. A comparison with the more successful national union confederations reveals the problems of organizing a transnational 'action set' of unions. We conceive an 'action set' as an alliance of interacting organizations for the sake of a common purpose (adapted from Aldrich and Whetten, 1981: 387); a transnational 'action set' is thus an alliance of national and transnational union organizations to achieve what cannot be attained via national routes. Seen in comparison with national union confederations, we ask to what degree has the ETUC authority over its member organizations ('hierarchical ordering'), and whether it can integrate the diverse functional, sectoral interest organizations ('functional differentiation'). Thus, we will also discuss developments at less inclusive levels, at the meso level (the transnational sectoral unionism) and at the micro level (the cross-frontier works councils).[1]

Given our interest in analysing the organizational obstacles to transnational organization of labour, we will not evaluate here in detail the (obviously meagre) opportunities and results of the 'social dimension' at the Community level (for recent accounts see: Bryant, 1991; Due et al., 1991; Goetschy, 1991; Rhodes, 1991; Streeck and Schmitter, 1991; Teague, 1989a). Instead we look at the two interlocutors of organized labour, the state and the employers, and the respective two fields of action, social and labour legislation and collective bargaining. Based on national union histories, we know how important these interlocutors are in shaping the organization of labour interests.

The structure of the chapter follows thus a simple exposition: from the national to the transnational level, and from macro to lower-level forms of transnational action. First, we consider the diversity at the national level, that is, the differences between the union actors whose capacity for transnational cooperation and coordination is at stake. We expect that 'structural equivalence' in the organizations which form the network of European trade unions and their peak associations, as well as a broad political and ideological similarity of views and purposes, contribute to international cooperation. However, we find large and persistent national diversity and even divergence in some aspects. Second, turning to the transnational level, we review the formation and organization process of a European 'action set' of peak federations and trade unions – the development of an interorganizational alliance between union movements of different nations for the purpose of a common cause. How much progress has been made compared to 20 or 30 years ago, when the first attempts were made to reply to the new realities of regional integration and the advance of multinational firms (Günther, 1972; Levinson, 1972; Roberts, 1973)? Is the declining role and power of peak associations in the national political and industrial arena (Baglioni and Crouch, 1990; Visser, 1990; Vos, 1991) an opportunity for a shift of attention and resources to the transnational level? Third, using the analogy of the formation of peak associations in the national arena, we argue that unless a third party or rival 'action set' of state actors or employer associations forces some degree of international coordination and centralization upon trade unions, internal obstacles are too large for the ETUC to become more than a weakly integrated 'go-between' of independent national units. The two relevant interlocutors are the European Commission and the employers, and in particular the European employer organizations and significant multinational firms. We first discuss the role of the Commission and argue that some (but not enough) movement towards transnational unionism has been triggered. Next, we consider the role of employers associations and multinational firms and the possibility of transnational collective bargaining of some kind. Is it possible that what until now has been a 'non-event' will become reality?

National Diversity in Union Organization

'Diversity, lack of general cooperation, and the absence of adequate supranational structures appear as the main drawbacks of the European trade union movement; and unless there are drastic changes these features will determine the outlook for future European labour relations' (Blanpain, 1972: 301). Twenty years have passed since this judgement was published, years of profound changes in the political, economic, social and cultural environments of union movements as sets of organizations. Have there been the drastic changes which Blanpain thought necessary?

There is little doubt that, however much the environments of trade unions have changed in the past 20 years and however similar these changes have been across Europe, trade unions and trade union movements have changed remarkably little. The cross-national diversity of these union movements is still as considerable as it was when described half a century ago by Sturmthal (1953) or almost a quarter of a century ago by Blanpain (1972) and Kendall (1975). Although individual unions have disappeared or merged, new unions organizing new groups of employees in the public sector and among managerial staffs have been created, yet the structure of union movements and the management style adopted in unions have remained the same. In (inter-)organizational terms union movements exhibit a remarkable degree of 'structural inertia' (Ebbinghaus and Visser, 1990).

Across European countries, union movements differ widely in terms of overall representation and support among workers (Table 7.2). These differences are larger than 20 years ago. The current level of union density in France and Spain is only around 10% of all employees in employment and in Greece, Switzerland and the Netherlands around 25%. At the other end of the scale we find some of the Scandinavian countries with a unionization level of 75% and more, whereas Germany, Italy and Britain – in the British case after a decade of falling membership levels – occupy the middle ground with one-third to two-fifths of the employed workforce joining a union. Considering only the private sector, cross-national differences are even more pronounced (Visser, 1991). These variations reflect the different levels of resources, of financial means, staff, research and information, as well as different degrees of power and independence vis-à-vis employers, political parties and governments.

The impression of diversity is reinforced when we consider two further aspects: whether union movements are united or divided in ideological and political terms, and whether they are internally concentrated or fragmented in industrial, occupational or political terms. The German union movement is united and concentrated; British unions combine in one peak federation, but within and between unions, members' interests are fragmented according to occupational and industrial labour markets; Italian, French and Spanish unions are ideologically divided, but in Italy members in the private sector are concentrated in few comprehensive sectoral unions. In a study of trade union movements in ten European countries, Visser (1990) has developed an index of horizontal and vertical integration of national union movements.

Horizontal integration is a composite measure of the unity, internal fragmentation, associational monopoly and external opposition in these movements. Following Schmitter's thesis concerning the structural preconditions for neo-corporatist policy-

Table 7.2 *The action set of trade union peak associations in Western Europe*

	EC-6							EC-9		EC-12				EFTA							EC and EFTA
	BE	FR	GE	IT	LU	NE	DE	IR	UK	GR	SP	PO	all	AU	FI	IC	NO	SZ	SW	all	
Union density	53	12	34	40	50	25	73	52	42	25	10	30	31	45	71	78	57	26	85	57	34
Peak centres	3	5+	4	3+	2	4	4	1	1	2	4	2	35+	1	4	2	3	4	3	17	52+*
Sector unions (%)	68		81	65		68	12	6	26					79			61	66	80		
ETUC																					
Affiliates	2	3	2	3	2	2	2	1	1	2	3	1	24	1	2	2	1	2	2	10	34*
Monopoly (%)	92	−50	87	−90	87	78	85	92	88	92	−96	48	84	100	77	77	65	60	93	84	84
Unions aff.	33	70+	18	61	−	31	86	61	84	77	−	−	−	15	40	−	33	27	45	−	−

Union density statistics and membership share are of 1988 or 1989. The number of peak associations and ETUC affiliation are as of 1 January 1991. Sector union percentage: percentage of total membership is sector unions (industrial and all grade unions).

+ more peak associations or unions exist, but number is unknown,

− associational monopoly (share in total membership) is lower but total membership is not known,

* there are a further eight peak associations of trade unions in Turkey, Cyprus and Malta, six of which are affiliated to the ETUC.

Sources: Union densities: Visser, 1991; union organization: Visser, 1989, 1990; and own data.

making (Schmitter, 1974, 1981), it was argued that the 'action set' (see above) of trade unions will be more cohesive if horizontal integration in the national union network is high, that is, first, if there is unity or at least coordination between union confederations; secondly, if a high degree of organizational concentration and little or no political rivalry exists within unions or between unions within confederations; thirdly, if the degree of associational monopoly of the main confederation(s) in terms of membership representation is large; and, fourthly, if pressures from rival or competing specialized interest groups are weak. Such highly representative, unified, concentrated and internally cohesive union confederations with no, little or placid outside opposition, exist in Germany, Sweden and Austria, and to a lesser extent in the other Scandinavian countries, although occupational unions fragment sectoral organizations and have created more players and bones of contention in Denmark and Norway. In Britain, Ireland, and Greece trade unions and trade unionists are unified in one major peak association, and outside opposition appears to be feeble, but on all other subdimensions horizontal integration is weak; there are still many unions competing for influence and members, internal cohesion is small, and political factionalism pervasive. In the remaining countries unions and their members are divided between different peak federations, but relations may differ from very conflicting (France, Portugal) to accommodative (Belgium, the Netherlands, Switzerland), though this may have changed from the former to the latter over time (Italy, Spain). Within confederations there is a high degree of domain consensus and organizational concentration in the Netherlands, Italy and Belgium, but in Italy and the Netherlands, as in France and Greece, established union centres experience considerable and growing opposition from specialized, sectionalist unions in the public sector.

A further dimension along which European trade union movements differ is the degree of authority invested in peak associations, or the degree of vertical integration in the national union network (Visser, 1990). Some peak associations, most notably ETUC's two largest affiliates – the Trade Union Congress (TUC) in Britain and the Deutscher Gewerkschaftsbund (DGB) in Germany – have no authority in matters of collective bargaining with employers (see also Köpke, 1990). In the other countries union confederations do have this right, within restrictions specified in union by-laws. These confederations can replace, join, assist or supervise affiliated unions in negotiations with governments and with central or sectoral employer associations. In the 1970s and early 1980s there have been spells of central economy-wide bargaining in many European

Table 7.3 *Integration and representation of union movements in Europe (average values), 1970–1989*

Country	Horizontal integration		Vertical integration		Union density	
	Index	Rank	Index	Rank	%	Rank
Austria	9.0	(1)	9.0	(1)	53	(4.5)
Belgium	5.0	(6)	5.5	(5)	53	(4.5)
Denmark	5.1	(5)	4.0	(7.5)	71	(2)
France	1.3	(12)	1.0	(11)	18	(12)
Germany	8.0	(2)	5.0	(6)	36	(9)
Ireland	4.3	(8)	3.0	(9)	51	(6)
Italy	3.9	(10)	4.0	(7.5)	43	(8)
Netherlands	4.0	(9)	6.0	(4)	33	(10)
Norway	5.3	(4)	8.0	(2)	55	(3)
Sweden	6.3	(3)	7.5	(3)	78	(1)
Switzerland	3.7	(11)	2.5	(10)	30	(11)
United Kingdom	4.9	(7)	0.5	(12)	46	(7)

Sources: Integration index: Visser, 1990: 152, 176 and updates from Ebbinghaus, Visser and Pfenning (1992); union density: Visser, 1991, see Table 1 (averages of net density rates employed dependent labour force 1970, 1975, 1980, 1985 and 1988/89)

countries, though with a varying degree of success. In the course of the 1980s central bargaining and the role of confederations in preparing the ground for such bargaining appear to have been declining, most notably in Sweden and the Netherlands, though it has not fully disappeared (namely, Italy, Spain, Portugal, Denmark, and Belgium: cf. Baglioni and Crouch, 1990).

Where wage and related negotiations are conducted at the central level over a considerable length of time, peak associations are able to build up resources and authority of their own (Blyth, 1979; Headey, 1970; Windmuller, 1975). The reverse is probably also true. Where collective bargaining has drifted to lower (workplace, firm, region or industry) levels, organizational resources and authority will also be relocated to that lower level (Clegg, 1976). Cases in point are the decentralization in British unions in the 1960s and 1970s, and the decline in authority and resources in the Dutch confederations during the 1980s. The index of vertical integration also takes into account the existence and importance of a central strike or solidarity fund as a possible inducement or sanction for unions to refrain from 'going it alone'. Our ranking of European countries showed the Austrian Confederation of Trade Unions (ÖGB) in the first place, followed by the Norwegian and Swedish confederations (Visser, 1990: 176–7). The TUC was lowest on this scale, as it is understaffed with only 230 officials and employees. There are currently less than three paid peak centre officials per 100,000 members in Britain, against 12 in Germany, 20 in Italy, Norway and Sweden, 25 in the Netherlands and more in Austria. The rate of paid officials in the average British union is also much lower than elsewhere in Europe, but tends to be supplemented by employer-supported senior shop stewards. The figures for France, Greece, Spain and Portugal are difficult to ascertain, but indicate a severe understaffing of unions, a concentration of all scarce resources at the confederal level, lack of specialization and a high degree of dependence on state political funding.

When involved in the formation and implementation of incomes policies in the national arena, a small and ideologically undivided set of unions will find it easier to adopt and maintain a policy of mutual cooperation (Scharpf, 1987; Swenson, 1989; Tarantelli, 1986; Visser, 1990). This reasoning can also be applied to the international level. With only one peak association per country, broadly similar in terms of representation and resources (as measured, for instance, by the overall union density level), with a similar interorganizational structure at the union level (preferably few encompassing unions), and a congruence in political and ideological views (preferably at some distance from direct party or state involvement), international cooperation might be easier to achieve than it is at present.

Towards a Transnational Peak Organization of European Unions

The European Trade Union Confederation (ETUC) is the major transnational 'action set' of European unions. The members of this alliance are, first and foremost, national peak associations (themselves action sets of unions from the same country but from different industries) and, in the second place, transnational sector committees or the so-called European Industry Committees (EIC, also action sets of unions, but *from the same industry* in *different countries*). Historically, the peak associations have been dominant in ETUC, underlying the mainly political, pressure group-orientated character of this transnational peak organization of national peak associations. Having its seat in Brussels, ETUC targets mainly – but not solely – the European Community and its institutions. From its conception in 1973, and unlike its predecessors, ETUC combines workers from EC and non-EC countries, on the understanding that the latter may one day apply and be admitted as members of the Community (as happened in the case of

Greece, Spain and Portugal). In the future, ETUC will become increasingly under pressure to open itself toward the new democratic union movements in Eastern and Central Europe, becoming thus an even more numerous, heterogeneous peak association. ETUC declares as its aim 'to jointly represent and promote the social, economic and cultural interests of workers at the European level in general and in particular in respect of all European institutions, including the European Communities and European Free Trade Association' (Preamble, ETUC, 1987: 8).

ETUC combines 40 peak associations from 21 countries with a total membership of about 44 million workers, employees, civil servants, professionals, unemployed, and retired workers (see Table 7.4). The number of affiliates is large. Member organizations differ considerably in terms of size, resources, domain, organization and ideology; their position in the 'home market' is also quite different. ETUC has achieved a remarkable degree of 'associational monopoly' in terms of membership, organizing 86% of the, roughly, 52 million unionized workers in Western Europe. There are some major union organizations outside ETUC, but with two exceptions (the French and Portuguese communist-led peak associations) those are union centres which serve special constituencies (public sector, managerial staff, in some cases white-collar employees). In addition to ETUC, there are two 'specialized' European peak associations – one of public service unions (CIF) and one for managerial staffs (CIC), both founded in the 1950s when the first steps towards regional integration were made.

It took 15 years from the establishment of the Common Market (1958) and the foundation of the main employer association, the Union of Industrial and Employers' Confederations of Europe (UNICE), before ETUC was established. Its predecessors were the regional organizations of the international socialist and Christian union movements. Regional European organizations had in fact developed in response to the extension of the free and Christian trade union internationals beyond the Western industrialized countries where they had been founded (Windmuller, 1976a). Initially, the regionalization process was slow and contested within the internationals; the new regional sub-units remained dependent upon their international parent organizations, and were mainly concerned with representation and lobbying at the seats of the European Coal and Steel Community (ESCS), the EEC, EFTA or the OECD (see Windmuller, 1980).

The creation of the European Economic Community in 1958 was accompanied by the establishment of a European Trade Union Secretariat, in which socialist unions from six EEC countries were

Table 7.4   *National union confederations affiliated to ETUC (and EFTUC)*

Abbrev.	Name	Country	Year	Domain	Orientation	Membership
TUC	Trades Union Congress	UK	1973	All	Labour	8,405,000
DGB	Deutscher Gewerkschaftsbund	GE	1969*	All	Socialist	7,861,000
CGIL	Confederazione Generale Italiana del Lavoro	IT	1974	All	Communist	5,014,000
CISL	Confederazione Italiana Sindacati Lavoratori	IT	1969	All	Catholic	3,210,000
LO	Landesorganisationen i Sverige	SW	1973	Manual	Socialist	2,023,000
ÖGB	Österreichischer Gewerkschaftsbund	AU	1973	All	Socialist	1,644,000
TÜRK-IS	Türkije Isçi sendikalari konfederasyonu	TU	1988	All		1,493,000
LOiD	Landsorganisationen i Danmark	DE	1973	Manual	Socialist	1,413,000
UIL	Unione Italiana del Lavoro	IT	1969*	All	Socialist	1,344,000
CSC	Confédération des Syndicats Chrétiens	BE	1974	All	Catholic	1,241,000
TCO	Tjänstemännens Centralorganisation	SW	1973	Non-manual		1,139,000
SAK	Suomen Ammattilittojen Keskusjärjesto	FI	1974	Manual	Socialist	1,081,000
FNV	Federatie Nederlandse Vakbeweging	NE	1981	All	Socialist	967,000
NVV	Nederlandse Verbond van Vakbeweging	NE	1969*	All	Socialist	
NKV	Nederlands Katholiek Vakverbond	NE	1974	All	Catholic	
FGTB	Fédération Générale du Travail	BE	1969*	All	Socialist	875,000
LOiN	Landsorganisasjonen i Norge	NO	1973	All	Socialist	782,000
UGT-P	Uniao Geral dos Trabalhadores	PO	1979	All	Socialist	700,000
UGT	Unión General de Trabajadores de España	SP	1973	All	Socialist	663,000
GSEE	Geniki synomospondia ergaton ellados	GR	1976	All		550,000
DAG	Deutsche Angestellten Gewerkschaft	GE	1991	Non-manual		506,000
CCOO	Confederacion Sindical de Comisiones Obreras	SP	1991	All	Communist	500,000
CFDT	Confédération Française Démocratique du Travail	FR	1974	All	Socialist	485,000
CGT-FO	CGT – Force Ouvrière	FR	1969*	All	Socialist	450,000

SGB	Schweizerischer Gewerkschaftsbund	SZ	1973	Manual	Socialist	441,000
ICTU	Irish Congress of Trade Unions	IR	1974	All	Labour	440,000
TVK	Toimihenkilö-ja Virkamiesjärjestöjen Keskusliitto	FI	1973	Non-manual		387,000
FTF	Fällesrådet for Danske Tjenestemands- og Funktionärorganisationen	DE	1973	Non-manual		320,000
CNV	Christelijk Nationaal Vakverbond	NE	1974	All	Christian	300,000
ELA-STV	Ezuko Langilleen Alkartasuna	SP	1974	Regional		110,000
CNG	Christlichnationaler Gewerkschaftsbund der Schweiz	SZ	1974	Manual	Christian	108,000
SVEA	Schweizerischer Verband evangelischer Arbeitnehmer	SZ	1974	All	Protestant	
CFTC	Confédération Française des Travailleurs Chrétiens	FR	1991	All	Catholic	106,000
ADEDY	Anotati Diikisis Enoseos Demosion Y pallilon	GR	1991	Public		100,000
ASI	Althydusamband Island	IC	1973	All	Socialist	62,000
CGT-L	Confédération Générale du Travail du Luxemburg	LU	1969*	All	Socialist	44,000
SEK	Synomospondia ergaton kypron	CY	1982			41,000
GWU	General Workers Union	MA	1975	Manual		29,000
LCGB	Lëtzebuerger Chrëschteche Gewerkschafts-Bond	LU	1974	All	Christian	21,000
BSRB	Bandalag Starfsmanna Rikis of Baeja	IC	1980	Public		17,000
CMTU	Confederation of Maltese Trade Unions	MA	1980			11,000
KTS	Kibris türk isci sendikalari i federasyonu	CY	1982			10,000
DISK	Turkiye devrimci isci sendikalari kondederasyonu	TU	1985		Labour	

Membership as of 1988 or 1989.
* Affiliation year to EFTUC, becoming ETUC in 1973.

Sources: Barnounin, 1987: 51–4 (Table 3.1–3); ETUC 1987: 11–2; Roberts and Liebhaberg, 1976: 273; Tuydka, 1983: 52; Visser, 1989.

Table 7.5 *Largest union confederations outside the ETUC (above 100,000 members)*

Abbrev.	Name	Country	Domain	Orientation	Membership
DGB	Deutscher Beamtenbund	GE	Public		794,000
CGTP-IN	Confederaçao Geral dos Trahalbadores Portugueses	PO	All	Communist	700,000
CGT	Confédération Générale du Travail	FR	All	Communist	600,000
FEN	Fédération de l'Education Nationale	FR	Education		335,000
CGB	Christlicher Gewerkschaftsbund	GE	All	Christian	305,000
Akava	Akava	FI	Staff		256,000
SACO	Sveriges Akademikers Centralorganisation	SW	Staff		244,000
HAK-IS	HAK-IS	TU	All	Islam	200,000
CGSL	Centrale Générale des Syndicats Libéraux de Belgique	BE	All	Liberal	181,000
YS	Yrkesorganisasjonenes Sentralforbund	NO	Non-manual		167,000
STTK	Suomen Teknisten Toimihenkilöjörjesöjen Keskoslitto	FI	Technicians		153,000
YURT-IS	YURT-IS	TU	All	Nationalist	150,000
VSA	Vereinigung Schweizerischer Angestelltenverbände	SZ	Non-manual		144,000
AF	Akademikernes Fellesorganisasjon	NO	Staff		130,000
MHP	Vakcentrale voor Middelbaar en Hoger Personeel	NE	Staff		124,000
CFE	Confédération Française de l'Encadrement	FR	Staff		108,000
AC	Ambtenarencentrale	NE	Public		107,000

Membership as of 1988 or 1989.

* Affiliation year to EFTUC, becoming ETUC in 1973.

Sources: Visser, 1989 and own data.

represented. Following the reorganization of the European Community in the late 1960s, the Secretariat was consolidated and became the European Free Trade Union Confederation in the Community (EFTUC) in 1969. The socialist confederations from countries belonging to the European Free Trade Association had formed a secretariat in Geneva in 1967. When in the late 1960s negotiations over Community membership began with Denmark, Norway, Ireland and Britain, union representatives of these countries were usually invited to attend EFTUC meetings (Blanpain, 1972: 283). The Christian confederations, affiliated with the World Confederation of Labour (WCL), formed their own regional organization, targeted at the Community, in 1958. The organization was reformed and strengthened in 1969 with the establishment of a Brussels-based office (Bouvard, 1972: 86–7). Finally, the French and Italian Communist union confederations, who had initially rejected the Community, and in the French case continued to do so, formed a *Comité Permanent* in Brussels in 1966. Until 1969 they had not been recognized by the Commission and both confederations had been excluded from national representation on the Economic and Social Committee, though the Italian government had from 1964 on demanded a seat for the CGIL (Roberts and Liebhaberg, 1976: 262).

In sum, the situation described by Blanpain as 'diversity, lack of general cooperation and . . . absence of adequate supranational structures' has changed considerably. ETUC succeeding EFTUC in 1973, has overcome the territorial split between EC and non-EC countries as well as between Northern and Southern, richer and poorer countries; has bridged most of the ideological and political cleavages which continued to exist at the national level, and has made substantial progress in completing its representation of white-collar employees. Compared to its predecessors, who were little more than semi-permanent coordination committees and hardly deserved to be called 'organizations', the foundation of ETUC was a major step forward in the direction of building a transnational organization. For the first time the rule of unanimity in voting was abandoned. Decisions became possible on the basis of a qualified, two-thirds majority, thus introducing some degree of supranationality, though the new organization did not acquire the rights and means to coordinate or supervise bargaining relations of affiliates. The two-third majority rule ensured that no decision could be taken against the will of one of the major affiliates, and also that the interests of unions from the EFTA bloc were taken into account.

With the benefit of hindsight we can say that the leaders who, in

1973, founded the ETUC and secured entry of the Christian unions the following year, made good use of a particularly favourable period in the post-war history of European labour. At the same time, developments since 1973 have been slow, especially in the area of internal organization building.

The Successful Extension of ETUC

The resurgence of militancy between 1968 and 1973 had brought trade unions to the centre of attention and had boosted their self confidence. At the time governments sought active cooperation and involvement of trade unions. The secularization of European societies, combined with the attenuation of the ideological and political tensions associated with the Cold War, helped the trade union movements to concentrate on common identities and problems, and in a number of countries – most notably in Finland, Italy and the Netherlands – unions overcame some century-old schisms. The opening of the European Community and the entry of Denmark, Ireland and the United Kingdom posed the necessity of a territorial overhaul of European union organization, while the growing presence and merger activities of multinational firms added urgency to the need for transnational coordination of union action. It should be noted that similar steps forward in transnational unionism did not occur in other world regions, and that unity proved easier to accomplish in Western Europe than elsewhere. For instance, the merger talks between the International Confederation of Free Trade Unions, to which in Europe mainly socialist confederations belong, and the Christian World Confederation of Labour, failed in the same year (Windmuller, 1976b, 1980).

The completion of ETUC took place in several steps. The *territorial* broadening was easiest and occurred right at the start in 1973, including the then illegal socialist confederation of Spain, mainly sponsored by the German and international socialist labour movement. ETUC extended its representation to Greece in 1976, to Portugal in 1979 with the membership of the Socialist UGT-P, and to Turkey in 1985 when DISK, at that time persecuted and illegal, was admitted. Turkey's largest union confederation, TÜRK-IS, was admitted three years later.

The *Christian* unions of the WCL became part of ETUC in 1974. Only the German Christian union confederation (CGB) was refused access by the dominant DGB, while the small Confédération Française des Travailleurs Chrétiens (CFTC) remained outside because of its quarrels with the Confédération Française Démocratique du Travail (CFDT), from which it had split ten years earlier. The 'secularized' CFDT had been one of the founding and leading organizations. Like the DGB in ETUC, it recently abstained from its veto, and the CFTC was finally admitted in 1991, while the CGB remained outside (see Table 7.5).

A much more contentious issue was the affiliation of the *communist-led* confederations. ETUC adopted a policy that membership is acceptable only if there is no opposition from an affiliate in the same country, if the organization cuts its ties with with the communist World Federation of Trade Unions (WFTU) and is independent from the Communist Party (Barnounin, 1976: 26–40; Debunne, 1987: 57–66; Roberts and Liebhaberg, 1976: 264–6). In the Italian case there were no objections to admit the CGIL in 1975. Two years earlier the organization had withdrawn as a member of the WFTU, its ties with the party had been loosened in the process of unification of Italian union confederations, and its application was supported by the other two Italian confederations. Yet, a minority of the DGB, Force Ouvrière and the Christian confederations in Belgium, Luxemburg and Switzerland were against admission. The French CGT and the Portugese Intersindical were refused affiliation in 1980. The demand of the Spanish communist-led Comisiones Obreras has long been blocked by the DGB, but in 1990 the organization was admitted. The expectation is that the Intersindical will follow soon, especially as it only held an associate membership with the now evaporating WFTU. Opposition from other French unions, and its close ties with the French communist party, will probably continue to close the door for the CGT, despite support for its admission from the TUC.

From the start, ETUC had admitted the peak associations of white-collar unions in Denmark, Sweden and Finland as its members, but in other countries the monopolistic claim of its affiliates to represent all white-collar employees (the case of the DGB in Germany), or, conversely, a conscious policy of abstinence on the part of white-collar federations (the case of the Swiss VSA) had forestalled full integration. It should be added that inclusion of *white-collar* unions was not a salient issue in the formative years of ETUC, especially since some of these white-collar organizations, most notably the Deutsche Angestellten Gewerkschaft (DAG), were indirectly represented through European Industry Committees, in particular the Euro-FIET (see below). In January 1991 the DAG was admitted, and with the exception of the Swiss VSA and the Norwegian YS all of the major white-collar peak federations are now members of ETUC.

In terms of 'associational monopoly', ETUC occupies the same position in Western Europe as the DGB holds in Germany. As a peak association ETUC clearly qualifies as an *encompassing organization* (Olson, 1982), combining white- and blue-collar workers with different levels of skills and education, from rising and declining industries, large and small firms, in the public and private sector, as well as retired workers, the unemployed, and workers depending on benefits. Like the DGB, ETUC is unrivalled, and there is no second organization of its kind. However, unlike the DGB the degree of horizontal integration within ETUC is weak, resembling the British TUC, as it cannot grow in terms of organizational resources above the lowest common denominator of its supporting member associations. The DGB has only 17 affiliates, more or less one for each industry; a comparable situation in ETUC would mean 12 affiliates from the EC countries and nine more to include the other Western European states.

The Lack of Internal Organization Building

Interorganizational cooperation is more readily achieved when the number of participants is small, one of the organizations is in a position to adopt a leadership role, the organizations share a common set of values and objectives, and a rival 'action set', whose superior capacity for action must be met, is present (Olson, 1965; Philipps, 1960). Comparing national union confederations, Visser (1990, Ch. 9) found that, other things being equal, the absence of internal political and organizational cohesion in an action set of unions tends to prevent the development of confederal authority. This finding can also be applied to ETUC. If we place ETUC on the scale of horizontal integration, it appears in the bottom range, somewhere near the TUC in Britain; united but fragmented and with little internal cohesion. The degree of vertical integration is probably even lower than in the British situation. ETUC has, like the TUC, no bargaining mandate. Its possibilities to influence the bargaining behaviour of its affiliates are remote; it holds no strike resources; the organization is lower on staff and resources than nearly all of its main affiliates, except those in very small countries (Malta, Cyprus, Iceland) or those working under extreme adverse conditions (DISK). ETUC counts 35 officials and staff members (a ratio of less than 1 per million members!) and is highly dependent on the European Commission for its financial revenue, research and information resources. Each member organization pays only a small percentage of its income as affiliation fees to ETUC; the TUC paid, for example, in the mid-1980s, before its financial crisis, less than 3% of its annual income (or about £150,000) to ETUC, 10% to the international union movement and about 0.6% to the OECD Trade Union Advisory Committee (TUAC). It thus seems that ETUC pays a price for its successful attempt to include the largest possible set of union organizations and to establish itself as the one and only voice of labour in Western Europe.

Recently, the issue of ETUC's authority has arisen and some steps have in fact been taken with the adoption, at the 1991 delegate conference in Luxemburg, of the 'Steekelenburg' plan 'for a more efficient ETUC'. The two main elements are the integration of the European Industry Committees and the creation of a 'comité de direction' between ETUC's executive council, which is far too large, political and cumbersome, and the secretariat, which lacks the political heavyweights to commit the organization on important issues. The idea is that the 40 confederations represented on the executive council will be represented through ten delegates on the new committee, thereby giving rise to some degree of coalition building and interest combination between confederations from different countries. The means of ETUC – its staff and finances in particular – are also to be enlarged in response to the much greater workload (drafting resolutions, advising on directives and communications, influencing deregulation proposals) in the preparation process for '1992'. Employers are engaged in similar attempts to draw on additional resources and to expand their staff in Brussels (Tyszkiewicz, 1990).

The reforms of 1991 stopped short of transforming ETUC from, in the words of CGIL leader Bruno Trentin, a 'coordination body between national centres' into a 'supranational organization'. Clearly, not all ETUC affiliates, especially the largest among them, are ready to make this move. Some, among them the TUC and the DGB, lack the mandate from their member organizations. The mundane question as to whether national union confederations will be forthcoming with additional financial contributions is also surrounded with uncertainty. Some of the major affiliates of ETUC, such as those in Britain, Belgium, France or the Netherlands, are in dire financial straits. Recently, the TUC announced a further cut of 15% of its spending, following a decline of revenue due to membership losses. The Dutch FNV also faces a further round of reductions. In France and Belgium confederal expenditure is propped up with public money. Thus, while the loss of power and functions of the national peak federations due to the demise of incomes policies and macro-economic concertation at home may encourage the national peak federations to redirect their activities to the international field and to Brussels, membership decline and lower revenues as well as the reluctance of national unions to maintain elaborate national confederations whose effectiveness and political role is declining, operate in the reverse direction.

In national union movements a dominant union may assume a

leadership role. Rather than through explicit and premeditated coordination, via the peak association, other unions adapt *post factum* to the policies chosen and conditions created by the dominant union, especially when the union is perceived as being effective. The IG Metal is probably the best example of a union which checks and prevents centralizing tendencies in the DGB, and at the same time provides for a leadership role in the German union movement. With one-third of the membership of the DGB and its location in industry and production, the dominance of the union is often envied by others, but not really questioned. Its resources outnumber those of the confederation by far. As important, perhaps, is the fact that the union was successful at some crucial stages – unlike many unions in industry in Europe – and despite growing unemployment, the union maintained its position (density, bargaining clout, sectoral agreements), and was one of the few unions which actually gained the 35-hour working week. There is no parallel in ETUC. Its two largest affiliates, the TUC and the DGB, each representing nearly 20% of ETUC's total membership (before the German unification), represent the converse in nearly all relevant aspects of trade union politics and policies. In recent years the TUC has abandoned its long-time opposition against European integration and the Common Market, but the confederation has anything but a proactive policy on European integration (see Teague, 1989b). With German unification, the DGB became the largest European union confederation with more than 12 million members, yet it faces the formidable challenge of integrating its new East German members and union branches into an established union movement more than 40 years old. While turning to its internal problems, the DGB may in fact become even less willing or capable to assume a European leadership role – not to speak of the reservations by other union movements about a German *Alleingang* (solo effort).

The Second Pillar: Multinational Unions at the Sectoral Level

Transnational sectoral cooperation of national trade unions has a long history. Craft and occupational unions with foreign branches preceded the formation of international union organizations. International Trade Secretariats (ITS) were formed after the turn of the century. Between the wars some of these secretariats, especially the International Transport Secretariat, were quite active but most of the ITSs were unstable and understaffed, highly dependent on the variable degree of support of, first, their German parent organizations and, after the annihilation of the German trade union movement, of the British and American movements. Though formed by unions whose peak associations were part of the International Confederation of Free Trade Unions (ICFTU), the ITSs remained autonomous from the confederation (Windmuller, 1980). Weak hierarchical ordering of sectoral union organization remained a characteristic of post-war unionism in Europe as well.

European sector organizations came about in two ways: as an effort of individual unions to coordinate their pressure group activities aimed at Community institutions, or as a result of the regional differentiation process of the ITSs, similar to events in the international peak associations. A first set of European sector organizations emerged following the shift in policy-making towards the supranational level with the foundation of the European Coal and Steel Community (ECSC), the European Economic Community (EEC) and Euratom in the 1950s. A rather peculiar example was the 'Committee of 21', formed in 1952, for the purpose of coordinating union representation at the ECSC in Luxemburg. It combined three international organizations (the ICFTU and the two ITSs in mining and metals), 12 sector unions from these industries, and six national confederations from the six member countries. Each participant retained full autonomy and all decisions required unanimity (Roberts and Liebhaberg, 1976: 261). With the 1958 reorganization only the national unions retained their representation on the ECSC committee. The establishment of the European Common Market in 1958 triggered the formation of Brussels-based offices for representation and lobbying purposes in some of the most affected sectors: agriculture (EFA), food (IUF), as well as building trades (EFBW) and chemicals (ICF, later CEF – see Table 7.6 for full names). The ICF, located in Hanover at the headquarters of its powerful and dominant German affiliate, claimed to organize energy workers as well. This claim was rejected by other German unions and the international organizations; it was the only ITS without formal ties with ETUC. Its recent reform into a European federation was followed by ETUC recognition. This first set of European sector organizations originally limited their scope to the six Common Market countries. In the 1980s they followed ETUC in regional scope.

For the second set of organizations, EC pressure group politics was less important until the 1980s. The establishment of European organizations must be seen as the result of a regional differentiation process after the ITS had grown far beyond the traditional core area of Western Europe and North America. Foundation years, organizational structure, location, membership, regional scope and

Table 7.6   *European Industry Committees (EICs) recognized by ETUC*

Abbreviation	Name (headquarters)	Foundation	Reorganized	in ETUC
Recognized immediately after foundation of ETUC				
ICFTU-ECSC	Metalworkers' and Miners' Inter Trade Committee (Luxemburg)	1952	1958	1973
EFA	European Federation of Agricultural Workers' Unions in the Community (Brussels)	1958	1971	1973
EMF	European Metalworkers Federation (Brussels)	1963	1971	1973
Euro-FIET	European Regional Organization of the International Federation of Commercial, Clerical and Technical Employees (Geneva/Brussels)	1964	1973	1973
PTTI	Postal, Telegraph and Telephone International – European Committee (Geneva)	1968	1973	1973
ECAKU	European Committee of Trade Unions in Arts, Mass Media, Entertainment (Vienna)			1973
Recognized later by ETUC				
ECF-IUF	European Committee of Food, Catering and Allied Workers within the IUF (Brussels)	1958	1975	1978
ELCTWU	European Liaison Committee of Transport Workers' Union (Brussels)	1962	1979	1979
EPSC	European Public Service Committee (Brussels)	1966	1981	1979
ETTUC	European Teachers Trade Union Committee (Luxemburg)	1956		1981
EFBW	European Federation of Building and Woodworkers in the EEC (Brussels)	1958	1974	1984
EGF	European Graphical Federation (Berne)	1973		1987
ECF	European Chemical and General Workers' Union (Brussels)	1958	1988	1988
TGLWU	European Committee of Textile, Garment and Leather Workers' Union (Brussels)	1964	1975	1988
EFJ	European Federation of Journalists	1988		1989

Sources: Barnounin, 1987: 54–6 (Table 3.4–7); Stöckl, 1986: 233–5; ETUC, 1987: 13; Rütters and Tuydka, 1990.

affiliation varies between these European sector organizations (see Table 7.6). Some of the regional organizations maintain parallel offices which target the European Community institutions in Brussels. Some of the European sector organizations have also developed ties with the Economic and Social Committee (ECO-SOC) and the European Parliament, mostly via a national representative of an allied affiliate. With the recognition of the European Federation of Journalists there are now 15 European Industry Committees (EICs) recognized by ETUC. Reflecting the very different historical foundation trajectories, these EICs are very different in membership size, organizational structure, strategy and potential (Rütters and Tuydka, 1990).

From the point of view of organizing an action set of unions at the sectoral level, or in multinational firms, multi-unionism and incongruous domain definitions pose serious difficulties. If we take the example of metal engineering, we find mainly one union in Germany; two (one for blue- and one for white-collar workers, but belonging to the same confederation) in Austria; two or three in Norway; three (of which the two white-collar unions belong to another federation) in Sweden; three or four in Finland, Italy, Switzerland and the Netherlands (each union belonging to a different confederation); four or five in Belgium (a blue- and a white-collar union for each of the two major confederations); five or more unions (divided by skill-level and status, but often competing for membership and influence with one another) in Denmark, Ireland, and in Britain often many more. In Spain and Portugal there are at least two unions, and in many regions more. These numbers do not yet include organizations of managerial staffs, who also claim a place on bargaining tables. Domains are also highly incongruous, making it difficult to define the proper 'task environment' (Thompson, 1967) of international unionism at the sectoral or firm level. In Belgium, Germany, Italy, Sweden and Switzerland 'metal engineering' is a union domain of its own, and the organizing union does not have to attend to interests of workers in other domains. But often 'metal' is included in a wider domain, including 'mining and energy' (Austria) or other industries such as chemicals or textiles (Norway, the Netherlands). Union domain definitions larger than the metal sector are found where unskilled manual workers' unions (Denmark, Britain, Ireland), allied occupational unions (Britain, Ireland), and catch-all white-collar unions (Austria, Belgium, Denmark, Norway) exist. In some cases, especially among craft unions, we find domain definitions smaller than the metal sector. Metal engineering may seem a sector of particular complexity, but the situation is not very different in other sectors with large and increasing cross-border trade and investment (for example, chemicals, food, banking and finance, telecommunications).

The role of the transnational sector unions has been a contentious issue ever since the foundation of ETUC (Stöckl, 1986: 29–30). At that time, the French and Belgian union confederations were in favour of a formal and hierarchical integration of the sectoral organizations. This was strongly opposed by the British TUC and the Scandinavian unions, who were afraid of a further weakening of the ITSs. Understandably, they gave higher priority to international union action against world-wide operating multinational firms than improved union cooperation with the Community. As a compromise, the ETUC Executive Committee was given the freedom to recognize European Industry Committees. Formally, EIC representatives previously had only information and consultation rights on the ETUC Executive Committee (Stöckl, 1986: 30). Organizational ties are loose and not highly formalized. The EICs do not pay affiliation fees or receive income from ETUC. Of course, indirectly ETUC is dependent upon the sectoral organizations, since its affiliated peak associations do in most cases receive 75% and more of their revenue from the affiliated unions. However, the dependency does not channel via the EICs, who are themselves often understaffed and underfinanced. The largest of the EICs, those of the metalworkers, has only six permanent staff members; powerful national unions have hundreds. Even those large unions with a reputation of internationalism, such as the IG Metal in Germany, the MSF in Britain, the FIOM in Italy or the IB–FNV in the Netherlands, spend only a tiny proportion of their revenue on international union organization.

In the preparation for '1992' and the consultation process over various pieces of technical and sector-related information, ETUC is increasingly dependent on the expertise and cooperation of the EICs. This is reflected in the recent ETUC reform, in which sectoral representatives are given a full vote (except on internal matters such as finance and statutes) in its governing body. By coopting the EIC's leadership it is hoped that the growing criticism mounted towards ETUC within some of the industry committees can be silenced, and the threat of transnational unionism at the sectoral in lieu of intensified peak level cooperation can be countered. Whether it will have the intended effect of greater integration and effective leadership of ETUC remains to be seen. Much depends on the importance given to the EICs by their national affiliates and the political and organizational weight of the representatives from the national unions. Until the recent reform, few leaders of the EIC affiliates were represented on the ETUC Executive Committee via their national union leaders. The same pressures seem to be at work in transnational aggregation of interests as those that were at stake in the history of the national integration of union movements, when most trade union confederations finally preferred a less politicized functional principle of representation (individual national unions) over a territorial principle (regional trade union councils).

The European Community: Access, Recognition and Concertation

Owing to its role of initiating and drafting EC directives, the Commission is the prime target for 'proactive' pressure group politics of both capital and labour. Given the limited number of officials and the absence of a national or regional administrative substructure, the Commission has to rely on working groups and consultative committees in order to acquire the necessary expertise to draft legislation. This makes the Commission relatively open to 'clientelism' (Averyt, 1975; Sargent, 1985), and has created a pluralist and competitive market of information transmission and pressure group politics (Streeck and Schmitter, 1991). It works at the disadvantage of comprehensive organizations of labour, who depend upon (rather than produce) information – especially information of a technical and de-politicized nature which is most helpful to the Commission's overall objective of integration through mutual recognition and deregulation of trade barriers. The compartmentalization of the Commission into as many as 23 Directorate Generals has also worked to the detriment of the unions. As a matter of fact, ETUC is reported to have regular contacts with only a number of directorates, particularly DG V (Social Affairs) and DG X (Information); access to recognition by other departments is not as easy. Working parties outside Social Affairs are kept deliberately technical, that is apolitical, and mainly limited to producer interests. For instance, in the process of drafting its directive on the deregulation of the finance sector, DG XV (Financial Institutions) refuses to consider employees' participation rights claimed by the European federation in this sector, Euro-FIET. It refers to the need of a general rather than sectoral solution via legislation drafted by DG V, where the matter is stalled because of the differential impact in nations and sectors. This division of labour reinforces the de-coupling of the internal market project from the social dimension; while the former passes relatively smoothly, the latter faces objections by national governments and European employer associations.

The Council of Ministers remains the most powerful decision-maker within the EC, unchanged by the Single European Act (1987). While the Commission is a supranational body with limited legislative power and control over policy implementation, the main decision-making bodies are the European Council (meeting twice a year), the sectoral Councils of Ministers and the Permanent Representative Committee (COREPER). These are inter-governmental institutions through which national interests are accommodated. Until the Single European Act, all legislation had to be passed by unanimity. After 1987, internal market decisions needed a qualified majority only (54 out of 76 votes). In other words, while until 1987 one (small) country alone could veto a proposal, now an alliance of some large and small countries (three to six depending on the size) is needed. In matters of social and labour law, however, unanimity is required, except in the case of measures of health and safety at the workplace (SEA, Article 118 A).

In social matters it thus remains possible that one country, following pressures of national employer associations and companies, can block Community legislation. Britain under Margaret Thatcher often fulfilled this role, though this may have relieved governments in other countries from the need to antagonize union constituencies at home. Thus, while unions are handicapped in the development of proactive social policy responses by the Commission's organization and priorities, the Council's continued primacy makes it much easier for employers to pressurize national governments and representatives and prevent what they do not like. The fate of the Fifth draft directive, the Vredeling proposal and the European Company Statutes has been sealed in each case by this inequality in action potential, and it is now near certain that the European Works Council directive will follow the same path, though in this case employer associations and multinational firms hardly needed to mobilize protest (Hall, 1991).

As long as harmonization or convergence in social legislation is out of the question, and as long as the principle of subsidarité and mutual recognition serves to deregulate the Single European Market without (higher level) EC regulation, unions must live with the threat of 'regime shopping' (Streeck, 1990b). The fear of 'social dumping', as expressed by German unions in particular, may be exaggerated, and has in fact been criticized by unions in less developed areas who stand to gain from capital transfers because of lower social and wage costs. It may be true that only sectors with high factor mobility are affected (cf. Due et al., 1991: 92). The paradox is that even uniform or, lest that be politically unfeasible, minimum standards will have a different impact in each national system, given the cross-national differences in the ability of unions, and of state agencies, to monitor and enforce these standards. Although the Social Charter of 1989 was merely a solemn declaration of 11 EC member states (EC minus the United Kingdom) and is not legally binding, the Third Action Programme of the Commission has used it as its base for proposing a number of draft directives. In doing so, the Commission bases its proposals on a broad legal interpretation of Articles 100 A and 118 A (both with qualified majority rule), which is challenged by the British government and the employer associations, and may lead to a case before the European Court of Justice (cf. Rhodes, 1991: 269–70). The Commission based its proposed European Works Council directive upon Article 100, requiring unanimity. This prudence may have been suggested by its wish not to weaken the case for political union at the intergovernmental conference in Maastricht in 1991 (see Hall, 1991), but it now seems that the Commission has gambled wrong on both accounts.

Prima facie, the advisory Economic and Social Committee (ECOSOC) is a 'Euro-corporatist' institution. Yet for various reasons, it has never developed into a major comprehensive advisory body or an inportant channel of influence for European trade unions. A recent evaluation by the EC interdepartmental working party put the facts rather bluntly: 'the Economic and Social Committee is still no more than a consultative body and despite the weight given to its opinions they play a relatively minor role in the Community decision-making process, particularly since the Committee's opinion is sought only after the Commission has adopted a position' (CEC, 1988c: 108). ECOSOC is a 'tripartite' body with representatives from producer, labour and consumer (and other various) interests. Labour and employers each occupy one-third of the seats, while the third component is heterogenous and unpredictable in its voting behaviour. Delegates are not appointed by their national or European organizations, but by the national governments as personal representatives. As a consequence, neither ETUC nor EICs are ex officio and directly committed. ETUC provides, however, the coordination and support that ECOSOC labour delegates need since resources are short and the workload is high. (ECOSOC, 1980: 179–83; Barnounin, 1987: 82–3). The 'associational monopoly' of influence is very low, despite ETUC's comprehensiveness in terms of membership. Indeed, ETUC, on the side of labour, and UNICE and CEEP (public employers), on the side of capital, are only three among 20 international affiliations that represent one-third of the delegates each, while rival unions

(CIF, CIC) and other business and professional interest groups compose the remainder of delegates (Sidjanski and Condomines, 1983: 25).

The Standing Committee on Employment is a truly tripartite body that coordinates and confronts the views on employment policies of the employers, the unions and the administrative and political leadership of the Community (Commission and Council). The Committee had a troubled history after it started in 1970, but it survived several boycotts (by ETUC) and deadlocks. Several annual conferences on social policy and economic (full employment) policy were held in Brussels and Luxemburg (CEC, 1988d: 108). These meetings were organized on an *ad hoc* basis and no commitments were made by either party. ETUC seemed interested in the existence of a tripartite forum but was unwilling to discuss nationally contentious issues, in particular the income policy proposals of the Commission (Grote, 1987: 245).

In response to the failure of the conferences and the rising unemployment figures, ETUC made an attempt to develop collective action on a European scale between 1978 and 1983. It organized in 1978 an action day, and in 1979 an action week in which some national union centres participated. Four times ETUC manifestations preceded or accompanied the European Council meetings (the summits of Brussels 1978, Venice 1980, Maastricht 1981 and Stuttgart 1983). In 1983, in preparation for the Stuttgart summit, leaders of ETUC and of national peak associations met with the heads of governments to press for ETUC's 'jobs now' programme; only Margaret Thatcher sternly refused to receive the ETUC delegation. Although the pressure may take some credit for the informal 'Val Duchesse' meetings of union, employer and EC representatives and the relaunching of the Social Dialogue, there was still no result for ETUC and the unions (Debunne, 1987: 156). With the new Commision under Jacques Delors, the Social Dialogue was continued in 1985, now more precisely focused on topics such as new technologies and EC employment policies. Two working groups were set up, on macro economics (1986) and on new technologies (1987), while the Standing Committee on Employment remained active. The former *ad hoc*, informal and private talks, were formalized and received wider public coverage. Yet, employers are adamantly opposed to the possibility of 'joint agreements', which can be construed as preparing the way for new EC regulation; they are only willing to sign non-binding 'joint opinions' on non-contentious issues, of which, in fact, a number have been reached between the social partners. This position, the current weakness of unions and remaining differences between national movements, combined with the continuing decoupling of the internal market project from the social policy project, have brought the strategy of Delors's 'l'éspace social européen' to a standstill (see also Spiropoulos, 1991; Teague, 1989a: 68–70).

Is the sectoral (meso) level an alternative arena for experiments with concertation and social dialogue? In response to the differential impact of deregulation, there have been initiatives and pressures to create sectoral rather than general forums. In addition to the formal joint committees which existed since the 1960s, primarily in agriculture and transport, new working parties in construction, banking and retail trade have been set up, and some informal activity has been stepped up in other sectors. However, given the problematic structure of access, the technical nature of the information and consultation process, the administrative and political weakness of the European Industry Committees, and the incongruity in position and structure of the national sector unions, sectoral (meso-level) concertation schemes are set against a whole series of obstacles.

Collective Bargaining and Transnational Unionism

When expectations of transnational collective bargaining were raised in the 1960s, following the advancement of multinational firms and the relaunching of the European Community, the only level expected to develop was that of the single multinational firm. A decade later most analysts were concerned with demonstrating why transnational firm-level collective bargaining had not made any significant headway. In their extensive overview Northrup and Rowan (1979) identified four major obstacles:

1 Different national legislation covering employment and labour relations.
2 Employer opposition because of potential costs.
3 Union opposition because of the threat to sovereignty of national union organizations.
4 Employee resistance based on what they called 'parochial' attitudes.

Other barriers, on the union side, include the political schisms, multi-unionism, and the cross-national diversity, and in some cases the absence of firm-level representation (see Hayworth and Ramsay, 1984). The absence of employer incentives to engage in transnational bargaining activity, except in the case of managing an employment crisis, is well documented (see Enderwick, 1982,

1984). Ulman has pointed out that the incentive of transnational bargaining for unions is strong – prompted by fear of job loss in relatively high-wage countries. But there is also a strong alternative – 'job bargaining' or 'the attempt to restrain investment patterns directly in order to avoid job loss rather than indirectly through international coordination of wage determination on the union side' (Ulman, 1975: 31).

Subsequent analysis has concentrated less on true collective bargaining than on the development of a joint labour–management forum within multinational firms (Gold and Hall, 1991). In a number of – mainly French – firms such information and consultation bodies ('comités de groupe') exist. Joint forums exist at Saint-Gobin (1983), Thomson-Grand Public (1985), BSN–Gervais Danone (1985) and Bull (1988); an uncertain start was made in 1990 at Volkswagen, Nestlé and Pechiney; Euro-FIET has targeted similar company-wide forums at Allianz, while ICEF appears to plan similar activities at Michelin and Proctor & Gamble. Gillette and Unilever are among the firms who have refused any contact or dialogue of this kind (Buda and Vogel, 1989: 12–5; Gold and Hall, 1991; Northrup et al., 1988: 530–7).

UNICE, Europe's main employer association in the private sector, rejects these initiatives, as it is squarely opposed to any kind of transnational collective bargaining at whatever level. Like ETUC, UNICE is not mandated to sign collective agreements on behalf of its affiliates. On the sectoral level there is no substitute; transnational employer (as distinct from business) organization is weak and in fact in many countries the sectoral level is under pressure (France, Italy, Netherlands) or has been abandoned (Britain) as the dominant level of collective bargaining over wages and employment levels.

Rather than true collective bargaining, we may witness the emergence of some degree of European coordination of national collective bargaining in order to achieve greater compatibility in national arrangements – especially arrangements of a procedural kind. Some development in this respect has occurred in sectors which are exposed to deregulation, privatization or loss of national protection, and where employers are fragmented and weak. The social dialogue on vocational training in retail and in insurance sectors has produced an agreement in the case of retail (IRE, 1/1991). In the public sector agreements have been reached in European railways and public utilities. It should be noted that in none of these cases are the employer associations members of UNICE, which strongly disapproves of the negotiations. These sectoral agreements constitute problems for unions as well. In the two mentioned private sectors, unions are notoriously weak; in the two semi-public sectors sectionalism is pervasive and ETUC's monopoly is far from established. There is indeed the danger of a rather sectionalist or occupational type of international unionism developing along the lines of narrowly defined interests. Euro-Cockpit, which appears to be Europe's first transnational union outside ETUC and claims to represent 20,000 aircrew members, is an example of this development. Clearly setting itself apart from the European and International Transport Workers' Federation, it has asked for separate EC recognition under the European Company Statute, and has threatened to pursue industrial action if necessary in obtaining bargaining recognition (IRE 2/1991). More sectionalism is to follow should British unions such as the GMB and MSF do what they have announced and attract merger partners among minor or major unions (or sections thereof) abroad in order to form European 'super-unions' (IRE 9/1988 and 4/1990).

It is possible that at the level of firms transnational bargaining of some kind will develop in the next decade. This presupposes that trade unions get around the practical and legal problem of organizing international strikes, that is, circumventing peace clauses in national sectoral (multi-employer) collective agreements and legal prohibition of solidarity strikes. Firm-level transnational bargaining is therefore likely to develop at the expense of sectoral national bargaining, with the strongest firms opting out of the existing national structures of employer and union solidarity. This is a scenario of union decline, since single-employer bargaining is associated with the emergence of dualism (Goldthorpe, 1984) and wage competition between unionized and non-unionized sectors, which unions cannot win (Blanchflower and Freeman, 1990; Visser, 1991).

Conclusions

Our overall conclusions in this chapter are threefold. First, the meso or micro level is not an alternative for macro-level coordination, even if in the short or medium run the prospects for transnational union organization and action seem better at lower and less-inclusive levels. Second, the prospects of a 'neo-corporatist' dynamic of organization building centred on Community institutions are remote. Third, there is no alternative, for European labour, but to take the debate on a 'social Europe' into the national arena.

We have identified a number of organizational and political

obstacles on the road to transnational unionism in the Community, both at the confederal and the sectoral level. The participants are numerous and unequal. No one appears to be capable, trusted or willing to fulfil a leadership role. Internally, within their own countries, the participating union organizations represent different domains, policies and ideologies. There is no target organization whose superior coordinating abilities can be imitated, or must be met. European employer associations – UNICE in particular – are too deliberately weak to assume a role as catalyst in transnational cooperation, like employer associations often did in the national arena (Sisson, 1987). The European Commission and its agencies have sometimes wanted to help for reasons of their own, but it must be doubted whether the Community institutions can ever assume the role which most European states had in the history of national union movements. European integration occurs without an elaborated central state in its middle (Streeck and Schmitter, 1991). The European Community lacks much of the democratic legitimation and the citizens' rights (Bryant, 1991) which played an important role in the political democratization of the nation state. In short, none of the three grand centralizing forces in the history of European union movements – that is, the struggle for universal suffrage from its early stages until the First World War, the struggle against depression and general wage cuts between the wars, or the post-war policies of macro economic demand management and central wage control – is available in the Europe of today.

The problem of constructing a viable form of transnational unionism at the European level is compounded by the fact that the deconstruction of the national level goes in two directions at the same time. The decomposition of national policies and regulatory capacities is the product of a shift towards the supranational level and a trend towards decentralized decision-making in politics and economics. The reawakening of intraregional political and economic cooperation, and of interregional competition, combined with the rediscovery of the firm as the central arena of industrial relations, tends to undermine the sectoral structure of union organization and workers' solidarity. In the European Community there are few signs of a remake at the transnational level of what is now disappearing at the national level.

Note

1. We do not analyse regional developments in international unionism because very little is known about the 'inter-regional trade union councils' which were formed in border regions from the mid 1970s on. In the mid 1980s there were eight councils,

five in the Benelux-Ruhr-Saar area, the others in the Basle-triangle, Lombardy-Ticino and the Pyrenees. According to Barnounin (1987: 65) these councils dealt with the social problems of frontier workers, problems of transport, housing and infrastrucure, vocational training and cultural exchange.

8
Conclusions: Evolving Patterns of Organizing Interests in the European Community

Justin Greenwood, Jürgen R. Grote and Karsten Ronit

A number of major themes feature prominently throughout the individual contributions of this book, and in turn give rise to some important questions.

1 Is it possible to detect variations in the forms and degrees to which social groups, sectors and territories manage to organize interests?
2 Are some sectors, particularly those of high tech, characterized by limited presence and action of private interest groups?
3 Do groups prefer to voice interests via interaction with their 'own' government or do they prefer to act alone or in concert with similar groups across member states vis-à-vis EC institutions?
4 Can elements of neo-corporatism be identified at the European level and is this theory applicable to a higher level than that of the nation state?

In what follows, the ambition is not simply to answer these questions in the affirmative or confirmative, but rather to seek some valid explanations.

In the introduction to this book we stressed that a very even process of organizing European-wide interests was hardly imaginable. Investigations of national political systems often display substantial variations, and at a higher and even more complex level we hypothesized the likelihood of a more mixed pattern. Social, sectoral and territorial cleavages have often been identified as important variables in explaining collective action, and our studies have clearly shown that they also count in a European context.

A commonly observed dividing line of industries or sectors is that between 'sun-rise' industries (such as new technologies) and the suffering 'sundowners'. Whether firms in high tech domains, given their relatively recent emergence and continuous innovation, have been able both to identify shared interests and accommodate rapidly in terms of some kind of collective action is highly pertinent.

A variety of avenues of political action of such sectors or clusters of industries have proved to be available. Existing associations integrate new interests, high tech industries establish brand new associations and single firms act alone and also by loose cooperation. Evidence from our studies certainly displays a variety of combined activity but neither public efforts of national governments nor the EC have generally made private action redundant.

Broadly speaking, interests may be represented along national and transnational channels in an EC context. Groups may induce their own government to forward their interests or choose the 'Euro strategy', that is, to represent interests directly or via relevant and often federated encompassing interest organizations. We have not argued that the two routes are mutually exclusive or that one has simply replaced the other. It is rather their changing role which has been interesting to examine. This gives us an idea of how interests manage to organize and to what extent the nation state or the embryonic state of the EC should be conceived of as the epicentre of policy processes.

Neo-corporatism is concerned about the relationship between organized interests and the state. This volume is also heavily engaged in problems of such private–public exchanges. While some arrangements may be characterized as neo-corporatist in character it would be premature to generalize by using broad labels such as 'corporatist' or 'pluralist' to describe interest group–EC relations. Patterns are too fragmented and do not lend themselves to such generalizations.

Social, Sectoral and Territorial Organization of Interests

Collective action varies between social groups, sectors and territories, resulting in a variety of problematiques in organizing interests at national and transnational levels.

The first and general conclusion to be drawn is that business has managed to organize interests more effectively than labour and from much earlier. The forums and means for labour to coordinate are still comparatively few and weak. This is not only attributable to the impact of the somewhat pluralistic pattern of organizing labour in at least some of the member states. The direct transnational challenges facing labour from employers' associations have not been a developmental factor and labour has not been dependent upon entering into transnational collective bargaining.

At the same time, organized labour has not found any clearly definable role. These 'missing links' may provide a clue as to why issues such as the social dimension have been put on the agenda relatively late, and why organized labour has played a modest role in raising the problem.

In contradiction to labour, business has 'always' been trans-national. The larger firms in particular have for decades been affiliated not only to domestic but also to host associations of the countries in which they operate. Therefore, it is to a certain extent somewhat illusory to speak of pure national business interest associations. Nevertheless, national associations have primarily organized domestic firms, and have been embedded in national political cultures and carry different legacies. Transnational coor-dination, or more advanced forms of collective action by groups beyond the nation state, has been achieved at other levels such as between national peak associations in UNICE. Sector associations or various informal groups are of far greater significance. Whereas labour relies primarily on such high- (peak-) level coordination, business has had a variety of coordination strategies to choose between. In this respect we are not only referring to the obvious fact that individual and comptetitive operations in the market place provide business with an additional type of action. From the early days of European integration it has been demonstrated, albeit with shifting intensity, that the associability of business has not been conditioned by substantial and prior pressures exerted by labour. Business is constituted by a relatively limited number of indepen-dent actors even at the transnational level, but business is not just drawing advantage from group size and the fewer steps to climb in aggregating interests. This latter advantage is present in national contexts too. Business also displays a distinct transnational mobil-ity, which makes transnational collective action easier.

Many firms, and not exclusively the giants, are already relatively experienced in handling different political challenges in member states. This kind of experience tends to create common responses across member states. Such moves are emphasized by the Single Market, which has brought a convergence of regulatory issues at national levels as well as at the European level. Therefore, the problem of finding appropriate answers to political challenges has become an urgent task in business, particularly since the mid 1980s. However, these challenges mainly seem to have been directed towards business as a producer group, and less towards business as employers.

Variation is not only found between different social groups. Differentiation within business can easily be identified and some cleavages found between territories and between firm size. This problematique is tackled in the chapter by Grote who has detected strong variation in the organization of small and medium-sized enterprises in Germany and Italy. These asymmetries at national levels are seen as complicating all kinds of transnational interest organization. The same problem is emphasized in the two studies on peak associations of labour and capital.

Business has not been challenged equally across sectors. However, the general conclusion to be drawn is that sector associations in recent years have been playing a greater role than peak associations. In some cases the Commission has deliberately expressed an interest in having appropriate negotiation partners below the peak level, and has encouraged their formation.

We may distinguish between sectors which have become objects of regulation at different periods of time. Agriculture and fishery were regulated at a relatively early stage, whereas telecommunication, consumer electronics and pharmaceuticals and biotechnologies occurred much later. Compared to agriculture and fishery for instance, high tech sectors are, as far as the individual firms are concerned, significantly less local in terms of plant localization, and less characterized by unilateral dependencies on a single government. In other words, one of the most significant features is the high degree of mobility attributed to firms in the sectors.

A comparison of sectors reveals, however, that the organization of interests follows a rather varied pattern. European-wide business associations have been established, in some cases without organizing all national sector associations. National production may be weak or simply missing, and national interest aggregations are for that simple reason vacant in Euro associations. This was most evident in the telecommunications study (chapter 2).

The existing sectoral associations can date their origin to different stages of European integration, or more precisely to attempts to adopt new policies and integrate new areas into the 92-process. The 1970s saw the regrouping of interests in the pharmaceutical landscape of associations, whereas the 1980s was a decade of regrouping in telecommunications and the initial formation of associations in consumer electronics and biotechnologies. These associations are by no means equally powerful. The term 'letterhead association' can also be applied to some, such as can be seen in the case of consumer electronics and telecommunications.

With the exception of the pharmaceuticals case (chapter 3), business has not, in each of the sectors analysed, finally achieved the formation of a single cohesive association managing substantial diversity and possessing a *de facto* monopoly of representing the sector concerned. A monopoly in representing a certain constituency of firms is present in the case of the consumer electronics industry, and even though Cawson sees the association as heavily under resourced, he points to the legitimizing functions it neverthe-less performs.

The situation in the telecommunication industry is less clear. Although a single association has been set up on the producer side, it carries no responsibility for the entire interest aggregation to the European level. What adds to the complexity of this sector is the distribution of influence between national and transnational groups, and the degree to which policy processes have hitherto been embedded in national settings.

We should like to emphasize that nowhere in this volume can an outright competitive and classical pluralist relationship between associations trying to organize precisely the same constituency in a European context be claimed. As far as the three studies on high tech industries are concerned the relationship between trans-nationally organized actors is more of a complementary nature.

Another interesting feature found in all sectoral studies is the political activity of individual firms. In some cases they consider it more fruitful to go on their own despite the greater legitimacy which group action often yields. On the other hand, this does not exclude their affiliation and active involvement in associational life. In fact, the sectors chosen consist of a limited number of firms and a high degree of economic concentration, which, according to much collective action theory, are factors that should provide these groups with ample opportunities of organizing interests. Not that they have failed to do so, but larger firms have also been politically active and have partly bypassed associations. This aspect is another piece of evidence suggesting that business is in an advantageous position compared to labour owing to opportunities of single firm action.

Interest Groups: Just Empty Shells?

An important question arising from our studies is whether a sort of interest-group-free zone of politics has materialized, and whether limited importance can be attached to the associations. This may sound somewhat contradictory to the conclusion drawn so far, as we have been pointing to the existence of a plethora of interest organizations and their mushrooming during the past decade. Therefore, the question raised does not so much address the mere existence and proliferation of associations, but rather their role and status. They might be empty shells deprived of any political value apart from the one which lies in entrepreneurial fraternity.

The Commission has played a significant role in identifying new issue areas and has put these into a more global context. A particular aim has been the improvement of European competitiveness in relation to the United States and Japan, such as the numerous research and development programmes adopted in the 1970s and 1980s. This, however, should not lead us to the hasty conclusion that private actions, in whatever form, are missing and that interest groups have failed to respond to new challenges. The sectors analysed in this book have only relatively recently undergone a more profound Europeanization. National agendas of regulation display commonalities, and the political ambition to adopt regulatory measures community-wide has increased considerably. Moreover, our sectors have become European in the sense that they are based on the application of 'new technologies', with firms applying these across member states. Both factors could be taken as arguments against the swift and timely formation of new and indispensable interest groups. The very identification and definition of new interests takes time, and the reliance of sectors upon traditional and tested national routes of interest representation might discourage European action. However, sector associations have been established and have become interlocutors with the Commission.

The studies of peak associations by both Visser and Ebbinghaus (chapter 7) and Lanzalaco (chapter 6) stressed in the case of labour and business that 'national legacies' are of utmost importance, and that the management of diversity is extreme at the peak level. From this perspective we also find some interesting arguments as to why associations below the peak level have important functions to perform. On the other hand, we should not underestimate the fact that some are still rather weak in terms of resources and collective political action.

Few would claim that the EC played a very dynamic role in forwarding European integration in the dark age of 'Eurosclerosis'. EC institutions, as well as governments of member states, were not seen as terribly succesful in this respect. The fact that the EC has come to play a greater role, however, cannot be seen without taking into account the role of organized interests. Both in cases where the process of integration has gained momentum, and where it has been hampered, we have seen that the interest group factor counts. So, the contribution by Visser and Ebbinghaus on organized labour stresses that questions pertaining to, for instance, the 'social dimension' have not been raised nor significantly furthered by organized labour at a transnational level. The lack of commitment of employers seems to have been detrimental to collective efforts of European labour, and to integration in this field. On the other hand, this has given the Commission and governments an opportunity to 'fill the gap' themselves and address problems related to the labour market. However, there are substantial limits to what the Commission can and will do on its own when organized interests are missing, split or if associations have limited autonomies to negotiate.

Evidence from the sectoral studies has shown that although business has responded in different ways it has nevertheless assumed a significant role in issue identification and policy formulation. But the relationship between organized business and the Commission is by no means characterized by simple unilateral pressures. Business is represented by various actors, and relationships are always of a reciprocal nature.

As a rule associations have been specializing in their own rather narrow domains, and interests have not really been engulfed by already established and encompassing European associations. Their political activity has generally been kept at the sectoral or sometimes even subsectoral level. UNICE, for instance, the voice of manufacturing industries at large, has not been involved in representing the sectors concerned, and Schneider suggests that the peak level should be regarded as consisting of 'horizontal coordination systems'. Effectiveness through smaller and less inclusive associations is preferred to broad compromises and representativeness through peak associations, as many vital issues are so unique that they are completely irrelevant and unknown to firms outside the sector itself. This strategy has led to the proliferation of a plurality of interest organizations.

However, the mere emergence of new technologies does not automatically lead to new associations. Technologies are often cross-sectoral and they are often not linked to a single and well-defined industry, a factor making associability much more difficult. Moreover, it takes time to find out whether older associations are willing to manage the representation of new interests. What has triggered off the formation of transnational associations and their regrouping, if there is any single event behind such 'ignition', often seems to be the initiatives of EC plans to regulate the sector, and the determined efforts of organized business to forestall such regulation or to influence plans and cooperate with the Commission. However, it is difficult to establish cause and effect between regulation and associability. The very formation of transnational associations in sectors or subsectors of new technologies is also driven by a combination of economic concentration, scientific progress, industrial development, representational factors, and last but not least by public policies.

The Commission has not only kept a watchful eye on sectors

because their regulation is somehow more manageable. Its interest has also been triggered because high tech sectors contribute to improved competitiveness. It is neccessary to emphasize that the active role of the Commission has not been a substitute for private activity. On the contrary, it has indeed encouraged not only the initial formation of relevant associations in all sectors analysed here, but has continuously sought to integrate them in policy processes. Indeed, the associations organizing the pharmaceutical industry, biotechnologies and producers of consumer electronics and the telecommunication industries have become recognized as the legitimate representatives of business within each of their domains. At the same time it has not been a difficult task for sector associations to identify the Commission and one or more of its DGs as relevant and strategic partners. Labour, consumers and environmental groups come far down the priority list.

On the other hand, this does not imply that all associations have become equally integrated. To date, the pharmaceutical industry seems to have achieved most, but its associational history is older, its resources are superior to the other sectors and it displays more cohesion. An indication of the more general lack of cohesion is the degree to which individual members feel challenged to act on their own and surpass the association when contacting EC institutions.

A common feature is thus that single large and global corporations (which are numerous in high tech industries) are political actors in their own right. Their attempts to establish links with EC institutions have by no means been futile. All the actors involved apparently seem to accept this specific kind of complementarity of interest representation.

It would, however, not be reasonable just to conclude that associations are incapable of controlling their members, or that associations are entirely letterhead associations with only a legal right to carry their names. The pattern outlined does show that associations are facing certain limits, and that firms act autonomously not only in the market sphere but also in politics. Where common denominators are sought and achieved, the appropriate actor is very often the association. But interactions with large corporations operating on a cross-sectoral basis may also prove to be of value to the Commission.

The Choice of Routes: National and Transnational Avenues

Although the adoption of the Single European Act was a major step forward, nobody can really claim that political integration has made the nation state obsolete and that national political systems with all their traditions have vanished.

The nation state does exist and there is still room for the political activity of interest organizations within this framework. Lanzalaco goes so far as to say that as long as the nation state exists it will remain the main focus of interest organizations, but all chapters emphasize that the choice of routes is a process. The individual contributions of this volume have, to the extent that the national level has been reviewed, also verified its importance. The interesting thing is that the process of integration is not directionless, and the relationship between the sovereign nation state and the emerging, embryonic and still very fragmented supranational EC state is shifting. The nation state has not vanished but the EC has obviously become an increasingly relevant target for private interests. Indisputably, the EC now contains a higher degree of competence than before the passage of the Single European Act.

But how are we to imagine the likely future scenarios of 'stateness' at different levels of political, administrative and institutional complexity and, is it possible to order them in terms of their probability? Answers to this question are difficult to give since analysing the 'stateness' is analysing a moving target. From the perspective of exchanges between interest groups and the EC the likelihood of a federative state, at least in the near future, is small and would undoubtedly require increased competences at the level of both European associations and the EC as such. At the same time the competences at national levels would have to be defined and maintained more clearly. Evidently, the most probable version of the 'EC state' is a state, far from static, that coexists with nation states. However, this is a kind of generalization that does not exclude an unequal distribution of competences across sectors and policy areas.

This is witnessed by the fact that interest groups have accommodated quite differently in choosing the national route (that is, interest representation vis-à-vis national governments in handling purely national problems or EC-related issues) and the transnational route (that is, interest representation vis-à-vis the Commission via transnational groups). Both routes do count, but in some cases the transnational has gained prominence.

Peak associations of both business and labour are still important devices in their national environments, and despite the fact that encompassing organizations in manufacturing industry and in labour were created decades ago in an EC context, national peak associations still seem to prefer the national route. A particular group of firms, the smaller and medium-sized enterprises, also prefer interactions with their paternal government instead of relying on collective action with similar firms in the other member states.

There is quite another story to be told from the sectoral level, although not all sectoral interest groups pay equal attention to the European channel. Some are still pretty much embedded in national arrangements, as shown in the study on telecommunications where strong consumer interests of both private and public nature somehow tied producers to specific national patterns of policy processes. This has in no way excluded the formation of European interest groups nor prevented a few individual but large corporations from entering the European scene, but national governments are after all important targets, not least because they are determining a number of limits and strongly contribute in defining a common telecommunications policy. In the pharmaceutical industry we do find specific national arrangements as well, but here a number of similar issues have reached the political agenda in the individual member states. Common issues and interests have not been hard to identify.

In some sectors transnational routes have proved far more valuable than in others, and become a more or less strong supplement to the traditional and well-entrenched national routes, if they have not surpassed them. The Europeanization of a sector may occur so fast that the formation of a European interest group without national affiliates may become neccessary, as seen in the study by Greenwood and Ronit of the biotechnology case. Here, the introduction of direct firm membership in the biotech association which was initially applied in the form of 'invitations', clearly illustrates the emphasis put on transnational groups and the importance attributed to the transnational route.

The reliance on direct firm membership is a radical new way of organizing interests. This model is hardly applicable everywhere. It seems to be conditioned by the fact that some industries are characterized by a high degree of economic concentration and significant mobility across member states in Europe, and the existence of a limited number of huge corporations with lots of mutual contacts. Federative structures then become slow and are rendered inappropriate. In some cases, organizing in Europe barely requires more than the organization of a few firms, partly because the degree of concentration is high, and because there is not always a need to organize the small and insignificant firms. This is a great advantage, not least to corporations based outside the EC as the Japanese (in the case of consumer electronics) and the Swiss (in pharmaceuticals). Transnational business interest associations generally seem to welcome the membership of such corporations where there is an absence of single paternalistic and nationalistic ties.

The pattern of routes suggests a shift over the past decade where transnational associations have proliferated, or have been revitalized, and where EC policies have been adopted and competences delegated from national governments. The traditional national route has not been abandoned, in that even at this level new groups are emerging trying to accommodate to new demands, but in many cases the importance attributed to this has declined. Nowhere, however, has the transnational route entirely replaced the national route yet, and the relationship between the two routes is still rather complementary. The interesting point, therefore, has been to identify the shifting and relative weight of routes according to such variables as peak and sector levels, social groups, the encompassingness or specialization of interests, and the size of groups. Taken as a whole, however, the weight of routes is shifting towards the transnational route but definitely not by sheer coincidence. Whereas the national route is in principle available to all interests, the transnational route, as an additional option, is a route with more substantial limitations.

A Complex Pattern of Exchanges

Both the formation of the EC in the late 1950s, and the more recent passing of the Single European Act, have posed substantial challenges to private interests, and have led to the burgeoning of European-wide associations. Together with the organizational systems of the individual member states, a plurality of interest groups exist beyond and above nation states. It therefore seems reasonable to ask what kind of interest intermediation has emerged. From our studies it is impossible to draw the conclusion that interest intermediation at the European level is clearly of either a corporatist or pluralist nature. A multitude of groups do exist but they are seldom attempting to organize and represent almost the same European-wide interest categories in interactions with the same parts of the EC apparatus. As Grote demonstrates the small and medium-sized enterprises have associations which partly stand in a competitive relationship to each other, although it must be taken into account that the formation of associations is still in a relatively early stage. A few coordinating forums have already been created which might compensate for fragmentation, and the Commission is not without influence upon such initiatives. The fact that both national and transnational groups sometimes negotiate directly with the EC is not indicative of a truly competitive relationship between various private actors, but should in most cases be interpreted as forming part of a 'dual strategy' of available routes.

At the European level, some evidence of a more corporatist style relationship, with encompassing associations holding a virtual monopoly in representing a certain interest category acknowledged and encouraged by the relevant EC bodies can be found, but again reservations have to be made. The peak associations are, for instance, characterized by a limited degree of hierarchical ordering.

As far as the sectoral level is concerned, some weaker signs of competition can actually be found amongst interests in the telecommunications sector and in biotechnologies, which can be characterized as relatively new industrial areas on the European scene. Their orientation has previously been either rather domestic, or the technology itself new and undeveloped. Thus, the formation of associations has taken place within the past few years, and there seems to have been too little time for finding the most appropriate forms of interest representation, although restructuring measures have continuously been taken to avoid fragmentation, particularly in biotechnologies. In the latter case these have been of an interorganizational nature and have later been followed by the formation of a more encompassing and transsectoral association. Consequently, it would be far more correct to characterize the organization of interests in these industries as partly inefficent, at least in the initial phases, rather than competitive and truly pluralist. In consumer electronics and in pharmaceuticals, single associations represent reasonably well-defined interest categories and are at least in this respect unchallenged.

Indeed, the Commission has not only challenged private interests to such an extent that associations have emerged and been regrouped at the European level. In some cases it has openly encouraged the formation of representative associations. The relationship has been built on reciprocity where associations have shared responsibility for the policies adopted, and in some cases (for example, in the pharmaceutical industry) the overseeing of self regulation has been offered and accepted as a viable alternative to public regulation.

All sector associations are, however, relatively specialized. Interest aggregation thus stops at a modest level. Affiliation to wider associations can be found, but preference is for independent actions. Newly emergent interests are represented by small and narrow associations, instead of being absorbed by already established ones. In this sense the demand of neo-corporatist studies that 'encompassingness' is a fundamental criterion cannot be met in any of our sector-related studies. We have been investigating various producer groups facing heavily specialized issues, closely related to particular articles. Under these circumstances it would be useless or even impossible to find any common denominator with other producer groups. The associations reviewed here seem to have recognized this banal fact.

Another problem is of course the degree of collective action and compliance-seeking among members. Most associations are of recent origin, and have had limited time to find their own style. Associations representing firms in biotechnologies, telecommunications and consumer electronics have been relatively under-resourced, and are weak in this respect when compared to the often large corporations they are supposed to represent, and the challenges they are facing. Hierarchical control is weak.

Sectors are sometimes heavily concentrated, and large firms are present in all the sectors studied in this volume. Therefore, it would be unrealistic to expect such members to be straightforwardly controlled by their association, a feature highlighted in neo-corporatist theory. Instead we should regard these relationships as voluntary, albeit the firms have been pressed by competitors and the political environment to enter into some sort of compromise.

It would also be unwise to consider the resources of an association as the only political potential of business. Firms, particularly the larger ones, possess these as well and associations can draw upon them. In other words, firms do replace associations or groups and enter into direct contacts with the Commission. Elements of such exchanges have been identified in some of the sector studies in this volume and are characterized as micro-corporatist in Cawson's analysis of the consumer electronics industry (chapter 4). Consequently, associations in the sectors concerned cannot be said to hold a monopoly in representing a particular industry, including its individual firms.

A number of larger firms take solo actions whereas smaller and middle-sized firms have to rely on associative action. The individual option is generally chosen in addition to the associational one, as free-riding is apparently not practised among large firms. This is particularly the case when the issue is too specific for an association to handle or where no proper association is yet available, as is the case with the consumer electronics industry. In such cases the firm can be considered a legitimate negotiation partner, although it lacks the broader legitimacy inherent in traditional associative action. However, the emergence of associations has not brought individual firm actions to a halt.

Although a number of the hallmarks typically associated with what has been termed meso and micro variants of corporatism can be found at the EC level, no sound macro corporatist arrangements appear to prevail. Once these arrangements belonged to the flagship of the theory, and much has been said and written about these. At the EC level collective bargaining has been wrapped up by much rhetoric and much optimism has been voiced too, but little progress has been achieved so far, although encompassing associations have organized labour and business for decades. Neo-corporatist arrangements at the EC level are often bilateral or sometimes even multilateral in character but nowhere, neither in the high tech sectors nor in regions, does the arrangement strictly depend on the simultaneous participation and consent of labour and capital. From a political point of view modest encouragement has been given, both historically and after the passing of the Single European Act.

In a period where emphasis has been put on other aspects of integration, other types of relationships between interest groups and EC institutions have emerged at lower and more manageable levels of interest intermediation. These arrangements may look less grandiose but nevertheless they all touch upon the major problem of creating a single European market from a very pragmatic point of view.

Concluding Remarks

A few years have passed since the project of creating a single European market was launched. Actually, the idea of a single market was part and parcel of the original plan behind the EC but it has certainly gained momentum since it was officially adopted in 1986 and put into a coherent framework.

It seems clear that the eventual success of such a project is hardly imaginable without interest groups organized beyond the nation state. Accordingly, associations have continuously proliferated, regrouped and coordinated interests during the last years in order to accommodate growing expectations from both members and EC institutions. A significant number of associations have recently emerged and joined those brought to life since the late 1950s, and the European route has been given higher priority both by national and transnational associations.

However, variations do exist in respect to the way interests are organized and the role they perform. Capital is easier to organize transnationally than is labour, but not all business groups are responding equally to new challenges. Peak associations of business are not playing the leading role in representing interests vis-à-vis the

Commission and its directorates. Sector associations generally seem to be far more important, and small worlds of partnerships or networks between state and interest groups of particular industries have emerged. Numerous initiatives have been launched at these levels by the EC, something which has not excluded private action. On the contrary, the formation and integration of interest groups have been given great encouragement. But again sectoral interests are not always easily manageable, and this paves the way for single firms bypassing associations or other groups, either because they prefer to act on their own or because they use associations as complementary units to mediate interests.

This pattern does not resemble typified standard versions of corporatism at national levels. However, the fact that corporatist-style exchange relations have indeed been established, primarily below the level of peak associations, suggests that rejections of their viability have been premature and have somewhat rested on speculation.

The fact that interactions between state and organized interests are now structured along several national and transnational lines, with actors equipped with unclear competences, complicates both the analysis itself and also the ability to 'corporatize' such interactions. Under these circumstances it must be taken into account that the maturation of this particular kind of arrangement takes time.

Alternatively, it requires that new coordinating mechanisms are created as either permanent or *ad hoc* solutions, which for their part need further conceptualization.

Bibliography

ACARD   Advisory Council for Applied Research and Development
API   Associazione delle Piccole Imprese
BIA   Bio Industry Association
CEC   Commission of the European Communities
CERVED   Societa Nazionale di Informatica delle Camere di Commercio,
               Industria, Artigianato, Agricoltura
CGIA   Confederazione Generale Italiana dell'Artigianato (Confartigianato)
CNA   Confederazione Nazionale dell'Artigianato
Confindustria Confederazione Generale dell'Industria Italiana
DIHT   Deutscher Industrie- und Handelstag (German Chamber of
               Industry and Commerce)
ECOSOC   Economic and Social Committee of the European Commission
ECPR   European Consortium for Political Research
EFPIA   European Federation of Pharmaceutical Industry Associations
ETUC   European Trade Union Confederation
EUI   European University Institute
IEA   Institute of Economic Affairs
IFPMA   International Federation of Pharmaceutical Manufacturing
               Associations
IIM   International Institute of Management
IIRA   International Industrial Relations Association
ILERI   Institut Libre d'Etude des Relations Internationales
IPSA   International Political Science Association
IRE   Industrial Relations Europe
ITU   International Telecoms Union
OECD   Organization for Economic Cooperation and Development
UACES   University Association for Contemporary European Studies
UEAPME   Union Europeene de l'Artisanat et des Petites et Moyennes
               Entreprises
UNICE   Union of Industrial and Employers Confederations of Europe
WZB   Wissenschaftszentrum (Social Science Centre), Berlin.

Official Documents

ACARD (1980) *Report of Joint Working Party of the Advisory Council for Applied Research and Development and the Advisory Board for the Research Councils and the Royal Society* (The Spinks Report). London: HMSO

API Toscana (1989) *La piccola impresa, l'associazionismo, i servizi avanzati in Toscana* (Rapporto 1989). Florence: API

API Toscana (1991) 'Piccole e medie imprese si uniscono', *Strategie. Periodico dell'API Toscana CONFAPI*, III (1–2), January–February 1991

BIA (1991) *BIA Bulletin: News from Europe* 10 March 1991. London: BIA

BIOFUTUR (1989) 'La bioindustrie s'organise', *BIOFUTUR*, 84 (November), pp.41–2

CEC (1986) SME Action Programme. COM(86)445 final. Brussels: CEC

CEC (1988a) 'An Enterprise Policy for the Community. Creating a Favourable Environment for Enterprise and Promoting Business Development in the Evolving European Market'. COM(88)241. Brussels: Task Force SME

CEC (1988b) 'The European Community and Cooperation among Small and Medium-Sized Enterprises', in *European File*, No.11, June–July

CEC (1988c) 'The Community and Business: the Action Programme for Small and Medium-Sized Enterprises', in *European File*, No.3, February, pp.32–7

CEC (1988d) 'The Social Dimension of the Internal Market. Interim Report of the Interdepartmental Working Party', in *Social Europe*, Special Edition. Brussels: DG V of the EC Commission

CEC (1989a) 'Proposal for a Council Decision Relating to the Improvement of the Business Environment and the Promotion of the Development of Enterprises, in Particular of Small and Medium-Sized Enterprises, in the Community'. COM(89)102 final. Brussels, 7 March

CEC (1989b) *The Rules Governing Medicinal Products in the European Community*, vol 1: *Rules Governing Medicinal Products for Human Use in the European Community*. Brussels: CEC

CEC (1989c) Preliminary Draft Proposal for a Council Directive on Pharmaceutical Advertising. Revision 2, 111/8118/89. Brussels: CEC

CEC (1989d) 'Future System for the Authorisation of Medicinal Products', in *European Biotechnology Information Service*, 4 (July). Brussels: CEC

CEC (1990a) Appendix to the 1990 Budget: SEC(90)2025 def.; 19.10.1990, part three/A

CEC (1990b) 'The Social Dimension', in *European Documentation*, 2/1990 (4th edn). Luxemburg: Office for Official Publications of the EC

CEC (1991a) *European Social Dialogue – Joint Opinions*. Brussels: DG V of the EC Commission

CEC (1991b) 'European Industrial Policy for the 1990s', in *Bulletin of the European Communities*, Suppl. 3/91. Brussels: CEC

CEC (1992) *Directory of European Trade and Professional Associations*. Luxembourg: Office for Official Publications of the EC.

CERVED (1989) 'Analisi della struttura imprenditoriale dell'artigianato. Un esempio di applicazione delle metodologie di cluster analysis ai dati dell'Albo delle Imprese Artigiane'. (Presented at La Conferenza Nazionale sull'Artigianato, Florence, 21–22 April, 1989)

CERVED (1991) *Movimprese – Varazioni Semestrali nell'Anagrafe delle Imprese Italiane*. No. 1, new series. Padua: Societa' Nazionale de Informatica delle Camere di Commercio, Industria, Artigianato, Agricolutra

CGIA (1990) *Confartigianato Riepilogo dati statistici associativi* (Direzione Centrale dell'Organizzazione). Rome: CGIA

CNA (1991) Confederazione Nazionale dell'Artigianato e delle Piccole e Medie Imprese. Rome: CNA

Confindustria (1980) *Le parti sociali in Europa: le organizzazioni dei datori di lavoro*. Rome: Confindustria

Democrazia Cristiana (1959) *Atti dei Congressi*. Rome: Cinque Lune

DIHT (1987) *Industrie – und Handelskammern in der Bundesrepublik Deutschland*. Bonn: DIHT

DIHT (1989) *Wegweiser zum EG-Binnenmarkt* (3rd edn). Bonn: DIHT

EBIS (1991) Eugreen Biotechnology Information Service, Issue No.4, Brussels: EBIS.

ECMA (1991) European Computer Manufacturers Association, Memento 1991, Geneva

ECOSOC (1980) *European Interest Groups and their Relationships with the Economic and Social Committee*. Published by the Economic and Social Committee of the European Communities. Westmead: Saxon House

EFPIA (1988) *Ten Years of EFPIA* (Annual Report 1988). Brussels: EFPIA

EFPIA (1990a) *European Code of Practice for the Promotion of Medicines*. Brussels: EFPIA

EFPIA (1990b) *A Brief Guide to the EEC Directives Concerning Medicines*. Brussels: EFPIA

ETUC (1987) *Profile of the ETUC* (info. no. 21,). Brussels: ETUC

Eurostat (1989) *Statistische Grundzahlen der Gemeinschaft*. Luxemburg: Office for Official Publications of the EC

IFPMA (1984) *Code of Pharamaceutical Marketing Practices*. Geneva: IFPMA

ITU (1990) International Telecom Union, Yearbook of Public Telecommunications Statistics, 17th edn, Geneva

OECD (1983) *Telecommunications. Pressures and Policies for Change*. Paris: OECD

OIE (Organisation Internationale des Employers) (1984), *Principles Caracteristiques de ses Federations Membres*, Bruxelles, mimeo.

Partito Socialista Italiano (1991) *Europa '93: Una strategia per l'artigianato* (Supplement to no.1, *Argomenti socialisti*). Rome: Edar Libri

Revue Internationale PME (1988) *Economie et gestion de la petite et moyenne entreprise*. 1 (1), Brussels, mimeo DGXXIII of the European Communities

UEAPME (1989) *EG–Entwicklung und Politik für Handwerk, Klein- und Mittelbetriebe: Jahresbericht 1989*. Brussels: UEAPME

UEAPME (1990) *Europaisches Sprachrohr des Handwerks und der Klein- und Mittelbetriebe*. Brussels: UEAPME

UNICE (1990) 'Bilan de quatre années de fonctionnement de la fiche d'impact. Proposition de l'UNICE pour l'amelioration du systèmes. Mimeo, Brussels

Literature

Agenzia Industriale Italiana (1986) 'Italy (Country report)', in Paul Burns and Jim Dewhurst (eds), *Small Business in Europe*. London: Macmillan, pp. 99–130

Aldrich, Howard and Ellen R. Auster (1986) 'Even Dwarfs Started Small: Liabilities of Age and Size and Their Strategic Implications', in H. Aldrich, E.R. Auster, U.H. Staber and C. Zimmer (eds), *Population Perspectives on Organizations*. Uppsala: Acta Universitatis Upsaliensis (Studia Oeconomiae Negotiorum 25), pp. 29–61

Aldrich, Howard and David A. Whetton (1981) 'Organization Sets, Action Sets, and Networks: Making the Most of Simplicity' in Paul C. Nystrom and William H. Starbuck (eds), *Handbook of Organizational Design*: Vol. 1, *Adapting Organizations to Their Environments*. Oxford: Oxford University Press, pp. 385–408

Aldrich, Howard and Catherine Zimmer (1986) 'Entrepreneurship through Social Networks', in Donald L. Sexton and Raymond W. Smiler (eds), *The Art and Science of Entrepreneurship*. Cambridge, Mass: Ballinger

Allen, Christopher S. (1989) 'Corporatism and Regional Economic Policies in the Federal Republic of Germany: the "Meso" Politics of Industrial Adjustment', *Publius: The Journal of Federalism*, 19 (Fall 1989): 147–64

Amin, Ash (1989) 'Flexible Specialization and Small Firms in Italy: Myths and Realities', *Antipode*, 21 (1): 13–34

Amin, Ash and Kevin Robins (1990) 'Industrial Districts and Regional Development: Limits and Possibilities', in F. Pyke, W. Sengenberger and G. Becattini (eds), *Industrial Districts and Inter-firm Cooperation in Italy*. Geneva: International Institute for Labour Studies (ILO)

Anderson, Jeffrey J. (1988) 'Territorial Networks of Interest in Britain and Germany: Regions and the Politics of Economic Decline'. PhD dissertation, Yale University. Ann Arbor: University of Michigan

Anderson, Jeffrey J. (1990a) 'When Market and Territory Collide: Thatcherism and the Politics of Regional Decline', *West European Politics*, 13 (2): 234–57

Anderson, Jeffrey J. (1990b) 'Skeptical Reflections on a Europe of Regions: Britain, Germany and the ERDF', *Journal of Public Policies*, 10 (4): 417–47

Anderson, Jeffrey J. (1991) 'Business Associations and the Decentralization of Penury: Functional Groups and Territorial Interests', *Governance*, 4 (1): 67–94

Andrews, W.G. (1991) 'Corporatist Representation in European International and Supranational Organizations'. Paper presented at the Panel on 'Changing Relations between Organized Business and Labour'. 15th World Congress of the International Political Science Association, Buenos Aires, 21–25 July 1991

Atkinson, Michael M. and William D. Coleman (1989) 'Strong States and Weak States: Sectoral Policy Networks in Advanced Capitalist Economies', *British Journal of Political Science*, 19: 47–67

Audretsch, D.B. (1989) *The Market and the State: Government Policy Towards Business in Europe, Japan and the USA*. New York: Harvester Wheatsheaf

Averyt, W. (1975) 'Eurogroups, Clientela, and the European Community', *International Organizations*, 29 (4): 949–72

Averyt, W. (1977) *Agro Politics in the European Community: Interest Groups and the Common Agricultural Policy*. New York: Praeger

Avorn, J.L. (1982) 'Scientific versus Commercial Sources of Influence upon the Prescribing Behaviour of Physicians', *American Journal of Medicine*, 73: 4–8

Baggott, R. (1986) 'By Voluntary Agreement: the Politics of Instrument Selection', *Public Administration*, 64: 51–67

Baglioni, Guido and Colin Crouch (eds) (1990) *European Industrial Relations. The Challenge of Flexibility*. London: Sage

Baglioni, Guido, Rinaldo Milani and Ettore Santi (1987) *Le relazioni sindacali in Italia*. Rapporto CESOS 1985/86. Rome: Edizioni Lavoro

Bagnasco, Arnaldo (1977) *Tre Italie. La problematica territoriale dello sviluppo italiano*. Bologna: Il Mulino

Bagnasco, Arnaldo (1988) *La costruzione sociale del mercato*. Bologna: Il Mulino

Balfour, C. (1972) *Industrial Relations in the Common Market*. London: Routledge and Kegan Paul

Barnounin, B. (1987) *The European Labour Movement and European Integration*. London: Frances Pinter

Bates, E. (1990) 'Outsiders Inside', *European Management Journal*, 8(4):4

Baun, Michael (1990) 'Europe 1992 and Trade Union Politics: Towards a European Industrial Relations System?'. Paper presented at the Seventh International Conference of Europeanists, Washington DC, 23–25 March 1990

Becattini, Giacomo (ed.) (1987) *Mercato e forze locali. Il distretto industriale*. Bologna: Il Mulino

Becattini, Giacomo (1989a) 'Riflessioni sul distretto industriale marshalliano come concetto socio economico', *Stato e Mercato*, 25: 11–29

Becattini, Giacomo (1989b) 'Sectors and/or districts: some remarks on the conceptual foundations of industrial economies', in E. Goodman, J. Bamford and P. Saynor (eds), *Small Firms and Industrial Districts in Italy*. London: Routledge.

Becattini, Giacomo (1990a) 'The Marshallian industrial district as a socio-economical notion', in F. Pyke, G. Becattini and W. Sengenberger (eds), *Industrial Districts and Inter-firm Cooperation in Italy*. Geneva: International Institute for Labour Studies (ILO), pp.37–52

Becattini, Giacomo (1990b) 'Italy (country report)', in Werner Sengenberger, Gary M. Loveman and Michael J. Piore (eds), *The Re-Emergence of Small Enterprises*, Geneva: International Institute for Labour Studies (ILO), pp.144–73

Bellini, Nicola (1990) 'The management of the economy in Emilia-Romagna: the PCI and the regional experience', in Robert Leonardi and Raffaella Y. Nanetti (eds), *The Regions and European Integration – The Case of Emilia-Romagna*. London and New York: Pinter, pp.109–24

Benson, J.K. (1982) 'A Framework for Policy Analysis', in D.L. Rodgers and D.A. Whetton (eds), *Interorganizational Coordination*. Ames: Iowa University Press

Berger, Suzanne (1975) 'Uso politico e sopravivenza dei ceti in declino', in F.B. Cavazza and S.R. Graubard (eds) *Il caso italiano*. Milan: Garzanti

Berger, Suzanne (1980) 'The traditional sector in France and Italy', in Suzanne Berger and Michael Piore, *Dualism and Discontinuity in Industrial Societies*. Cambridge: Cambridge University Press

Berger, Suzanne (ed) (1981) *Organizing Interests in Western Europe*. Cambridge: Cambridge University Press

Berghahn, Volker (1984) 'Ideas into Politics: the Case of Ludwig Ehrhard', in R. Bullen, M. Pogge von Strandmann and A.B. Polonsky (eds), *Ideas into Politics: Aspects of European History 1880–1950*. London: Croom Helm, pp.178–92

Bianchi, Giuliano (1990) 'Innovating in the Local Systems of Small and Medium Sized Enterprises', in *Entrepreneurship and Regional Development*, 2

Bianchi, Giuliano and Jürgen R. Grote (1991) 'Come creare ordine dalla confusione? Progettazione e attuazione dei Programmi Integrati Mediterranei', in Flavio Boscacci and Gianluigi Gorla (eds), *Economie locali in ambiente competitivo*. Milan: Franco Angeli, pp.309–39

Bianchi, Patrizio (1990) 'Le politiche industriali per le piccole e medie imprese e il riorientamento delle politiche comunitarie', in *Rivista di Politica Economic*, LXXX, serie III, fascicolo V: 171–203

Bieber, R., R. Dehousse, J. Pinder and J. Weiler (eds) (1988) *1992: One European Market? A Critical Analysis of the Commission's Internal Market Strategy*. Baden-Baden: Nomos Verlagsgesellschaft

Birkinshaw, P., I. Harden and N. Lewis (1990) *Government by Moonlight*. London: Unwin Hyman

Blanchflower, D.G. and R. Freeman (1990) 'Going Different Ways: Unionism in the US and Other Advanced OECD Countries'. London: LSE–Centre for Economic Performance. Discussion Paper no.5

Blanpain, R. (1972) 'Efforts to Bring About Community-level Collective Bargaining in the Coal and Steel Community and the EEC', in H. Günther (ed.), *Transnational Industrial Relations. The Impact of Multinational Corporations and Economic Regionalism on Industrial Relations*. London: Macmillan–St Martin's Press, pp.275–308

Blim, Michael L. (1990) *Made in Italy. Small-Scale Industrialization and its*

Consequences. New York and London: Praeger

Blyth, C. (1979) 'The Interaction between Collective Bargaining and Government Policies in Selected Member Countries', in OECD (ed.), *Collective Bargaining and Government Policies*. Paris: OECD

Bonnett, Kevin (1985) 'Corporatism and Thatcherism: Is There Life After Death?', in Alan Cawson (ed), *Organized Interests and the State*. London: Sage

Bornschier, Volker and Hanspeter Stamm (1990) 'Transnational Corporations', in Alberto Martinelli and Neil J. Smelser (eds), *Economy and Society. Overviews in Economic Sociology*. London: Sage, pp.203–29

Bosso, C.J. (1988) 'Transforming Adversaries into Collaborators – Interest-Groups and the Regulation of Chemical Pesticides', in *Policy Sciences*, 21:3–22

Bouvard, M. (1972) *Labour Movements in the Common Market: The Growth of a Pressure Group*. New York: Praeger

Bowman, J.R. (1982) 'The Logic of Capitalist Collective Action', *Social Science Information*, 21 (4–5)

Braithwaite, J. (1984) *Corporate Crime in the Pharmaceutical Industry*. London: Routledge and Kegan Paul

Braunthal, G. (1965) *The Federation of German Industry in Politics*. Ithaca, NY: Cornell University Press

Brunetta, Renato and Carlo Dell'Aringa (eds) (1990) *Labour Relations and Economic Performance*. Proceedings of a Conference held by the International Economic Association in Venice. London: Macmillan

Brusco, Sebastiano (1989) *Piccole imprese e distretti industriali*. Turin: Rosenberg and Sellier

Brusco, S. and M. Pezzini (1990) 'Small-scale enterprise in the ideology of the Italian left', in F. Pyke, G. Becattini and W. Sengenberger (eds) *Industrial Districts and Inter-firm Cooperation in Italy*. Geneva: International Institute for Labour Studies (ILO), pp.142–60

Bryant C.G.A. (1991) 'Europe and the European Community 1992', *Sociology* 25(2): 189–207

Buda, Dirk (1991) *Auf dem Weg zum europaischen Betriebsrat*. Reihe Eurokolleg 6. Bonn: Friedrich Ebert Stiftung

Buda, Dirk and Jean Vogel (1989) *L'Europe Sociale 1992. Illusion, Alibi où Réalité?* Rapport no.2 (Etude pour le Secretatiat d'Etat à l'Europe 1992). Brussels: Université Libre

Burns, Paul and Jim Dewhurst (eds) (1986) *Small Business in Europe*. London: Macmillan

Burstall, M.L. (1985) 'The Community's Pharmaceutical Industry', Commission of the European Communities. Luxemburg: CEC

Burstall, M.L. (1990) *1992 and the Regulation of the Pharmaceutical Industry*. London: IEA

Busch, Peter and Donald Puchala (1976) 'Interests, Influence and Integration: Political Structure in the European Communities', *Comparative Political Studies*, 9 (3): 223–54

Butt Philip, Alan (1983a) 'Pressure Groups and Policy-Making in the European Community', in J. Lodge (ed.), *Institutions and Policies of the European Community*. London: Frances Pinter, pp.21–7

Butt Philip, Alan (1983b) 'Pressure Groups and European Community Decision-making', in J. Lodge (ed.), *The European Community. Bibliographical Excursions*. London: Frances Pinter, pp.47–56

Butt Philip, Alan (1985a) *Pressure Groups in the European Community*. London: UACES Occasional Papers, 2

Butt Philip, Alan (1985b) 'Corporatism and Accountability in the European Community'. Mimeo, University of Bath, prepared for ESRC Corporatism and Accountability Research Programme. *ESRC/CA News – Corporatism and Accountability*, 1:10

Cameron, David R. (1990) 'Sovereign States in a Single Market: Integration and Intergovernmentalism in the European Community'. Paper presented at the Conference on European Political Institutions and Policy-Making after 1992, the Brookings Institution, 29–30 March 1990

Campbell, John L. and Leon N. Lindberg (1991) 'The Evolution of Governance Regimes', in John L. Campbell, J. Rogers Hollingworth and Leon N. Lindberg (eds), *Governance of the American Economy*. Cambridge, Mass.: Cambridge University Press

Campbell, John L., J. Rogers Hollingworth and Leon N. Lindberg (eds) (1991) *Governance of the American Economy*. Cambridge, Mass.: Cambridge University Press

Caporaso, James A. (1974) *The Structure and Function of the European Community*. Pacific Palisades: Goodyear Publishers

Caporaso, James A. (1979) 'The Emergent European Community: Problems of Interest Group Hedonism'. Paper presented at ECPR Joint Sessions of Workshops. Brussels, April 1979

Cawson, Alan (1982) *Corporatism and Welfare: Social Policy and State Intervention in Britain*. London: Heinemann Educational Books

Cawson, Alan (1985a) 'Corporatism and Local Politics in Britain', in Wyn Grant (ed), *The Political Economy of Corporatism*. London: Macmillan

Cawson, Alan (ed.) (1985b) *Organized Interests and the State*. London: Sage

Cawson, Alan (1991) 'Running a High Tech Industry: Consumer Electronics'. Unit 13 for Open University Course D212 'Running the Country'

Cawson, A., K. Morgan, D. Webber, P. Holmes, and A. Stevens, (1990) *Hostile Brothers: Competition and Closure in the European Electronics Industry*. Oxford: Clarendon Press

Cecchini, Paolo (1988) *1992 – The Benefits of a Single Market*. Aldershot: Wildwood House

Cerny, Phil (1991) 'The Limits of Deregulation: Transnational Interpenetration and Policy-Change', *European Journal of Political Research*, 19 (2): 173–96

Chrisaffis, T. (1988) 'Intra-European Trade in Consumer Electronics Products'. Draft chapter for DPhil thesis, University of Sussex

Clegg, H.A. (1976) *Trade Unions under Collective Bargaining. A Theory Based on Comparisons of Six Countries*. Oxford: Basil Blackwell

Colebatch, H. (1991) 'Getting Our Act Together: A Case Study in Regulation and Explanation'. Paper presented to the Government/Business Study Group at the XVth World Congress of the International Political Science Association, Buenos Aires, 21–25 July, 1991

Coleman, James S. (1972) 'Systems of social exchange', *Journal of Mathematical Sociology*, 2:145–63

Coleman, William D. and Wyn Grant (1988) 'The Organizational Cohesion and Political Access of Business: a Study of Comprehensive Associations', *European Journal of Political Research*, 16: 467–87

Coleman, William D. and Henry J. Jacek (eds) (1989a) *Regionalism, Business*

Interests and Public Policy. Sage Series in Neo-Corporatism. London: Sage (in association with European University Institute, Florence)

Coleman, William D. and Henry J. Jacek (1989b) 'Capitalists, Collective Action and Regionalism: an Introduction', in William D. Coleman and Henry J. Jacek (eds) _Regionalism, Business Interests and Public Policy_. London: Sage, pp.1–13

Collins, Randall (1988) _Theoretical Sociology_. New York: Harcourt Brace Jovanovich

Commons, J. (1932) 'Labour Movement', in _Encyclopedia of the Social Sciences_, vol. III. London: Macmillan

Cooke, P. (1988) 'Flexible Integration, Scope Economies, and Strategic Alliances: Social and Spatial Mediations', _Environment and Planning D: Society and Space_, 6: 281–300

Coombes, David (1981) 'Consultative Machinery for the Social Policy of the European Community'. Paper presented at the meeting of the International Political Science Association's Research Committee on European Unification, Brussels, 1981

Cordaro, G. (1990) 'Towards 1992: The European Community Telecommunications Policy', _Telecommunications_, January 1990, pp. 33–5

Crouch, Colin (1985) 'Corporatism in Industrial Relations – A Formal Model', in Wyn Grant (ed.), _The Political Economy of Corporatism_. London: Macmillan, pp. 63–89

Crouch, Colin (1986) 'Le origini storiche dei rapporti tra stati e interessi nell'Europa Occidentale', _Stato e Mercato_, 18

Crouch, Colin (1990a) 'Generalized Political Exchange in Industrial Relations in Europe during the Twentieth Century', in Bernd Marin (ed), _Governance and Generalized Exchange. Self-Organizing Policy Networks in Action_. European Centre for Social Welfare Policy and Research, Campus Westview, pp 69–117

Crouch, Colin (1990b) _Corporatism and Accountability: Organized Interests in British Public Life_. Oxford: Oxford University Press

Crozier, Michel and Ehrhard Friedberg (1980) _Actors and Systems_. Chicago: Chicago University Press

Dang N'guyen, G. (1985) 'Telecommunications: A Challenge to the Old Order', in Margeret Sharp (ed), _Europe and the New Technologies. Six Case Studies in Innovation and Adjustment_. London: Frances Pinter, pp. 87–133

Dang N'guyen, G. (1988) 'Telecommunications in France', in J. Foreman-Peck and J. Muller (eds), _European Telecommunications Organizations_. Baden-Baden: Nomos Verlagsgesellschaft pp. 131–54

Debunne, G. (1987) _Les syndicats et l'Europe. Passé et devenir_. Brussels: Labor

Dehousse, Reynaud, (1989) '1992 and Beyond: the Institutional Dimension of the Internal Market Programme', in Reynaud Dehousse and Joseph Weiler (eds), _Legal Issues of European Integration_. Berlin and New York: De Gruyter

Deppe, Frank, J. Huffschmid and K.P. Weiner (eds) (1989) _1992 – Projekt Europa. Politik und Oekonomie in der Europaeischen Gemeinschaft_. Cologne: Pahl-Rugenstein Verlag

Denton, G. (1968) 'Germany', in G. Denton et al. (eds), _Economic Planning and Policies in Britain, France and Germany_. London: Allen and Unwin

De Vroom, B. (1987) 'El desarollo de un nuevo "estado" y la evolucion de las asociaciones de interes. El caso de las asociaciones de intereses empresariales a nivel de Comunidad Europea', in Carlota Sole (ed.), _Corporatismo y Diferenciacion Regional_. Madrid: Ministerio de Trabajo y Seguridad Social, pp. 55–69 di Palma, Guiseppe (1987) 'The Available State: Problems of Reform', in Peter Lange and Sydney Tarrow (eds), *Italy in Transition. Conflict and Consensus*. London: Frank Cass, pp. 149–65

Dore, Ronald (1990) 'Two Kinds of Rigidity: Corporate Communities and Collectivism', in Renato Brunetta and Carlo Dell'Aringa (eds) *Proceedings of a Conference held by the International Economic Association in Venice (Italy)*. London: Macmillan, pp. 92–114

Duchene, F. and G. Shepherd (eds) (1987) *Managing Industrial Change in Western Europe*. London and New York: Frances Pinter

Due, J., J.S. Madsen and C.S. Jensen (1991) 'The Social Dimension: Convergence or Diversification of IR in the Single Market?', *Industrial Relations Journal*, 22 (2): 85–102

Dunleavy, P. (1990) *Democracy, Bureaucracy and Public Choice*. London: Harvester Wheatsheaf

Dyson, K. (1991) 'Die Entwicklung der Telekommunikation in Westeuropa', in E. Grande, R. Kuhlen, G. Lehmbruch and H. Mading (eds) *Perspektiven der Telekommunikationspolitik*. Opladen: Westdeutscher, pp. 43–68

Dyson, K. and P. Humphreys (eds) (1990) *The Political Economy of Communications. International and European Dimensions*. London and New York: Routledge

Ebbinghaus, Bernhard and Jelle Visser (1990) 'Where does Trade Union Diversity Come From?'. Paper presented at the XIIth World Congress of Sociology – Working Group on Labour Movements, Madrid, 10–14 July 1990

Ebbinghaus, B.O., J. Visser and W. Pfenning (1992) *The Structure of Trade Union Systems in Western Europe. A Data Handbook*, vol. 1. Frankfurt and New York: Campus

Elias, D. (1980) 'Die Nutzung der Fernmeldedienste', in E. Witte (ed), *Telekommunikation fur den Menschen. Individuelle und gesellschaftliche Wirkungen*. Berlin: Springer, pp. 92–106

Ellwein, Thomas, Joachim Jens Hesse, Renate Mayntz and Wolfgang F. Scharfp (eds) (1990) *Jahrbuch zur Staats- und Verwaltungswissenschaft*, vol. 4. Baden-Baden: Nomos Verlagsgesellschaft

Emerson, Michael (1988) 'The Economics of 1992', *European Economy*, 35 (March)

Enderwick, Peter (1982) 'Labour and the Theory of the Multinational Corporation', *Industrial Relations Journal*, 13 (Summer): 32–43

Enderwick, Peter (1984) 'The Labour Utilisation Practices of Multinationals and Obstacles to Multinational Bargaining', *Journal of Industrial Relations*, 26 (September): 345–64

Farry, Catherine and Wolfgang Streeck (1991) 'Polities Without Borders: Unions and Industrial Relations in the Regional Economies of the European Internal Market'. Mimeo. Madison: University of Wisconsin

Fennema, M. and H. Schijf (1985) 'The Transnational Network', in F. Stokman, R. Ziegler and J. Scott (eds), *Networks of Corporate Power*. Cambridge: Polity Press, pp. 267–88

Forndran, Ehrhard (1983) 'Interessenvermittlung und internationale Beziehungen. Zur Relevanz von Neokorporatismus in der internationalen Politik', in U. von Alemann and E. Forndran (eds), *Interessenvermittlung und Politik*. Opladen: Westdeutscher

Franzmeyer, Fritz (1988) 'Economic, Social and Political Costs of Completing the Internal Market', in R. Bieber, R. Dehousse, J. Pinder and J. Weiler (eds) *One*

European Market? A Critical Analysis of the Commission's Internal Market Srategy, Baden-Baden: Nomos Verlagsgesellschaft

Freeman, Gary P. (1985) 'National Styles and Policy Sectors: Explaining Structured Variation', *Journal of Public Policy*, 5 (4): 467–96

Freeman, R.P. (1990) 'On the Divergence in Unionism among Developed Countries', in Renato Brunetta and Carlo Dell'Aringa (eds) *Proceedings of a Conference held by the International Economic Association in Venice (Italy)* London: Macmillan

Garmise, Shari Orris and Jürgen R. Grote (1990) 'Economic Performance and Social Embeddedness: Emilia-Romagna in an Interregional Perspective', in Robert Leonardi and Raffaella Y. Nanetti (eds), *The Regions and European Integration: The Case of Emilia-Romagna*. London and New York: Frances Pinter, pp. 59–83 (Italian version published 1991, Milan: Franco Angeli Editori)

Genschel, P. and R. Werle (1992) 'From Hierarchical Coordination to International Standardization in Telecommunications'. MPFG Discussion Paper 1992/1. Cologne: Max Planck Gesellschaft für Gesellschaftsforschung

Goetschy, J. (1991) '1992 and the Social Dimension: Normative Frames, Social Actors and Content', *Economic and Industrial Democracy*, 12: 259–75

Goetschy, J. and D. Linhard (1990) *Le crise des syndicats en Europe occidentale*. Paris: La documentation française

Gold, M. and M. Hall (1991) 'Information and Consultation in European Multinational Companies and Evaluation of Practice'. Paper presented at Nordic Council Conference, Copenhagen

Goldthorpe, John H. (1984) 'The End of Convergence: Corporatist and Dualist Tendencies in Modern Western Societies', in John H. Goldthorpe (ed.), *Order and Conflict in Contemporary Capitalism. Studies in the Political Economy of Western European Nations*. Oxford: Clarendon Press, pp. 315–44

Grabher, Gernot (1990) 'The Weakness of Strong Ties: The Ambivalent Role of Inter-firm Cooperation in the Decline and Reorganization of the Ruhr'. Paper presented at the conference on 'Networks – On the Socio-Economics of Inter-Firm Cooperation', organized by WZB Research Area Labour Market and Employment, Berlin, 11–13 June 1990

Grabher, G. (1991) 'Against De-Industrialization: A Strategy for Old Industrial Areas', in Egon Matzner and Wolfgang Streeck (eds), *Beyond Keynesianism: The Socio-Economics of Production and Full Employment*. Aldershot: Edward Elgar, pp. 62–81

Grande, Edgar (1989) *Vom Monopol zum Wettbewerb. Die neokonservative Reform der Telekommunikation in Grossbritannien und der Bundesrepublik Deutschland*. Wiesbaden: Deutscher Universitatsverlag

Grande, Edgar and Volker Schneider (1991) 'Reformstrategien und staatliche Handlungskapazitaten. Eine vergleichende Analyse institutionellen Wandels in der Telekommunikation in Westeuropa', *Politische Vierteljahresschrift*, 32: 452–78

Granovetter, M. (1973) 'The Strength of Weak Ties', *American Journal of Sociology*, 78 (6): 1360–80 (reprinted in S. Leinhardt) (ed.), *Social Networks. A Developing Paradigm*. New York: Academic Press, 1977)

Grant, Wyn (ed.) (1985) *The Political Economy of Corporatism*. London: Macmillan

Grant, Wyn (1989) *Pressure Groups, Politics and Democracy in Britain*. London: Philip Allan

Grant, Wyn (1990) 'Organized Interests and the European Community'. Paper presented at the 6th International Colloquium of the Feltrinelli Foundation: 'Organized Interests and Democracy – Perspectives on West and East', Cortona, Italy, 29–31 May 1990

Grant, Wyn and Jane Sargent (1987) *Business and Politics in Britain*. London: Macmillan

Grant, Wyn and Wolfgang Streeck (1985) 'Large Firms and the Representation of Business Interests in the UK and West German Construction Industry', in Alan Cawson (ed.) *Organized Interests and the State*. London: Sage

Grant, W., W. Paterson and C. Whitston (1989) *Government and the Chemical Industry: A Comparative Study of Britain and West Germany*. Oxford: Clarendon Press

Greenwood, Justin (1988) 'The Market and the State: The Pharmaceutical Representative and General Medical Practice'. PhD thesis University of Nottingham, May 1988

Greenwood, Justin (1989) 'The Regulation of Pharmaceutical Marketing by National Governments: Toward a Transnational Private Interest Government?'. Paper presented at workshop on 'Deregulation, Reregulation and the Transnational Dimension' at the ECPR Joint Sessions, Paris, April 1989

Greenwood, Justin (1991) *Marketing Medicines*. London: Remit

Greenwood, Justin, Jürgen R. Grote and Karsten Ronit (1990) 'Organized Interests and the Internal Market: Associational Responses to the "Decomposition" of the Nation State'. Paper presented at the Conference of the ECPR on 'The New Europe', Rimini, September 1990

Greenwood, Justin and A.G. Jordan (forthcoming) 'The UK: A Changing Kaleidoscope', in M.C.P.M. van Schendelen (ed.), *Lobbying in Brussels*. Aldershot: Dartmouth.

Greenwood, Justin and Karsten Ronit (1991a) 'Pharmaceutical Regulation in Denmark and the UK: Reformulating Interest Respresentation to the Transnational Level', *European Journal of Political Research*, 19 (2): 327–59

Greenwood, Justin and Karsten Ronit (1991b) 'Organised Interests and the European Internal Market', in *Government and Policy*, 9: 467–84

Grote, Jürgen R. (1986) 'Voraussetzungen, Verlaufsformen und Ergebnisse konzertierter Politik auf EG-Ebene'. Paper prepared at interdisciplinary conference of the Arbeitskreis Europaische Integration on 'Europeanisation of Trade Unions in the Crisis Years. The Impact of EC Integration on Structure and Strategies of Trade Unions in a Period of Mass Unemployment', Hamburg, 29–31 May 1986

Grote, Jürgen R. (1987) 'Tripartism and European Integration: Mutual Transfers, Osmotic Exchanges, or Frictions between the "National" and the "Transnational"?' in Georges Spiropoulos (ed.), *Trade Unions Today and Tomorrow*, vol.1, *Trade Unions in a Changing Europe*. Maastricht: Presses Interuniversitaires Européennes, pp. 231–59

Grote, J.R. (1989a) 'Rent Seeking "Without Frontiers": on Institutional Supply and Organizational Demand for EC Regulatory Policies'. Paper presented at the panel on 'Deregulation, Regulation and the International Dimension' of the ECPR Joint Sessions, Paris, April 1989

Grote, J.R. (1989b) 'Guidance and Control in Transnational Committee Networks. The Associational Basis of Policy Cycles at EC Level'. Paper presented at the Conference of the Structure and Organization of Government (SOG) Research Committee of IPSA on 'Government and Organised Interests', Zurich, Switzerland, September 1989

Grote, J.R. (1990) 'Steuerungsprobleme in transnationalen Beratungsgremien: uber soziale Kosten unkoordinierter Regulierung in der EG, in Thomas Ellwein, Joachin Jens Hesse, Renate Mayntz and Fritz W. Scharpf (eds), *Jahrbuch zur Staats- und Verwaltungswissenschaft*, vol.4. Baden-Baden: Nomos Verlagsgesellschaft, pp.227–54

Grote, J.R. (1991) Politiche di rete per il sud del sud: obiettivi, concetti e metodi. Florence: Istituto Ricerche Economiche e Sociali (IRES-TOSCANA), unpublished report

Grote, J.R. (1992a) 'Diseconomies in space: traditional sectoral policies of the EC, the European Technology Community and their effect on regional disparities', *Regional Politics and Policies*, 2(1): 14–46.

Grote, J.R. (1992b) 'Networking: un nuovo approccio all'analisi delle interdependenze tra attori locali', *Il Nuovo Governo Locale*, No. 1/1992: 3–37

Grunert, Thomas (1987) 'Decision-Making Processes in the Steel Crisis Policy of the EEC: Neocorporatist or Integrationist Tendencies?' in Yves Meny, and Vincent Wright (eds), *The Politics of Steel: Western Europe and the Steel Industry in the Crisis Years (1974–1984)*. Berlin and New York: De Gruyter, pp. 222–308

Günther, H. (ed.) (1972) *Transnational Industrial Relations. The Impact of Multinational Corporations and Economic Regionalism on Industrial Relations.* London: Macmillan–St Martin's Press

Haas, Ernst B. (1958) *The Uniting of Europe: Political, Economic and Social Forces 1950–1957*. Stanford, Ca: Stanford University Press

Haas, Ernst B. (1964) *Beyond the Nation State: Functionalism and International Organisation*. Stanford, Ca: Stanford University Press

Hall, M. (1991) 'Employee Participation and the European Community: the Evolution of the European Works Council Directive'. Paper presented at Third International Industrial Relations Association European Regional Conference, Bari–Naples (Italy), 23–26 September 1991

Hancher, L. (1990) *Government, Law and the Pharmaceutical Industry in the UK and France*. Oxford: Clarendon Press

Hartmann, J. (1985) *Verbande in der westlichen Industriegesellschaft. Ein international vergleichendes Handbuch*. Frankfurt: Campus

Hayworth, N. and H. Ramsay (1984) 'Grasping the Nettle: Problems with the Theory of Trade Union Internationalism', in P. Waterman (ed.) *For a New Labour Internationalism*. The Hague: ILERI

Headey, B.W. (1970) 'Trade Unions and National Wage Policies', *Journal of Politics*, 32: 407–38

Hellmann, M.F. and I. Stockl (1981) 'Die Organisation und Koordination der Industrien durch den europaischen Unternehmerverband UNICE und seine Einflussnahme auf europaische Politik', *WSI Mitteilungen*, 7: 447–54

Hernes, G. and A. Selvik (1981) 'Local Corporatism', in Suzanne Berger (ed.), *Organizing Interests in Western Europe*. Cambridge: Cambridge University Press

Hilpert, Ulrich (1989) 'High Technology in der Region', in: *Perspektiven des Sozialismus*, 6(3): 160–71

Hilpert, U. (1991) *Neue Weltmarkte und der Staat. Staatliche Politik, technischer Fortschritt und internationale Arbeitsteilung*. Opladen: Westdeutscher

Holecombe, A. (1911) *Public Ownership of Telephones on the Continent of Europe*. Cambridge, Mass.: Harvard University Press

Holland, Stuart (1989) 'Competition, Cooperation and the Social Dimension: Reviewing the 1992 Proposals', in John Storm Pedersen and Bernt Greve (eds),

The Internal Market in EEC: A Debate on Eurotrends. Roskilde: Forlaget Samfundsoekonomi og Planaegning, pp.43–57

Holland, Stuart (1990) 'Europe of the Regions: The Scope for Networks'. Paper presented at conference on 'Networks – On the Socio-Economics of Inter-Firm Cooperation', organized by the Social Science Centre (WZB) Berlin, Research Area Labour Market and Employment, Berlin, 11–13 June 1990

Hrbek, Rudolf and Hans Platzer (1981) 'Interest Representation within the EC System'. Paper presented at Workshop on 'Interest Representation in Mixed Polities', ECPR Joint Sessions, Lancaster, April 1981

Humphreys, P. (1990) 'The Political Economy of Telecommunications in France: A Case Study of "Telematics"', in K. Dyson, and P. Humphreys (eds), *The Political Economy of Communications. International and European Dimensions*. London and New York: Routledge, pp. 198–228

Hyman, Richard and Wolfgang Streeck (eds) (1988) *New Technology and Industrial Relations*. Oxford: Basil Blackwell

Jackson, P. and K. Sisson (1981) 'Employers Confederations in Sweden and the United Kingdom and the Significance of Industrial Infrastructure', *British Journal of Industrial Relations*, 3(14): 306–23.

Jacobi, Otto (1990) 'Elements of a European Community of the Future: a Trade Union View', in Colin Crouch and David Marquand (eds), *The Politics of 1992*. Oxford: Basil Blackwell, pp. 23–37

Jordan, A.G. (1990) 'The Pluralism of Pluralism: An Anti Theory?', *Political Studies*, XXXVIII: 286–301

Jordan, A.G. and McLaughlin, A.M. (1991) 'The Logic of Participation in Euro-Groups: Some Evidence from the Car Industry'. Paper presented to a Workshop on 'Pressure Groups and Policy-Making in the European Community', Nuffield College Oxford, 17–19 May 1991

Jordan, A.G. (1991b) 'The Rationality of Lobbying in Europe: Why are Euro Groups so Numerous and so Weak?'. Mimeo, University of Aberdeen

Kaplinsky, Raphael (1990) 'From Mass Producton to Flexible Specialisation: A Case Study from a Semi-industrialised Economy'. Mimeo, Institute of Development Studies, University of Sussex, June

Keman, Hans and Dietmar Braun (1987) 'Economic Interdependence, International Regimes, and Domestic Strategies of Industrial Adjustment', *European Journal of Political Research*, 15: 547–59

Kendall, W. (1975) *The Labour Movement in Europe*. London: Allen Lane

Kenis, Patrick (1986) 'Industrial Restructuring: the Case of the Chemical Fibre Industry in Europe', in European University Institute, EUI Working Paper No. 86/191, Florence

Kenis, Patrick and Volker Schneider (1987) 'The EC as an International Corporate Actor: Two Case Studies in Economic Diplomacy', *European Journal of Political Research*, 15: 437–57

Keohane, Robert O. (1984) 'The World Political Economy and the Crisis of Embedded Liberalism', in J.H. Goldthorpe (ed.), *Order and Conflict in Contemporary Capitalism*. Oxford: Oxford University Press, pp. 15–39

Keohane, Robert O. (1986) 'Reciprocity in International Relations', *International Organization*, 40(1): 1–29

Keohane, Robert O. and Stanley Hoffman (1990) 'Conclusion: Community Politics and Institutional Change', in William Wallace, (ed.), *The Dynamics of European Integration*. London: Frances Pinter

Kerr, Clark, John T. Dunlop, Frederick H. Harbison and Charles A. Myers (eds) (1960) *Industrialism and Industrial Man. The Problems of Labour and Management in Economic Growth*. Cambridge, Mass.: Harvard University Press

King, R. (1985) 'Corporatism and Local Economy', in Wyn Grant (ed.), *The Political Economy of Corporatism*. London: Macmillan

Kirchner, Emil J. (1977) *Trade Unions as a Pressure Group in the European Community*. Westmead: Saxon House

Kirchner, Emil J. (1980a) 'Interest Group Behaviour at Community Level', in L. Hurwitz (ed.), *Contemporary Perspectives of EEC Integration*. London: Aldwych Press

Kirchner, Emil J. (1980b) 'International Trade Union Collaboration and the Prospects for European Industrial Relations', *West European Politics*, 3 (1): 124–30

Kirchner, Emil J. (1983) *Public Service Unions and the European Community*. Westmead: Gower

Kirchner, Emil J. (1986a) 'Interest Group Development at European Community Level as an Indicator of Integration'. Paper presented to the Fifth International Conference of Europeanists, Washington, DC, 18–20 October 1986

Kirchner, Emil J. (1986b) 'Interessensverbande im EG–System und der Integrationsprozess', *Integration*, 9 (4): 156–65

Kirchner, E.J. and H. Schwaiger (1981) *The Role of Interest Groups in the European Community*. (Published by the Economic and Social Committee of the EC.) Aldershot: Gower Publishing

Klinge, G. (1990) *Niederlassungs- und Dienstleistungsrecht fur Handwerker und andere Gewerbetreibende in der EG*. Baden-Baden and Düsseldorf: Nomos Verlagsgesellschaft and Verlagsanstalt Handwerk

Kogut, Bruce, Weijan Shan and Gordon Walker (1990) 'The structuring of an industry: cooperative agreements in the biotechnology industry'. Paper presented at conference on 'Networks: On the Socio-economics of Inter-firm Cooperation', Science Centre Berlin (WZB), Research Area Labour Market and Employment, Berlin, 11–13 June 1990

Kohler-Koch, B. (1990) 'Vertikale Machtverteilung und organisierte Wirtschaftsinteressen in der Europaischen Gemeinschaft' in U. von Alemann, R.G. Heinze and B. Hombach (eds), *Die Kraft der Region: Nordrhein Westfalen in Europa*. Bonn: Dietz, pp. 221–35

Köpke, G. (1990) 'Tarifpolitische Perspektiven im europaischen Binnenmarkt: Hemmnisse und Chancen', *Gewerkschaftliche Monatshefte*, 12: 757–66

Koshiro, Kazutoshi (1990) 'Japan (country report)', in Werner Sengenberger. Gary M. Loveman and Michael J. Piore (eds), *The Re-emergence of Small Enterprises*. Geneva: International Institute for Labour Studies (ILO), pp. 173–223

Kreile, Michael (1978) 'Neo-corporatism in Foreign Economic Policy: A Comparative Perspective'. Paper presented at ECPR Joint Sessions of Workshops on 'Corporatism in Liberal Democracies', Grenoble, 6–12 April 1978

Kriesi, Hans-Peter and Peter Farago (1989) 'The Regional Differentiation of Business Interest Associations in Switzerland', in William D. Coleman and Henry J. Jacek (eds), *Regionalism, Business Interests and Public Policy*. London: Sage

Kubler, Klaus-Joachim, Hans-Jurgen Aberle and Helmut Schubert (1982) *Die Deutsche Handwerksordnung: Kommentar, Mustersatzungen und Materialien*. Bonn: Erich Schmidt

Lange, Peter (1983) 'Politiche dei redditi e democrazia sindacale in Europa occidentale', *Stato e Mercato*, 9: 425–75

Lange, Peter (1990) 'The Politics of the Social Dimension: Interests, States and Redistribution in the 1992 Process – A Sketch'. Mimeo, Duke University, Wisconsin

Lanzalaco, Luca (1989) 'L'elezione di Pininfarina alla presidenza della Confindustria e i problemi dell'associazionismo imprenditoriale', in Raimondo Catanzaro and Raffaella Y. Nanetti (eds), *Politica in Italia*. Bologna: Il Mulino, pp. 237–67

Lanzalaco, Luca (1990) *Dall'impresa all'associazione. Le organizzazioni degli imprenditori: la Confindustria in prospettiva comparata*. Milan: Franco Angeli

Lanzalaco, Luca and Philippe C. Schmitter (1988) 'L'organizzazione degli interessi imprenditoriali a livello regionale', *Stato e Mercato*, 1: 63–97 (English version in William D. Coleman and Henry J. Jacek (eds) (1989) *Regionalism, Business Interests and Public Policy*. London: Sage

Lanzalaco, Luca and Philippe C. Schmitter (1992) 'The Prospective Impact of Europe's Internal Market upon Business Associability and its Implications for the Labour Movement', in Marino Regini (ed.), *The Future of Labour Movements*. London: Sage

Lash, Scott and John Urry (1987) *The End of Organized Capitalism*. Cambridge: Polity Press

Lehmbruch, Gerhard and Philippe C. Schmitter (1982) *Patterns of Corporatist Policy-Making*. London and Beverly Hills, Ca: Sage

Leonardi, Robert and Raffaella Y. Nanetti (eds) (1990) *The Regions and European Integration – the Case of Emilia-Romagna*. London and New York: Pinter

Levinson, Ch. (1972) *International Trade Unionism*. London: Allen and Unwin

Lewin, L. (1991) *Self Interest and Public Interest in Western Politics*. Oxford: Oxford University Press

Lindberg, Leon N. (1990) 'Towards a New European Style of Catpitalism? Financial Integration and Monetary Policy Coordination in the European Community'. Mimeo, Madison: University of Wisconsin, 4 April

Lindberg, Leon N. and Stuart A. Scheingold (1970) *Europe's Would-Be Polity: Patterns of Change in the European Community*. Englewood Cliffs, NJ: Prentice Hall

Lipset, Seymour M. and Stein Rokkan (1967) 'Cleavage Structures, Party Systems, and Voter Alignments: an Introduction', in S.M. Lipset and S. Rokkan (eds), *Party Systems and Voting Alignments*. New York: Free Press

Lodge, Juliet and Herman Valentine (1980) *The Economic and Social Committee in EC Decision-Making*. Westmead: Saxon House

Loinger, Guy and Veronique Peyrache (1988) 'Technological Clusters and Regional Economic Restructuring', in Philippe Aydalot and David Keeble (eds), *High Technology Industry and Innovative Environments – The European Experience (GREMI)*. London and New York: Routledge, pp. 121–38

Loveman, Gary W. and Werner Sengenberger (1990) 'Economic and social reorganisation in the small and medium-sized enterprise sector', in Werner Sengenberger, Gary W. Loveman and Michael J. Piore (eds), *The Re-emergence of Small Enterprises*. Geneva: International Institute for Labour Studies (ILO), pp. 1–62

Lowi, Theodore (1964) 'American Business, Case Studies, Public Policy and Political Theory', *World Politics*, 16: 677–715

Maier, Ch. (1981) 'Fictious Bounds . . . of Wealth and Law: on the Theory and Practice of Interest Representation', in Suzanne Berger (ed.), *Organizing*

Interests in Western Europe. Cambridge: Cambridge University Press

Majone, Giandomenico (1989a) 'Regulating Europe: Problems and Prospects', in Thomas Ellwein, Joachim J. Hesse, Renate Mayntz and Wolfgang F. Scharpf (eds) *Jahrbuch zur Staats- und Verwaltungswissenschaft*. Baden-Baden: Nomos Verlagsgesellschaft, pp. 159–78

Majone, Giandomenico (1989b) *Evidence, Argument and Persuasion in the Policy Process*. New Haven, Conn. and London: Yale University Press

Majone, Giandomenico (ed.) (1990) *Deregulation or Reregulation? Regulatory Reforms in Europe and the United States*. London: Frances Pinter

Marin, Bernd (ed.) (1990a) *Governance and Generalized Exchange. Self-Organizing Policy Networks in Action*. European Centre for Social Welfare Policy and Research. Frankfurt: Campus/ Boulder, Col.: Westview

Marin, Bernd (ed.) (1990b) *Generalized Political Exchange. Antagonistic Cooperation and Integrated Policy Circuits*. European Centre for Social Welfare Policy and Research. Frankfurt: Campus/Boulder, Col.: Westview

Marin, Bernd and Renate Mayntz (eds) (1991) *Policy Networks. Empirical Evidence and Theoretical Considerations*. Frankfurt: Campus

Martinelli, A. (ed.) (1991) *International Markets and Global Firms. A Comparative Study of Organized Business in the Chemical industry*. London: Sage

Matzner, Egon and Wolfgang Streeck (eds) (1991) *Beyond Keynesianism: The Socio-economics of Production and Full Employment*. Aldershot: Edward Elgar

Mayntz, Renate (1989) 'Interest representation at the level of the German Lander'. Paper presented on occasion of the Structure and Organization of Government (SOG) Conference on 'Government and Organized Interests' of the International Political Science Association, Zurich, Switzerland, 27–30 September 1989

Mayntz, Renate (1990) 'Organisierte Interessenvertretung und Föderalismus: Zur Verbändestruktur in der Bundesrepublik Deutschland', in Thomas Ellwein, Joachim J. Hesse, Renate Mayntz and Wolfgang F. Scharpf (eds), *Jahrbuch zur Staats- und Verwaltungswissenschaft*. Baden-Baden: Nomos Verlagsgesellschaft, pp. 145–57

Mazey, Sonia and Jeremy Richardson (1991) 'British Pressure Groups in the EC: Changing Lobbying Styles?'. Paper presented to the Joint Sessions of the European Consortium for Political Research, University of Essex, 22–28 March 1991

Meynaud, J. and D. Sidjanski (1971) *Les Groupes des Pression dans la Communauté Européenne 1958–1969*. Brussels: Université Libre

Moravcsik, A. (1991) 'Negotiating the Single European Act: National Interests and Conventional', *International Organization*, 45 (1): 19–56

Müller-Jentsch, W. (ed.) (1987) *Zunkunft der Gewerkschaften. Ein internationaler Vergleich*. Frankfurt: Campus

Mytelka, L.K. and M. Delapierre (1987) 'The Alliance Strategies of European Firms in the Information Technology Industry and the Role of ESPRIT', *Journal of Common Market Studies*, 26.

Nello, S.S. (1989) 'European Interest-Groups and the CAP', *Food Policy*, 14 (2): 101–6

Nerb, G. (1988) 'The Completion of the Internal Market: A Survey of European Industry's Perception of the Likely Effects', in *Documents: Cecchini Report*, vol. 3. Documents Series CB-52-88-502-EN-C. Luxemburg: Office for Official Publications of the EC

Neu, W., K.-H. Neumann and T. Schnoring (1987) 'Trade Patterns, Industry

Structure and Industrial Policy in Telecommunications', *Telecommunications Policy*, March: 31–44

Neunreither, Karlheinz (1968) 'Wirtschaftsverbände im Prozess der europaischen Integration', in Carl J. Friedrich (ed.), *Politische Dimensionen der europäischen Gemeinschaftsbildung*. Cologne and Opladen: Westdeutscher, pp. 358–443

Nora, S. and A. Minc (1978) *L'Informatisation de la Société*. Paris: La Documentation Française

Northrup, H.R., D.C. Campbell and B.J. Slowinski (1988) 'Multinational Union-Management Consultation in Europe: Resurgence in the 1980s?' *Industrial Labour Review*, 125 (5): 525–43

Northrup, H.R. and P. Rowan (1979) *Multinational Collective Bargaining Attempts*. Philadelphia: University of Pennsylvania Press

Oeschlin, J. (1980) 'Employers' Organizations', in R. Blanpain (ed.), *Comparative Labour Law and Industrial Relations*. Dordrecht: Kluwer

Offe, Claus and Helmut Wiesenthal (1980) 'Two Logics of Collective Action: Theoretical Notes on Social Class and Organizational Form', in *Political Power and Social Theory*, 1: 67–115

Olson, Mancur (1965) *The Logic of Collective Action. Public Goods and the Theory of Groups*. Cambridge, Mass: Harvard University Press

Olson, Mancur (1982) *The Rise and Decline of Nations. Economic Growth, Stagflation and Social Rigidities*. New Haven, Conn.: Yale University Press

Orsenigo, L. (1989) *The Emergence of Biotechnology*. London: Frances Pinter

Parri, Leonardo (1988) 'Dimension territoriale de la politique et dynamiques d'échange', *Revue Française d'Administration Publique*, 48: 111–24

Parri, Leonardo (1989) 'Territorial Political Exchanges in Federal and Unitary Countries', *West European Politics*, 12 (3): 197–219

Parri, Leonardo (1990a) 'Le politiche subnazionali per l'innovazione tecnologica nelle piccole imprese: le Regioni Rhone-Alpes ed Emilia-Romagna a confronto', *Piccola Impresa – Small Business*, 2: 63–105

Parri, Leonardo (1990b) 'Territorial Politics and Political Exchange: American Federalism and French Unitarianism Reconsidered', in Bernd Marin (ed.), *Governance and Generalized Exchange*. European Centre for Social Welfare Policy and Research. Frankfurt: Campus/Boulder, Col: Westview pp. 211–35

Parri, Leonardo (1991) 'Politiche locali per l'innovazione tecnologica: Rhone-Alpes ed Emilia-Romagna', *Stato e Mercato*, 31: 77–115

Pestoff, V. (1988) 'The Politics of Private Business. Co-operatives and Public Enterprise in a Corporate Democracy: The Case of Sweden'. European University Institute, Florence: colloquium papers

Peters, Guy (1990) 'The Institutions of Governance in the European Community'. Mimeo, Pittsburgh: University of Pittsburgh

Peterson, J. (1991) 'Technology Policy in Europe. Explaining the Framework Programme and Eureka in Theory and Practice', *Journal of Common Market Studies*, 29 (3): 269–91

Philipps, A. (1960) 'A Theory of Interfirm Organization', *Quarterly Journal of Economics*, 74: 602–13

Piore, M.J. (1990) 'Work, Labour and Action: Work Experience in a System of Flexible Production', in F. Pyke, G. Becattini and W. Sengenberger (eds), *Industrial Districts and Inter-firm Cooperation in Italy*. Geneva: International Institute for Labour Studies (ILO), pp. 52–75

Piore, Michael J. and Charles F. Sabel (1984) *The Second Industrial Divide:*

Possibilities for Prosperity. New York: Basic Books

Pizzorno, Alessandro (1975) 'I ceti medi nei meccanismi di consenso', in F.B. Cavazza and S.R. Graubard (eds), *Il caso italiano*. Milan: Garanti

Pizzorno, Alessandro (1977) 'Scambio politico e identita' collettiva nel conflitto di classe', in Colin Crouch and Alessandro Pizzorno (eds), *Conflitti di classe in Europa – Lotte di classe, sindacati e stato dopo il '68*. Milan: ETAS libri

Platzer, H.W. (1984) *Unternehmensverbande in der EG. Ihre nationale und transnationale Organisation und Politik*. Kehl am Rhein and Strasbourg: N.P. Engel

Puchala, Donald J. (1972) 'Of Blind Men, Elephants and International Integration', *Journal of Common Market Studies*, 10(3): 267–85

Pyke, F., G. Becattini and W. Sengenberger (eds) (1990) *Industrial Districts and Inter-firm Cooperation in Italy*. Geneva: International Institute for Labour Studies (ILO)

Renaud, J. -L. (1990) 'The Role of the International Telecommunication Union: Conflict, Resolution and the Industrialized Countries', in K. Dyson and P. Humphreys (eds) *The Political Economy of Communications*. London and New York: Routledge, pp. 33–59

Rhodes, Martin (1991) 'The social dimension of the Single European Market: National versus transnational regulation', *European Journal of Political Research*, 19: 245–80

Ridolfi, Mauro (1985) *Premesse per una teoria delle imprese minori*. Milan: Franco Angeli

Roberts, B.C. (1973) 'Multinational collective Bargaining: a European prospect?', *British Journal of Industrial Relations*, 11 (1): 1–19

Roberts, B.C. (1989) 'The Social Dimension of European Labour Markets', in Institute of Economic Affairs (ed.), *Whose Europe? Competing Visions for 1992*. London: IEA

Roberts, B.C. and B. Liebhaberg (1976) 'The European Trade Union Confederation: Influence of Regionalism, Detente and Multinationals', *British Journal of Industrial Relations*, 14 (3): 261–73

Rowan, R.L., K.J. Pitterle, and Ph.A. Miscimara (1983) *Multinational Union Organizations in the White-Collar, Service, and Communications Industries*. Philadelphia: Industrial Relations Unit, Wharton School

Rütters, P. and K.P. Tuydka (1990) 'Internationale Gewerkschaftsbewegung – Vorbereitung auf den europaischen Binnenmarkt', in M. Kittner (ed.) *Gewerkschafts-Handbuch 1990*. Cologne: Bund pp. 566–606

Sabel, Charles F. (1990) 'Flexible specilization and the re-emergence of regional economies', in Paul Hirst and Jonathan Zeitlin (eds), *Reversing Industrial Decline? Industrial Structure and Policy in Britain and Her Competitors*. Oxford and New York: St Martin's, pp. 17–70

Salaman, J.A. (1979) *Work Organizations*. London: Longman

Sandholtz, W. and J. Zysman (1989) 'Recasting the European Bargain', *World Politics*, 42: 95–128

Sargent, Jane (1982) 'Pressure Group Development in the EC: the Role of the British Bankers Association', *Journal of Common Market Studies*, 20: 269–85

Sargent, Jane (1983) 'British Finance and Industrial Capital and the European Communities', D. Marsh (ed.) *Capital and Politics in Western Europe*. London: Frank Cass

Sargent, Jane (1985) 'Corporatism and the European Community', in Wyn Grant (ed.), *The Political Economy of Corporatism*. London: Macmillan, pp. 229–55

Sargent, Jane (1987) 'The Organization of Business Interests for European Community Representation', in Wyn Grant and Jane Sargent (eds), *Business and Politics in Britain*, London, Macmillan

Sartori, Giovanni (1969) 'From the Sociology of Politics to Political Sociology', in Seymour M. Lipset (ed.), *Politics and the Social Sciences*. New York: Oxford University Press

Saunders, Peter (1983) 'The "Regional State": A Review of the Literature and Agenda for Research'. Working Paper 35. Brighton: University of Sussex

Scharpf, Fritz W. (1985) 'The Joint-Decision Trap: Lessons from German Federalism and European Integration'. Discussion Paper of the International Institute of Management–Labour Market Policy Division, IIM/LMP 85/1. Berlin: WZB

Scharpf, Fritz W. (1987) *Crisis and Choice in European Social Democracy*. Ithaca NY: Cornell University Press

Scharpf, Fritz W. (1988) 'Regionalisierung des europaischen Raumes. Die Zukunft der Bundeslander im Spannungsfeld zwischen EG, Bund und Kommunen'. Lecture at the 24th Cappenberger Colloquium of the Freiherr-vom-Stein Society, Ettlingen, 27 September

Schlencker, L.H. (1987) 'France: The Business State', in M.C.P.M. van Schendelen and R.J. Jackson (eds), *The Politicisation of Business in Western Europe*. London: Croom Helm, pp. 114–33

Schmitter, Philippe C. (1974) 'Still the Century of Corporatism?', *Review of Politics*, 36: 85–131. Reprinted 1979 in Philippe C. Schmitter and Gerhard Lehmbruch (eds) *Trends Towards Corporatist Intermediation*. London and Beverly Hills: Sage

Schmitter, Philippe C. (1977) 'Modes of Interest Intermediation and Models of Societal Change in Western Europe', in Philippe C. Schmitter and Gerhard Lehmbruch (eds), *Trends Towards Corporatist Intermediation*. London and Beverly Hills: Sage

Schmitter, Philippe C. (1981) 'Interest Intermediation and Regime Governability in Contemporary Western Europe and North America', in Suzanne Berger (ed.), *Organizing Interests in Western Europe. Corporatism and the Transformation of Politics*. Cambridge: Cambridge University Press

Schmitter, Philippe C. (1983) 'Organizzazione degli interessi e rendimento politico', in Gianfranco Pasquino (ed.), *Le societa complesse*. Bologna: Il Mulino

Schmitter, Philippe C. (1985) 'Exchange Theories of Integration: "Exit", "Voice" and "Suffrance" as Strategies in Regional Organizations'. Mimeo, Florence: European University Institute

Schmitter, Philippe C. (1988) 'Corporative democracy: oxymoronic? Just plain moronic? Or a promising way out of the present impasse?'. Mimeo, Stanford, Ca: Stanford University Press, March

Schmitter, Philippe C. (1990) 'Sectors in Modern Capitalism: Modes of Governance and Variations in Performance', in Renato Brunetta and Carlo Dell'Aringa (eds) *Labour Relations and Economic Performance*. London: Macmillan, pp 3–40

Schmitter, Philippe C. (1991) 'The European Community as an Emergent and Novel Form of Political Domination', in Estudio/Working Paper 1991/26, September 1991. Madrid: Instituto Juan March de Estudios e Investigaciones

Schmitter, P.C. and D. Brand (1979) 'Organizing Capitalists in the United States: The Advantages and Disadvantages of Exceptionalism'. Paper presented at the

Annual Meeting of the American Political Science Association

Schmitter, Philippe C. and Luca Lanzalaco (1989) 'Regions and the Organization of Business Interests', in William D. Coleman and Henry J, Jacek (eds), *Regionalism, Business Interests and Public Policy*. London: Sage

Schmitter, Philippe C. and Gerhard Lehmbruch (eds) (1979) *Trends Towards Corporatist Intermediation*. London and Beverly Hills: Sage

Schmitter, Philippe C. and Wolfgang Streeck (1981) 'The Organization of Business Interests'. Discussion Paper of the International Institute of Management–Labour Market Policies Division, IIM/LMP 1981/13. Berlin: WZB

Schmitter, Philippe C. and Wolfgang Streeck (1990) 'Organized Interests and the Europe of 1992'. Paper presented at a conference on 'The United States and Europe in the 1990s: Trade Finance, Defense, Politics, Demographics and Social Policy'. American Enterprise Institute, Washington, DC, 6–8 March 1990

Schneider, Volker (1988) *Politiknetzwerke in der Chemikalienkontrolle*. Berlin and New York: Walter de Gruyter

Schneider, Volker (1990) 'Control as a Generalized Exchange Medium within the Policy Process? A Theoretical Interpretation of a Policy Analysis on Chemical Control', in Bernd Marin (ed.) *Governance and Generalized Exchange. Self-Organizing Policy Networks in Action*. European Centre for Social Welfare Policy and Research. Frankfurt: Campus/Boulder, Col: Westview, pp. 171–89

Schneider, Volker (1991) 'The Governance of Large Technical Systems: The Case of Telecommunications', in T.R. La Porte (ed.), *Social Responses to Large Technical Systems. Control or Anticipation*. Dordrecht: Kluwer, pp. 19–41

Schneider, Volker and Raimund Werle (1990) 'International Regime or Corporate Actor? The European Community in Telecommunications Policy', in K. Dyson and P. Humphreys (eds), *The Political Economy of Communications*. London and New York: Routledge, pp. 77–106

Schneider, Volker and Raimund Werle (1991) 'Policy Networks in the German Telecommunications Domain', in Bernd Marin and Renate Mayntz (eds), *Policy Networks*. Frankfurt: Campus, pp. 97–136

Scott, Richard and John W. Meyer (1983) 'The Organization of Societal Sectors', in John W. Meyer and W. Richard Scott (eds), *Organizational Environments. Ritual and Rationality*. Newbury Park and London: Sage, 129–53

Sengenberger, Werner, Gary W. Loveman and Michael J. Piore (eds) (1990) *The Re-emergence of Small Enterprises: Industrial Restructuring in Industrialized Countries*. Geneva: International Institute for Labour Studies (ILO)

Sforzi, Fabio (1989) 'The geography of industrial districts in Italy', in E. Goodman, J. Banford and P. Gaynor (eds), *Small Firms and Industrial Districts in Italy*. London: Routledge, pp. 153–73

Sforzi, Fabio (1990) 'The Quantitative Importance of Marshallian Industrial Districts in the Italian Economy', in F. Pyke, G. Becattini and W. Sengenberger (eds), *Industrial Districts and Inter-firm Cooperation in Italy*. Geneva: International Institute for Labour Studies (ILO), pp. 75–108

Shalev, M. (1980) 'Industrial Relations Theory and the Comparative Study of Industrial Relations and Industrial Conflict', *British Journal of Industrial Relations*, 18 (1): 26–44

Shankley, S. (1991) Regulating a New Technology in the EC: The Case of Biotechnology, typescript, Science Policy Research Unit, University of Sussex

Sharp, M. (1985a) 'The New Biotechnology: European Governments in Search of a Strategy', in *Sussex European Papers*, no. 15, Brighton: University of Sussex

(Science Policy Research Unit)

Sharp, M. (1985b) *Europe and the New Technologies: Six Case Studies in Innovation and Adjustment*. London: Frances Pinter

Sharp, M. (1991a) 'Technological Trajectories and Corporate Strategies in the Diffusion of Biotechnology', in E. Deiaco, E. Hornell and G. Vickery (eds), *Technology and Investment: Crucial Issues of the 1990s*. London: Frances Pinter

Sharp, M. (1991b) 'Pharmaceuticals and Biotechnology: Perspectives for the European Industry', in C. Freeman, M. Sharp and W. Walker (eds), *Technology and the Future of Europe*. London: Frances Pinter

Sharp, M. and P. Holmes (eds) (1989) *Strategies for New Technologies: Case Studies from Britain and France*. London: Philip Allan

Sharp, M. and C. Shearman (1987) *European Technological Collaboration*. London: Routledge and Kegan Paul

Shearman, C. (1989) 'European Technological Collaboration: An Overview of Some of the Issues Arising'. Paper presented at the European Community Studies Association's Inaugural Conference, George Mason University, Fairfax, Virginia, 24–25 May 1989

Sidjanski, Dusan (1982) 'Les Groupes des Pression dans la Communauté Européenne', *Il Politico*, 43 (3): 539–60

Sidjanski, D. and J. Condomines (1983) 'Le profil du comité économique et social des communautés européennes en 1982–1983, *Revue d'integration européenne*, 7 (1): 9–40

Siemens (1991) International Telecom Statistics. Munich: Siemens

Sisson, K. (1979) 'The Organization of Employers' Associations in Five European Countries: Some Comments on their Origin and Development'. Paper presented at the International Institute of Management Workshop on 'Employers' Associations as Organizations'. Berlin: WZB.

Sisson, K. (1987) *The Management of Collective Bargaining. An International Comparison*. Oxford: Basil Blackwell

Sorge, Arndt and Wolfgang Streeck (1988) 'Industrial Relations and Technical Change: the Case for an Extended Perspective', in Richard Hyman and Wolfgang Streeck (eds), *New Technology and Industrial Relations*. London: Basil Blackwell, pp. 19–47

Spiropoulos, Georges (1991) 'Between European Legislation and Social Dialogue. Diverging Views on Future European Industrial Relations'. Paper presented at Third IIRA European Regional Congress, Bari–Naples (Italy), 23–26 September 1991

Stöckl, I. (1986) *Gewerkschaftsausschüsse in der EG*. Kehl and Strasbourg: N.P. Engel

Streeck, Wolfgang (1983) 'Between Pluralism and Corporatism: German Business Associations and the State', *Journal of Public Policy*, 3 (3): 265–84

Streeck, Wolfgang (1988) 'Interest Variety and Organizing Capacity: Two Class Logics of Collective Action?' Paper presented at the International Conference on 'Political Institutions and Interest Intermediation', University of Konstanz, Germany, 20–21 April 1988

Streeck, Wolfgang (1989a) 'The Territorial Organization of Interests and the Logic of Associative Action: The Case of Handwerk Organization in West Germany', in William D. Coleman and Henry J. Jacek (eds), *Regionalism, Business Interests and Public Policy*. London: Sage

Streeck, Wolfgang (1989b) 'The Social Dimension of the European Firm'. Revised version of a paper presented at the Annual Meeting of the Andrew Shonfield Association, Florence, European University Institute, 14–15 September 1989

Streeck, Wolfgang (1990a) 'More uncertainties: West German Unions Facing 1992'. Paper presented to a panel on 'One big union? Organized Labour and 1992'. Seventh Conference of Europeanists, Washington, DC, 23–25 March 1990

Streeck, Wolfgang (1990b) 'La dimensione sociale del mercato unico europeo: verso un'economia non regolata?' *Stato e Mercato*, 28 April: 29–69

Streeck, Wolfgang (1990c) 'Interest Heterogeneity and Organizing Capacity: Two Class Logics of Collective Action?' in Roland Czada and Adrienne Windhoff-Heretier (eds), *Rational Actors in Institutional Settings*. Boulder, Col.: Westview

Streeck, Wolfgang (1991) 'On the social and political conditions of diversified quality production', in Egon Matzner and Wolfgang Streeck (eds) *Beyond Keynesianism*. Aldershot: Edward Elgar.

Streeck, Wolfgang and Philippe C. Schmitter (eds) (1985) *Private Interest Government. Beyond Market and State*. Sage Series in Neo-Corporatism. London: Sage

Streeck, Wolfgang and Philippe C. Schmitter (1991) 'From National Corporatism to Transnational Pluralism: Organized Interests in the Single European Market', *Politics and Society*, 19 (2): 133–65

Strickland-Hodge, B. (1979) 'The Impact of Drug Information on the Prescribing of Drugs'. PhD thesis presented at the University of Aston

Sturmthal, A. (1953) *Unity and Diversity in European Labor*. Glencoe, Ill.: The Free Press

Swenson, P. (1989) *Fair Shares, Unions, Pay, and Politics in Sweden and West Germany*. Ithaca, NY: Cornell University Press

Tarantelli, Ezio (1986) *Economia politica del lavoro*. Turin: UTET

Teague, P. (1989a) *The European Community: The Social Dimension – Labour Market Policies for 1992*. London: Kogan Page

Teague, P. (1989b) 'The British TUC and the European Community', *Millenium: Journal of International Studies*, 18 (1): 29–45

Thompson, J.D. (1967) *Organizations in Action*. New York: McGraw Hill

Traxler, Franz (1987) 'Klassenstruktur, Korporatismus und Krise. Zur Machtverteilung in Osterreichs "Sozialpartnerschaft" im Umbruch des Weltmarkts', *Politische Vierteljahresschrift*, 28 (1): 59–79

Trigilia, Carlo (1986) *Grande partiti e piccole imprese*. Bologna: Il Mulino

Trigilia, Carlo (1989a) 'Small firm development and political subcultures in Italy', in E. Goodman, J. Bamford and P. Saynor (eds), *Small Firms and Industrial Districts in Italy*. London: Routledge and Kegan Paul

Trigilia, Carlo (1989b) 'Il paradosso della regione. Regolazione economica e rappresentanza degli interessi', *Meridiana*, 6: 173–98

Trigilia, Carol (1990a) 'Work and Politics in the Third Italy's Industrial Districts', in F. Pyke, G. Becattini and W. Sengenberger (eds), *Industrial Districts and Inter-firm Cooperation in Italy*. Geneva: International Institute for Labour Studies (ILO), pp. 160–85

Trigilia, Carlo (1990b) 'Italian Industrial Districts: Neither Myth Nor Interlude'. Paper presented at Conference on 'Industrial Districts and Local Economic Regeneration', organized by the International Institute for Labour Studies and the Commission of the European Communities, Geneva, 18–19 October 1990

Tuydka, K.P. (1983) 'Europaischer Gewerkschaftsbund (EGB)', in Siegfried Mielke (eds) *Internationales Gwerkschaftschandbuch*. Opladen: Leske and Budrich

Tyszkiewicz, Z.J.A. (1990) 'UNICE: The Voice of European Business and Industry in Brussels'. Paper presented at the IREC Conference on 'Employers' Associations in Europe', Trier, 28–30 September 1990

Ulman, L. (1975) 'Multinational Unionism: Incentives, Barriers, and Alternatives', *Industrial Relations*, 14 (2): 1–31

Ullmann, Hans-Peter (1988) *Interessenverbande in Deutschland*. Frankfurt am Main: Edition Suhrkamp

Ungerer, Herbert (1989) *Telecommunications in Europe*. Luxemburg: Office for Publications of the Commission of the European Communities

Ungerer, Herbert and Nicholas P. Costello (1988) *Telecommunications in Europe*. European Perspective Series. Luxemburg: Office for Official Publications of the European Communities

van der Pilj, K. (1989) 'The International Level', in T. Bottomore and R.J. Brym (eds), *The Capitalist Class: An International Study*. London: Harvester Wheatsheaf

van Schendelen, M.C.P.M. (forthcoming) 'Dutch Private and Public Lobbying in the European Community: The Vice or the Virtue of Multiple Lobbies', in M.C.P.M. van Schendelen (ed.), *Lobbying in Brussels*. Aldershot: Dartmouth

van Tulder, Rob and Gerd Junne (1988) *European Multinationals in Core Technologies*. Chichester: Wiley

Vaughn, W.M. (1972) 'Transnational Policy Programme Networks in the EC: the Example of European Competition Policy', *Journal of Common Market Studies*, 10, September: 36–61

Visser, Jelle (1988) 'Trade Unions in Western Europe: Present Situation and Prospects', *Labour and Society* (Geneva), 13 (2): 125–82

Visser, Jelle (1989) *European Trade Unions in Figures: 1913–1985*. Deventer and Boston: Kluwer

Visser, Jelle (1990) *In Search of an Inclusive Unionism*. Deventer and Boston: Kluwer

Visser, Jelle (1991) 'Trends in Union Membership', in Organisation of Economic Co-operation and Development (ed.), *Employment Outlook 1991*. Paris: OECD, pp 97–134

von Voss, R. (1980) 'Arbeitgeberverbande und Europaische Integration – Zur Vertretung Wirtschaftlicher Interessen in Europa', in K. Meessen (ed.), *Verbande und Europaische Integration*. Baden-Baden: Nomos Verlagsgesellschaft

Vos, P.J. (1991) 'Trade Unions and a Social Europe', in W.J. Derkcksen (ed.), *The Future of Industrial Relations in Europe*. Proceedings of a conference in honour of Prof. W. Albeda. The Hague: SDU/WRR, pp. 57–62

Wallace, William (1990) 'Introduction: the Dynamics of European Integration', in William Wallace (ed.), *The Dynamics of European Integration*. London: Frances Pinter

Wallace, William, Helen Wallace and and Carole Webb (eds) (1983) *Policy-Making in the European Communities* (2nd edn). Chichester: Wiley

Wassenberg, Arthur F.P. (1982) 'Neo-corporatism and the Quest for Control: The Cuckoo Game', in Gerhard Lehmbruch and Philippe C. Schmitter (eds), *Patterns of Corporatist Policy-Making*. London and Beverly Hills, Ca: Sage

Wassenberg, Arthur F.P. (1990) 'Games within Games: On the Politics of Association and Dissociation in European Industrial Policy-Making', in Bernd Marin (ed.), *Governance and Generalized Exchange*. European Centre for Social Welfare Policy and Research. Frankfurt: Campus/Boulder, Col.: Westview, pp.

255–89

Weber, H. (1987) *Unternehmerverbande zwischen Markt, Staat und Gewerkschaften. Zur intermediaren Organisation von Wirtschaftsinteressen*. Frankfurt: Campus

Weimer, Stephanie (1990) 'Federal Republic of Germany (country report)', in Werner Sengenberger, Gary W. Loveman and Michael J. Piore (eds), *The Re-emergence of Small Enterprises*. Geneva: International Institute for Labour Studies (ILO), pp. 98–144

Weiner, Klaus Peter (1989) 'Gewerkschaftsbewegung und Binnenmarkt', in Frank Deppe, Joerg Huffschmid and Klaus Peter Weiner (eds), *1992 – Projekt Europa. Politik und Oekonomie in der Europaeischen Gemeinschaft*. Cologne: Pahl-Rugenstein, pp. 83–110

Weiss, Linda (1988) *Creating Capitalism: The State and Small Business since 1945*. London: Basil Blackwell

Werle, Raimund (1990) *Telekommunikation in der Bundesrepublik. Expansion, Differenzierung, Transformation*. Frankfurt: Campus

Wessel, H.A. (1982) 'Der deutsche Schwachstromkabel-Verband – Vorgeschichte und Grundung sowie Entwicklung in den ersten Jahren seines Bestehens (1876–1917)', *Zeitschrift fur Unternehmensgeschichte*, 27 (1): 22–44

Williamson, Peter, J. (1989) *Corporatism in Perspective. An Introductory Guide to Corporatist Theory*. Sage Studies in Neo-Corporatism. London: Sage

Willis, D. and W. Grant (1987) 'The United Kingdom: Still a Company State?', in M.C.P.M. van Schendelen and R.J. Jackson (eds), *The Politicisation of Business in Western Europe*. London: Croom Helm, pp. 158–83

Windmuller, J.P. (1975) 'The Authority of National Trade Union Confederations: a Comparative Analysis', in D.B. Lipskey (ed.), *Power and Public Policy*. Ithaca, NY: Cornell University, pp. 91–107

Windmuller, J.P. (1976a) 'European Regionalism: a New Factor in International Labour', *Industrial Relations Journal*, 7 (2): 36–48

Windmuller, J.P. (1976b) 'Realignment in the ICFTU: The Impact of Detente', *British Journal of Industrial Relations*, 14 (3): 247–260

Windmuller, J.P. (1980) *The International Trade Union Movement*. Deventer and Boston: Kluwer

Windmuller, J.P. and A. Gladstone (1985) *Employers' Associations and Industrial Relations*. Oxford: Oxford University Press

Ypsilanti, D. and R. Mansell (1987) 'Reforming Telecommunications Policy in OECD Countries', *OECD Observer*, 148 (October/November): 18–23

Zysman, J. (1983) *Governments, Markets and Growth: Financial Systems and the Politics of Industrial Change*. Oxford: Martin Robertson

Index